hapi.js in Action

hapi.js in Action

MATT HARRISON

MANNING

SHELTER ISLAND

For online information and ordering of this and other Manning books, please visit www.manning.com. The publisher offers discounts on this book when ordered in quantity. For more information, please contact

Special Sales Department
Manning Publications Co.
20 Baldwin Road
PO Box 761
Shelter Island, NY 11964
Email: orders@manning.com

Manning Publications Co.
20 Baldwin Road
PO Box 761
Shelter Island, NY 11964

Development editor:	Susanna Kline
Technical development editor:	Nickie Buckner
Project editor:	Janet Vail
Copyeditor:	Corbin Collins
Proofreader:	Elizabeth Martin
Technical proofreader:	Matt Merkes
Typesetter:	Marija Tudor
Cover designer:	Marija Tudor

ISBN: 9781633430211
Printed in the United States of America
1 2 3 4 5 6 7 8 9 10 – EBM – 21 20 19 18 17 16

brief contents

v

contents

foreword

At the heart of any development framework is the idea that by sharing patterns and code, we tap into the collective wisdom and build on each other's success. Frameworks are, after all, a common foundation shared by like-minded developers solving similar problems. They are also the core building block of team collaboration and effective engineering communications.

What started as a small collection of utilities around the same time as Node.js's conception grew and evolved into the hapi.js framework. As we learned more from our collective experiences, built more large-scale production systems, grew our engineering teams, and increased our collaboration complexity, the framework evolved to reflect it and internalize these lessons learned.

The hapi.js community documentation is an excellent source of reference material, but it does not (and cannot) encompass the significant amount of knowledge and experience gained over the years from actual use. This is where *hapi.js in Action* comes in—an extensive collection of knowledge that has been, until recently, only available to a select few early adopters.

As a hapi.js core project maintainer, Matt Harrison brings a unique combination of insider know-how and community leadership. A big part of being a core maintainer involves interacting with new and experienced developers, answering questions, and investigating issues. It is this experience and body of work spread over hundreds of issues and questions that guides and makes this book invaluable.

Getting started with hapi.js is trivial. You can bring up a working web application in a couple of hours with just a few methods. However, hapi.js is a constantly evolving framework with its own terminology and best practices. From servers, connections, plugins, and routes to realms, extensions, and schemes, there are many ways the framework can make your life easier and your products better. But they can't help you if you don't know they exist.

As with any technology, moving from being a beginner to becoming an expert takes time. With this book, Matt has organized a largely undocumented and scattered knowledge into an easy-to-follow narrative that both beginners and experts would benefit from.

As you begin (or continue) your experience with the hapi.js framework, you will join an engaged and rich community of application developers working together on the best-in-class tools and patterns. These tools already power an impressive array of products and services. From payment services and online retailers to cloud and music providers, you are probably already using at least one hapi.js based application today. Tomorrow we might use something you created.

With this book in hand, you have taken your first step toward becoming a hapi.js expert. Whether you use that experience to build innovative products, create your own open source components to share with others, or join the hapi.js community as an active contributor, I hope you find working with the framework fun and empowering. It was built with love and dedication by dozens of open source developers looking to make application development better every day.

It's called hapi for a reason.

ERAN HAMMER
HAPI.JS CREATOR

preface

When I was 16, I was having a ball, secretly recording my friends' catchphrases and turning them into Flash soundboards. I was slicing and dicing garish designs in Photoshop and putting together websites with HTML tables in Dreamweaver.

I spent a long time away from the web, training to become an architect. But I always really missed the buzz of building websites, creating something from just my own code and having it appear on screen and do stuff, so when I finally graduated I made a U-turn—I decided I wanted to get back into the web.

But, boy had things changed! We had CSS, web standards, and JavaScript, and PHP was the hot server technology of the day. I voraciously learned everything I could about WordPress, Joomla, Zend, CodeIgniter, and all the big frameworks and content management systems of the time. I made some pretty decent sites and landed a job as a junior developer. The truth is that I had no idea what I was really doing. My understanding of what was really happening was minimal. These frameworks did *so* much magic for me . . . and were so big that I felt totally lost.

This all began to change when I discovered Node.js. I started by writing a few small scripts that did things like spin up a mini HTTP server and serve a file to a browser from my hard drive. No magic, no heavy framework, just a few lines of the same humble JavaScript I knew from the browser. I knew what every line of code was doing. The lack of distance between my code and the inner workings was much more satisfying to my mind.

Everything started to fall into place for me after that. All these heavy frameworks I'd been using in the past were just obscuring the simplicity and beauty that was at the heart of all this web stuff. I vowed never to use something again in my work again without understanding how it worked.

Naturally, like everyone in the Node world, I started to use Express to build my web apps. Express was a joy to use for the kind of small projects I was working on at the time. As I started to work on larger, more serious projects, though, I kept running into problems with Express. Things like scaling to many developers, several teams, and large apps were a pain with Express. I started to wonder if I'd been so naïve to think that I could build serious apps with Node, sticking together a few dependencies by myself. Perhaps those big, heavy frameworks like Zend and ASP.NET with all their classes and abstractions were like that because that's what's needed for complex projects?

About the time I found out about hapi. These guys over at Walmart had the audacity to power the mobile traffic of world's biggest retailer on Black Friday with . . . a Node.js app. They were a big team, they had a lot of users, and their systems were complex. It sounded like they'd shared the same kind of frustrations that I'd had with Express and built their own framework. The best thing was that they'd open sourced it all. Maybe you *could do* enterprise-scale apps successfully in Node. I had to check this out!

The transition to using hapi for me was quick and painless. I loved the simple configuration-driven APIs and the powerful plugin system. My code was cleaner than ever. What's more, it was fast and secure. I decided hapi was somewhere I wanted to stay. I started contributing to the project on GitHub, improving documentation and writing my own blog posts evangelizing hapi.

I found the community extremely helpful, quickly responding to issues and fixing bugs. The project was and still is in a very healthy state. The policy of only releasing code that is tested to 100% coverage shows their commitment to quality.

When Manning approached me about writing a hapi book, I was a little intimidated by the prospect but I knew I would say yes. hapi needed a book, and I wanted to be the one to write about it. I'm honored to be able to share with you everything that I've learned about hapi. After almost 18 months of writing, I've learned so much more about the framework than I originally knew, yet my opinions have stayed the same. I believe it has that perfect balance of rich features and unlimited customizability but also remains easy to get up and running and stays out of your way in complex apps.

acknowledgments

I feel slightly guilty that it's my name emblazoned on the cover of this book. In reality this is the culmination of work and effort by many, many people. I didn't quite get the scale of this until I embarked on this journey. Every author says this in their acknowledgments and it's not out of modesty or humility—it's a fact.

First of all, I would like to thank my developmental editor Susanna Kline, with whom I've exchanged many, many hours of conversation on Skype. We've talked about everything from the weather (a lot, I think) to flying planes, cowboys (she's originally from Texas), and occasionally this book. Without Susanna's infinite capacity for good advice and insight, this would have been a different and lesser book altogether. Thanks also to Cynthia Kane for helping out as my editor on the first chapter.

Big thanks to Michael Stephens who was my first contact at Manning. Thanks, Mike, for your encouragement in our first chats and believing that I could take on this project. The confidence you gave me early on kept me going right till the end.

Thanks to Corbin Collins whose comments have been invaluable to keeping the quality and accuracy high. Thanks to Nickie Buckner for his eagle-eye and technical review of the manuscript, catching some very subtle mistakes in the text. Also a big thanks to Elizabeth Martin for picking up on lots of issues during the final stages of production. The following reviewers gave generously of their time and improved this book: Davide Fiorentino lo Regio, Earl Bingham, Gavin Whyte, Gonzalo Huerta-Canepa, Jeff Smith, Jeroen Benckhuijsen, Jerry Tan, Jonathan Whittington, Margriet and Nikander Bruggeman, Matt Hernandez, Nick McGinness, Philippe Charrière, Ryan Pulling, Stephen Byrne, and Thomas Peklak.

Thanks also to all the hapi contributors for creating hapi in the first place and making it such a pleasure to work with and write about. Without your brilliant work, this book wouldn't exist. Special thanks to Eran Hammer for starting the hapi project and your cooperation with reading this manuscript and writing a great foreword for us.

Thanks to my girlfriend, Yi Ching, for always supporting me and really believing in my abilities, even when I didn't.

Thanks to my parents, Gail and David, for giving me the love, encouragement, and resources I need to find my own path in this world, even when it looked like there was no path at all.

about this book

hapi.js in Action is a guide to hapi for total beginners, designed to ease you in at first with some simple but functional examples. Later the text builds on your theoretical knowledge with in-depth coverage of all the important features within hapi and the various plugins and modules in its rich ecosystem. By the end of the book, you should be comfortable with building maintainable, fast, secure production-ready web applications.

Who should read this book

Anyone who has an interest in building websites, APIs, single-page application servers, or any kind of networked HTTP service in JavaScript should read this book. Whether you've already used Node.js in your career or are just getting started, this book gives you a 360-degree view of the hapi world.

Even if you're familiar with hapi, I've no doubt there's material in this book that will be new and useful to you. Experienced hapi developers can use this book as a reference—the examples of how to use some of the more esoteric features will be useful to you.

How this book is organized

This book is split into three parts and eleven chapters.
Part 1: First Steps doesn't dilly-dally around. This gets you writing code in no time.

- *Chapter 1: Introducing hapi* does exactly that. You'll see what hapi is useful for and some of the key building blocks used to create apps.

- *Chapter 2: Building an API* gathers some requirements and helps you build a fully functional hapi app.
- *Chapter 3: Building a website* looks at some of the more front end-oriented hapi features like serving static content.

Part 2: Expanding your toolbox is all about building upon your basic knowledge from part 1 with a deeper understanding of the key building blocks. Mixed in with that, I teach you a few extra superpowers like validation and caching.

- *Chapter 4: Route and handlers in depth* explores in-depth two of the key components in all hapi apps.
- *Chapter 5: Understanding requests and responses* looks at the lifecycle of a request and how to modify it.
- *Chapter 6: Validation with Joi* teaches you how to lock down your APIs against bad input data by using the expressive and powerful Joi library.
- *Chapter 7: Building modular applications with plugins* shows you both how to extend hapi and how to split your apps into small, maintainable packages called plugins.
- *Chapter 8: Cache me if you can* teaches you how to make use of both browser and server-side caching to supercharge your apps.

Part 3: Creating rock-solid apps is where we get very serious and make sure your apps are secure, well tested, and free of bugs.

- *Chapter 9: Authentication and security* looks at various ways of authenticating users and some common security exploit mitigation techniques.
- *Chapter 10: Testing with Lab, Code, and server.inject()* teaches you the art of writing simple yet powerful tests to probe every inch of your apps.
- *Chapter 11: Production and beyond* helps you get your app on the road to production and gives you some advice and techniques for when things go awry.

There are two appendices. *Appendix A: Getting started with Node.js and npm* provides supplemental information, including downloading and installing Node and npm. *Appendix B: npm packages used in this book* explains version numbers and, as the title reads, contains an explanation of packages used in the book

About the code

This book contains many examples of source code both in numbered listings and in line with normal text. In both cases, source code is formatted in a `fixed-width font` `like this` to make it stand out from ordinary text. Sometimes code is also in **`bold fixed-width font`** to highlight code that is particularly important or relevant to the surrounding discussion.

In many cases, the original source code has been reformatted; we've added line breaks and reworked indentation to accommodate the available page space in the book. In rare cases, even this was not enough, and listings include line-continuation markers ➥. Additionally, comments in the source code have often been removed from the listings when the code is described in the text. Code annotations accompany many of the listings, highlighting important concepts.

All the source code for the examples and listings in this book can be found on GitHub at https://github.com/mtharrison/hapi.js-in-action. The code is organized hierarchically to match the chapter and subheading format used in the book. This is designed to make it as easy as possible for you to look up the working code for whichever section on the book you're working through.

The code samples in this book and on GitHub are written to work only with Node.js versions above 4.0.0, as several ES2015 features are used, such as `let`, `const`, and arrow functions.

Author Online

The purchase of *hapi.js in Action* includes free access to a private forum run by Manning Publications where you can make comments about the book, ask technical questions, and receive help from the author and other users. To access and subscribe to the forum, go to www.manning.com/books/hapi-js-in-action. This page provides information on how to get on the forum once you're registered, what kind of help is available, and the rules of conduct in the forum.

Manning's commitment to our readers is to provide a venue where a meaningful dialogue between individual readers and between readers and the author can take place. It's not a commitment to any specific amount of participation on the part of the author, whose contribution to the book's forum remains voluntary (and unpaid). We suggest you try asking him some challenging questions, lest his interest stray!

The Author Online forum and the archives of previous discussions will be accessible from the publisher's website as long as the book is in print.

Other online resources

- There is full API documentation along with several tutorials on the official hapi website at http://hapijs.com/.
- For any questions about how to use hapi or about the project in general, you can post issues on the discuss repo at https://github.com/hapijs/discuss.
- There's the hapijs tag on Stack Overflow too at http://stackoverflow.com/questions/tagged/hapijs.

About the author

Matt Harrison is a freelance web developer and consultant. He's a core contributor to hapi.js, a frequent blogger, and an active member of the Node.js community. In a former life, he was an architect. He likes to eat ramen and drink Guinness, though never at the same time.

about the cover illustration

The figure on the cover of *hapi.js in Action* is captioned "Sauvage de la Nouvelle Zee-lande" (a savage of New Zealand). The illustration is taken from a collection of dress costumes from various countries by Jacques Grasset de Saint-Sauveur (1757–1810), titled Costumes de Différents Pays, published in France in 1797. Each illustration is finely drawn and colored by hand.

The rich variety of Grasset de Saint-Sauveur's collection reminds us vividly of how culturally apart the world's towns and regions were just 200 years ago. Isolated from each other, people spoke different dialects and languages. In the streets or in the countryside, it was easy to identify where they lived and what their trade or station in life was just by their dress.

The way we dress has changed since then, and the diversity by region, so rich at the time, has faded away. It's now hard to tell apart the inhabitants of different continents, let alone different towns, regions, or countries. Perhaps we have traded cultural diversity for a more varied personal life—certainly for a more varied and fast-paced techno-logical life.

At a time when it's hard to tell one computer book from another, Manning cele-brates the inventiveness and initiative of the computer business with book covers based on the rich diversity of regional life of two centuries ago, brought back to life by Grasset de Saint-Sauveur's pictures.

Part 1

First steps

This first part of *hapi.js in Action* is all about laying the foundations for the rest of the book and introducing many of the core concepts in hapi.

Chapter 1 introduces hapi and explains what it is and what it can do for you. You'll also see—at a very high level—how apps can be put together.

In chapter 2, you'll jump right in and build a JSON API using hapi. You'll discover how to translate business requirements into working code and you'll touch upon many key concepts including routing, handlers, authentication, and working with a database.

Chapter 3 focuses on the front end, building a simple website for the API you built in chapter 2. You'll also learn all about static file serving and how to organize your markup into layouts, partials, and views using templating languages.

Introducing hapi

This chapter covers

- What hapi.js is
- The problem hapi.js solves
- The philosophy behind hapi.js
- The architecture of hapi.js

If you've built web applications, in any language or platform, you'll know that what sometimes starts out as a simple vision can quickly become complicated. There are numerous things to consider when building a web app, including how to go about caching, validating, and authenticating. You also need to decide how to structure your code into files and directories in a way that makes sense.

The decisions one needs to make up front are often difficult and can become overwhelming, even for experienced developers. This is one of the reasons we use frameworks rather than start from scratch every time.

There are many frameworks for building web applications with Node.js. The more minimal ones like Express.js offer relatively little out of the box, with the aim of flexibility, and still require you to make a lot of decisions about infrastructure. Other, more focused API-only frameworks like Restify are limited in their scope of applications.

3

TERMINOLOGY   Sometimes I write hapi.js and other times just hapi. In general, when I use hapi.js, I'm referring to the project, ecosystem, or community as a whole. When I use hapi, I'm talking about the core hapi package. hapi is always written with a lowercase "h." I'll use Node.js and Node interchangeably, referring to the same thing. Likewise, I may use Express.js, or simply Express, to refer to the other popular Node framework.

hapi.js lets you have your cake and eat it too. Its configuration-centric approach means it is flexible and can be tweaked to your desire. But if you only want to get up and running writing your business logic, the framework makes sensible decisions for you.

hapi's plugin system and rich module ecosystem means there's usually a module available that's been created by the hapi.js core team to solve your problem, and you can be sure it's secure and has been tested extensively.

1.1   *What is hapi?*

hapi is an open source framework for building web applications with Node, created by the mobile web team at Walmart Labs. If you've ever used a Walmart mobile app or browsed the company's website from your phone, you've been using hapi and probably didn't know it.

hapi's most common use case is building web services such as JSON APIs, but it can also be used to build HTTP proxies and as the server component of single page apps or websites. Figure 1.1 shows a few examples of these applications. If you need to build software that speaks HTTP, hapi's going to make your life a lot easier.

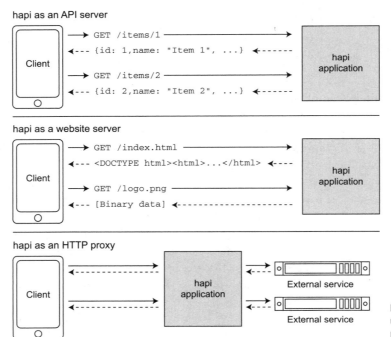

Figure 1.1   **hapi can be used to build all sorts of networked applications.**

Node already provides a way of building web servers with its built-in http module, but building anything serious using http alone is complicated and fraught. Thankfully, that's where frameworks like hapi step in.

To understand where hapi fits in, look at figure 1.2. You can see that hapi sits between Node and your own application's code, providing an abstraction layer for working with HTTP requests and responses.

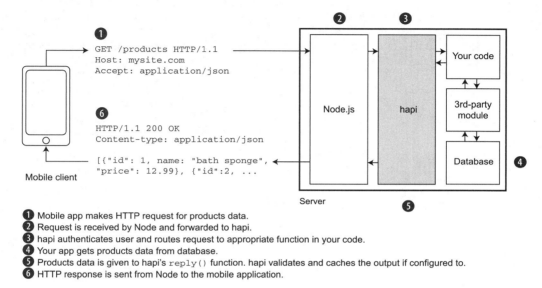

❶ Mobile app makes HTTP request for products data.
❷ Request is received by Node and forwarded to hapi.
❸ hapi authenticates user and routes request to appropriate function in your code.
❹ Your app gets products data from database.
❺ Products data is given to hapi's `reply()` function. hapi validates and caches the output if configured to.
❻ HTTP response is sent from Node to the mobile application.

Figure 1.2 Where hapi fits into an example application

If you've ever worked with Node, it's likely you've either used or are aware of projects with similar functionality to hapi. Express.js, Restify, Director, Loopback, and Sails are all examples of other frameworks that can be used to build web applications.

This section looks at what makes hapi different from these other frameworks and discusses the main building blocks that you'll need to know to be successful with hapi. It also considers the kinds of applications hapi is suited to and the kinds it isn't. Then it takes a look at the best places to go for help when you need it.

Node.js

Node is a platform for writing applications in JavaScript that run on a server. It's powered by the same, blazingly fast V8 JavaScript engine inside the Google Chrome browser. What Node offers on top of V8 is a set of APIs that you would expect to find in other languages used to write apps on the server side. There are APIs for working with TCP, HTTP, filesystems, and many more. These APIs are exposed as built-in JavaScript modules using the CommonJS module system.

(continued)

Because the http module in Node is fairly low level, building web applications from scratch every time can be tedious and involve writing a lot of boilerplate code. That's where frameworks like hapi find their place, offering a higher-level, more convenient API that suits many applications you might want to build.

If you come from a different server-side programming background like PHP or Ruby you may not be used to working so directly with HTTP requests in your application. You might be more familiar with using Apache or NGINX as a web server. Things are quite different in the Node world—the web server is actually part of your application, as highlighted here.

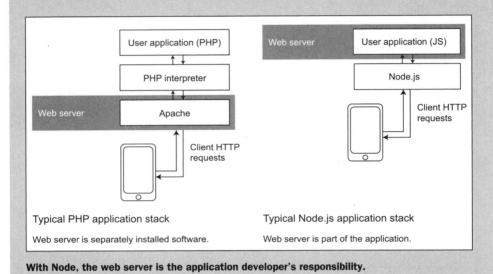

Typical PHP application stack

Web server is separately installed software.

Typical Node.js application stack

Web server is part of the application.

With Node, the web server is the application developer's responsibility.

1.1.1 What makes hapi special?

If there are so many other frameworks with similar features available, why should you choose hapi? The team members who developed hapi did so as a last resort, growing it out of their experience and frustration with other existing frameworks. As developers in charge of the mobile web infrastructure of Walmart, the world's biggest retailer, they might be considered a somewhat picky customer, but their collective effort has led to a framework that we can all benefit from.

Walmart has experienced doubling of mobile traffic and revenue year after year, as more people pick up their mobile devices to do their shopping, constantly presenting fresh challenges for its engineers. The mobile web team at Walmart Labs, led by senior architect Eran Hammer, chose Node as the platform to build out its future infrastructure. This decision was based on Node's efficient scaling model, the engineers' familiarity with the JavaScript language, and the healthy and vibrant community around Node.

Walmart's team of developers is geographically distributed. This meant they needed a framework that was highly modular and thus made it simple for many people to collaborate on large projects in a productive and safe manner.

The developers ran into problems using Express; the specific ordering of middleware and the possibility of conflicting routes in Express meant that an update by one team member could have adverse effects on another's work. The team solved this problem in hapi by creating the plugin architecture (discussed in depth in chapter 9) and a deterministic routing algorithm, which creates a more isolated and safer environment for each developer's work.

On Black Friday 2013, hapi.js was serving 100% of Walmart.com's mobile traffic. That was probably one of the biggest deployments of Node to date, and it was a great success, leading many other businesses to open their eyes to the potential of both Node and hapi for building enterprise-scale web services.

#nodebf

During Black Friday 2013, the Walmart Labs team shared their experiences with using Node in production with the world using the Twitter hashtag #nodebf. The team posted samples of code showing how parts of their infrastructure were put together. Some tweets showed graphs of flat lines for memory and CPU

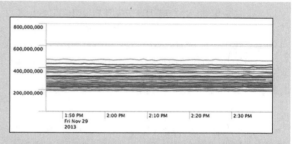

Flat memory charts from #nodebf (from @eranhammer on Twitter)

consumption throughout the day. These tweets caught the attention of everyone interested in learning how production-ready Node was for enterprise-scale applications.

IT'S NODE

Node is a great choice for building APIs. JSON has become the de facto standard encoding for transferring data over the web. Working with JSON in JavaScript is a natural choice. The low-level implementation details of Node's runtime let you scale your API to thousands of concurrent users without using expensive hardware.

STRONG FOCUS ON MODULARITY HELPS TEAMS

For me and many other users, modularity is perhaps the greatest strength of hapi. The plugin system lets you join isolated chunks of applications like Legos and have them run as a single application. These individual chunks or plugins can be developed, tested, and distributed (as npm packages) totally independently, maybe by different developers or teams in a large organization. Plugins also let developers create functionality to share with the entire open-source community. Chapter 7 covers hapi plugins.

CONFIGURATION-DRIVEN FEATURES

The hapi philosophy of configuration-over-code means that there aren't a lot of methods to remember to perform commonly required tasks, such as managing file uploads to a server. Instead complex behaviors are wrapped into simple configuration-driven APIs. You don't need to start learning all these configuration options until you need them because sensible defaults are always chosen for you by the framework.

IT'S REALLY QUICK TO GET STARTED

One of hapi's goals is to reduce the amount of boilerplate code that's required for writing Node apps. With hapi, you can get started writing your application's business logic in almost no time at all. This means you can try hapi quickly and decide if it's for you.

IT'S OPEN SOURCE

When you use an open source framework, the code is available online for the whole world to see and contribute to. If there's a feature missing, you can submit a feature request or even a pull request to add the functionality yourself. If you get stuck figuring out how a particular feature works, you can dive into the code and see for yourself or post an issue on GitHub.

IT'S BEEN BATTLE-TESTED IN PRODUCTION

Walmart runs all of its mobile website traffic and a number of other services with hapi.js. You don't get much higher-demand scenarios than that, and hapi has proven its worth. Other big names using hapi include PayPal, Yahoo!, Mozilla, and Disney.

1.1.2   *What kind of framework is hapi.js?*

There are highly opinionated frameworks that require you to do things in a predictable and consistent way, such as always naming your database tables according to a set format. *Opinionated frameworks* reduce the number of decisions required of you by making the decisions for you up front and then providing useful behavior without your needing to write code. With opinionated frameworks you usually trade convenience for flexibility.

An obvious example of an opinionated framework is Ruby on Rails, which makes several assumptions about the way you'll structure your application and the format of the data you'll work with. Defying these assumptions and doing something your own way can be anything from difficult to almost impossible.

Opinionated frameworks are often monolithic, offering a lot of features in a single library or package. When using a large framework like this, there's often little need for external software, provided you do everything the way the framework dictates.

At the other end of the spectrum are micro-frameworks that do very little and make almost no decisions for you; they're very thin wrappers around some native capability of the platform to offer convenient APIs for common tasks. A good example of such a framework is Express.js, a Node web framework. Express doesn't offer its own solution for organizing code, input validation, or working with databases. All those things are possible but require you to make decisions yourself or interface with other bits of software.

hapi treads a delicate line between offering rich functionality out of the box and staying unimposing. The core library of hapi provides only the essential features you will need when creating almost any modern web application. Anything additional, like authentication, is available but offered as a plugin module on npm. hapi apps are pieced together using these modules, along with your own code, through hapi's plugin system. Figure 1.3 compares these approaches.

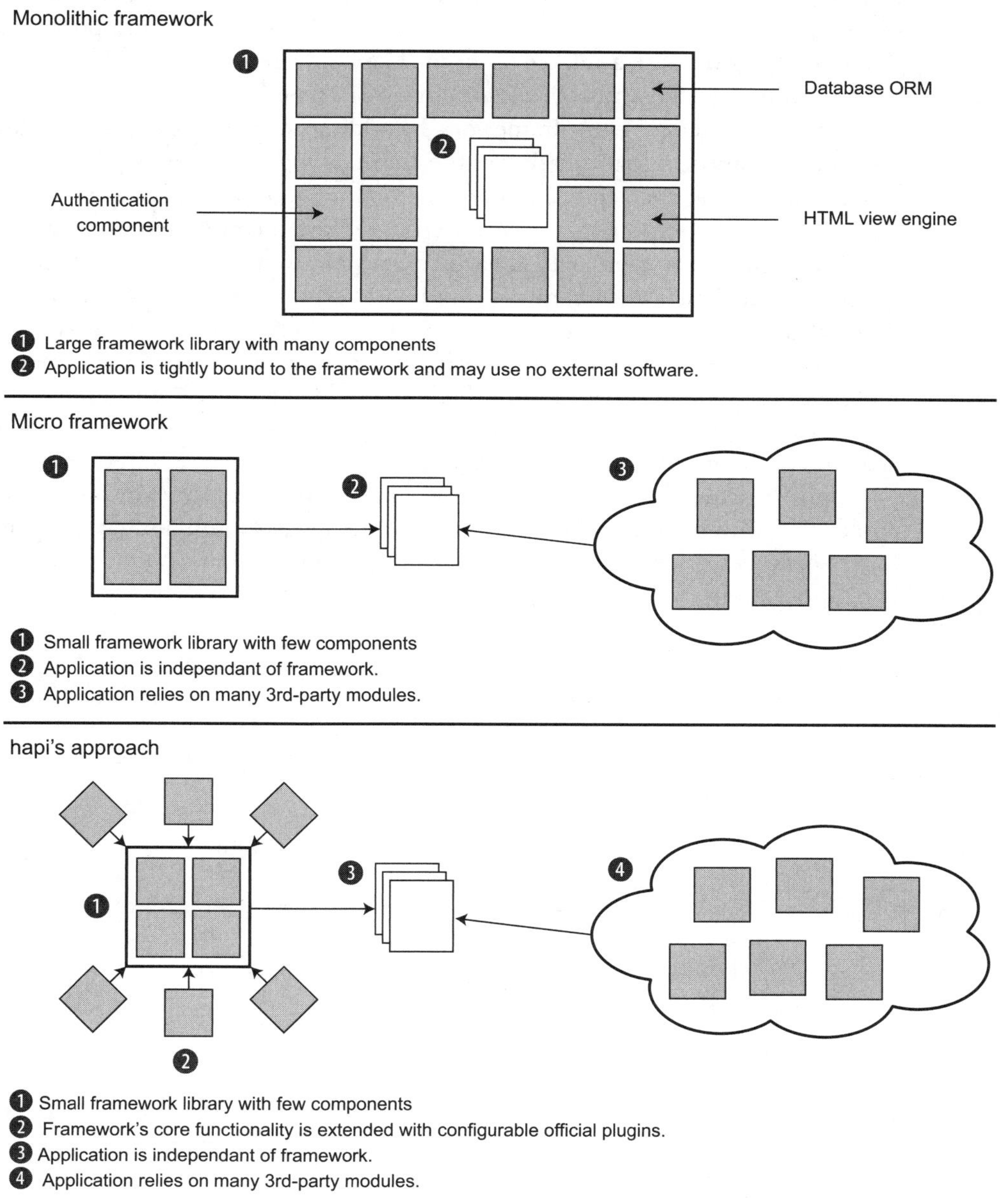

Figure 1.3 **Comparing different framework types**

hapi definitely has opinions, but it lets you have your own opinions too. When you want to do something different from the way hapi offers, you simply load a different plugin that works the way you want—or write your own plugin.

MODULAR, PLUGIN-BASED ARCHITECTURE

Building anything but the most simple apps with hapi usually involves some curation of modules to do the work for you. There's usually more than one popular module that does any given task available on npm. The hapi team has made this process easier by publishing a whole array of modules that work seamlessly with hapi.

As well as extending the framework by adding features like logging, plugins are used in hapi apps to logically divide the business logic of your application. Imagine we're building the back-end API of an e-commerce website. There are probably a few different logical components to that. We might have a component for payments, one for related products (similar to Amazon's Frequently Bought Together feature), and another for analytics. With hapi, we could build each of these as a separate plugin and then load those plugins into our server as needed. This can be a very powerful approach. If one particular component of our API needs scaling, we only need to load that plugin into more servers rather than duplicate our entire application. This modular approach also means that as our application grows, we can form dedicated teams around each component of our application, and they can work independently.

Figure 1.4 shows all of the elements that might be involved in building such an application with hapi. Don't worry if some of the terms are unfamiliar at the moment. Later sections explain them all in detail. Right now it's important to recognize that hapi applications are typically composed from many different parts.

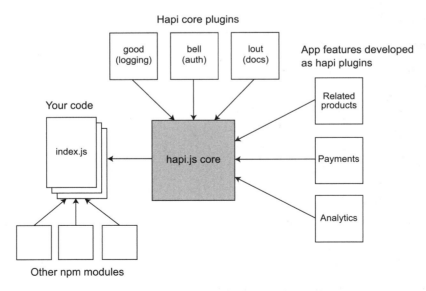

Figure 1.4 How an e-commerce API might be structured as a hapi app

CONFIGURATION-CENTRIC

The hapi framework's philosophy is that writing configuration is better than writing code. For this reason, much of the functionality in hapi is available through rich configuration options on a small set of available methods rather than through many available methods. What that means is you should end up writing less code to express your ideas than with other frameworks. And less code usually means an application that's easier to maintain and understand.

But why is configuration better than code? To illustrate the difference between a configuration-centric and code-centric API, imagine we're making a JavaScript library for an automated production line of jellybeans. An example of such a library that is code-centric or rich in methods might look like this code.

Listing 1.1   A jellybean library rich in methods

```
const Jellybean = require('jellybean');

const bean = new Jellybean.Bean();

bean.setName('Coffee');
bean.setColor('brown');
bean.setSpeckles(false);
bean.setHumanReaction('yuck!');
```

The code in the previous listing is quite verbose—five method calls on the bean object to create the jellybean. This next listing shows an alternate API that's more configuration-oriented.

Listing 1.2   A jellybean library rich in configuration options

```
const Jellybean = require('jellybean');

const options = {
    name: 'Tutti Frutti',
    color: 'mixed',
    speckles: true,
    humanReaction: 'yum!'
};

const bean = new Jellybean.Bean(options);
```

This example doesn't require any method calls to create the `jellybean` object. Instead the constructor accepts a configuration object with all the options. The second example is more flexible because it separates the configuration from the code.

We could place all the configurations of jellybeans in a separate file and include them. If we wanted to change the configurations later, we wouldn't need to change any code—we could simply update the config.

Many methods in hapi work on the same principle. You will find that this approach helps you write cleaner code and more maintainable applications.

Next, I introduce the main pieces of the hapi jigsaw puzzle that you'll need to know about to start building applications.

1.2   *The building blocks of hapi*

hapi is a full-featured framework, and there will be parts of it that you'll probably never use in your applications. A few key components, however, underpin every single hapi app. This section introduces you to servers, connections, routes, handlers, and plugins, illustrated in figure 1.5.

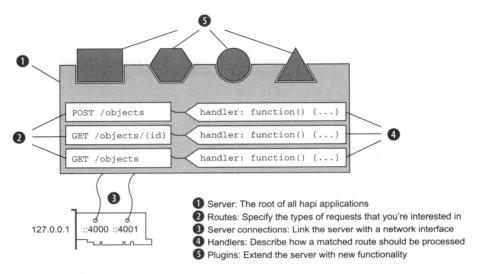

Figure 1.5   The building blocks of hapi

Every request your application receives will go through a lifecycle that interacts with these elements to form a response that is sent back to the client. Figure 1.6 shows a basic overview of this process. Once you grasp what these central building blocks are all about, you'll understand the overall process that you'll follow with hapi, no matter what you're building.

Let's start looking at code now. If you want to run this code, you'll need to make sure you've installed Node and npm. If you need help with that first, flip to appendix A. Please come back, though!

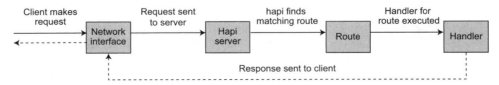

Figure 1.6   How the building blocks fit together

Let's install hapi now. Run `npm install hapi@13` to install hapi into your home directory. This isn't the ideal approach, but it's a quick way to get started. You'll learn how to better manage dependencies soon by making them local to a project.

Listing 1.3   A simple hapi app that uses all the building blocks

```
const Hapi = require('hapi');

const server = new Hapi.Server();           ← Create a server
server.connection({ port: 4000 });          ← Create a connection from
                                               the server to port 4000

server.route({
    method: 'GET',                          Create a route that responds
    path: '/en',                            to GET requests to /en
    handler: function (request, reply) {

        reply('Hello!');                    Define a handler
    }                                       for the route
});

const plugin = function (server, options, next) {

    server.route({
        method: 'GET',
        path: '/cn',
        handler: function (request, reply) {

            reply(' 你好 !');               Define a plugin, which
        }                                   internally creates
    });                                     another route

    next();
};

plugin.attributes = {
    name: 'My plugin'
};

server.register(plugin, (err) => {

    if (err) {                              Load the plugin
        throw err;                          into the server
    }

    server.start((err) => {                 ← Start the
                                               server
        if (err) {
            throw err;
        }
        console.log('Server running at:', server.info.uri);
    });
});
```

The previous listing is a code sample for a simple hapi app that uses all the building blocks. By the end of this section, you should understand what each part does, even if you don't yet understand all the code.

> **NOTE**   This book assumes you are running a version of Node greater than 4.0.0. The version of hapi that this book is written for relies on several ES2015 features such as let, const, and arrow functions, which aren't available in earlier versions.

1.2.1   Servers

Everything starts with a *server*, the container for your hapi application. Every other object in this list is created or used in the context of a server. A hapi server doesn't directly listen on a network port, instead you make *connections* from your server so you can speak to the outside world.

1.2.2   Connections

You use connections to attach a hapi server to a network interface so it can start accepting incoming requests. By using connections, you can have a single hapi server listen on multiple ports, which can be useful for applications that use TLS.

1.2.3   Routes

Routes in hapi are your way of telling the framework that you're interested in certain types of requests. You create a route with a set of options, including the HTTP verb (such as GET, POST, and PATCH) and path (for example /about) that you want to respond to, and add it to a server.

When a new request arrives at your server, hapi will attempt to find a route that matches the request. If it successfully pairs the request with one of your routes, it will look to your route *handler* for how to handle the request.

1.2.4   Handlers

Every time you create a route, you will also specify a handler. *Handlers* are the way you tell hapi how it should respond to an HTTP request. A handler can take several forms. The most flexible handler is defined as a JavaScript function with access to a request object and a reply interface. You can examine the request object to get details about the request. You can then use the reply interface to respond to the request however you want. For example, you might respond with an image file or a JSON response to an API request.

Using hapi plugins, you can add new handler types with behavior pre-programmed, so you don't need to write any code to use them. An example is the directory handler from the Inert plugin:

> **NPM PACKAGE**   inert v3 (http://npmjs.com/package/inert)

By using the directory handler, you can serve static files from a directory without needing to write any code. You'll be seeing how that works in chapter 3.

1.2.5 Plugins

Plugins are a way of extending servers with new functionality. They can extend a server with some global utility, such as logging all requests or adding caching to responses. Many plugins are available as npm packages that deal with things like authentication and logging, written by the hapi core team and community.

It's also possible to create your own plugins that divide your application into smaller logical chunks that are easier to maintain or even replace or remove altogether at a later date. Chapter 6 is devoted to looking at how you can use plugins in this way.

1.3 When you should (and shouldn't) use hapi

hapi is a flexible framework and can be used to build many kinds of applications, although some application types are a better fit than others. This section discusses some of the more common use cases for hapi and also the cases where it might not be the best choice for you.

1.3.1 When you should use hapi

Although I've already discussed APIs, hapi isn't limited to just this use case. It has support for functionality you might be used to from more general web application frameworks too, like HTML template rendering and static file serving.

It also has some more general networking features like HTTP request proxying that expand its reach even further. This section looks at some application types that hapi is suited to.

JSON APIS

JSON APIs are the classic use case for hapi. hapi's extensive feature set—including routing, input and output validation, authentication, caching, and automatic documentation—makes building APIs with hapi a pleasurable experience. You can build APIs that serve all kinds of clients, such as mobile applications, single-page apps, or even other services.

STATIC OR DATABASE-DRIVEN WEBSITES

hapi works with several HTML-templating languages like Handlebars and Jade so you can easily create HTML documents from dynamic data. You can find packages on npm for working with practically any database you can name. hapi also makes it simple to deploy apps with cookie-based authentication and sessions to maintain state between page requests.

SINGLE-PAGE APPLICATIONS

You can use hapi with front-end frameworks like Backbone, React, and AngularJS to create impressive single-page applications (SPAs). SPAs are usually constructed from modular page components. Using hapi, you can easily serve chunks of HTML or JSON as a response to AJAX requests initiated by user actions in the app.

PROXIES

hapi is also a good choice for building proxies and reverse proxies. A hapi plugin named h2o2 provides a handler type for proxying HTTP requests to other endpoints. Walmart uses hapi in this way to forward requests from its mobile API to a number of legacy Java apps. Using this approach, its developers can transparently replace these services with others when their useful lifetime comes to an end.

1.3.2 When you shouldn't use hapi

hapi is great for building HTTP applications, and because it's built on Node, it's super-fast at doing I/O and network operations. The same inappropriate use cases for Node are inherited by hapi, though. Because your JavaScript code in a Node app runs in only a single OS thread, it's not the right choice for CPU-intensive applications, so it wouldn't make sense to write things like video encoders, AI software, or 3D-rendering applications with hapi. There's nothing stopping you from writing such an application in a more suitable environment like C++, though, and using hapi as a web front end to those systems, or from using native modules for node.js.

Although originally designed to respond only to standard HTTP requests, the nes plugin has extended hapi with real-time capabilities via layering websocket communication over the hapi routing system. This is designed for what are often called *soft real-time applications*, where timing isn't absolutely critical. So it's perfect for things like chat applications, real-time feeds, and social apps. Using hapi or Node for hard real-time applications like avionics, nuclear power, or high-frequency financial trading systems wouldn't be recommended.

1.4 How it works

Now that I've covered some of the theory and background of hapi, let's look at how it works. The first step in building any hapi.js application is to create a server and make a connection to that server.

1.4.1 Installing hapi

Create and navigate to a directory anywhere on your machine to store this example. I will place mine in a directory under my home directory (~) called hapi-example:

```
mkdir ~/hapi-example && cd ~/hapi-example
```

Next let's create a package.json file in our project directory. npm uses this file to keep track of your project's dependencies. npm can create this file for you by running:

```
npm init
```

You can accept all the defaults that npm suggests, and once you have, npm will create the package.json file for you. Next you need to install hapi itself. In this book, you'll be working with hapi version 13. You can install this by typing the following into your console:

```
npm install --save hapi@13
```

This will create a node_modules directory under your current directory and download and place hapi inside there. It will also update the package.json file to reference hapi as a dependency of your project.

NPM PACKAGE hapi v13 (http://npmjs.com/package/hapi)

The final part of this setup is to create a JavaScript file to hold the code for the example. I will follow the convention of naming my file index.js.

If you've followed these steps, you should be ready to start writing code.

1.4.2 Creating a server

A *server* is an object in hapi that can receive and route requests. Before it can accept new requests it must be *connected* to at least one network socket using a connection.

HAPI API server.connection([options]) (http://hapijs.com/api#server connectionoptions)

The following listing creates a server that is connected to port 4000.

Listing 1.4 Creating a hapi server

```
const Hapi = require('hapi');                          Load hapi
                                                       module
const server = new Hapi.Server();       Connect server
server.connection({ port: 4000 });      to port 4000
```

Create a hapi server object → (points to const server line)

For this server to do something useful, I must add a route. A route pairs a path and an HTTP verb, such as GET or POST, with some desired output behavior. You tell hapi what the desired behavior for the route is using a handler.

1.4.3 Adding routes

The code in listing 1.5 adds two routes to the server using the server.route() method.

HAPI API server.route(options) (http://hapijs.com/api#serverrouteoptions)

The first route responds to GET requests to the path / with the text "Hello World!". The second route responds to GET requests for the path /json with a JSON response.

Listing 1.5 Adding routes to the server

```
server.route([{                              Call server.route() with an array
    method: 'GET',                           of route configuration objects
    path: '/',
    handler: function (request, reply) {     Respond to requests
                                             that match the / path
        reply('Hello World!');       Respond with a plain
    }                                text response
```

Respond to GET requests → (points to method: 'GET')

Define a handler function that runs for matching requests → (points to handler function)

```
}, {
    method: 'GET',
    path: '/json',
    handler: function (request, reply) {

        reply({ hello: 'World' });        ◁─┐ Respond with a
    }                                        │ JSON response
}]);
```

Note that in the listing, my two routes call the `reply()` function with different data types.

HAPI API `reply()` (http://hapijs.com/api#reply-interface)

The first route calls `reply()` with a string and the second with an object. hapi is smart enough to know that I want the first case to be a response type of `text/plain` and the second case to be a response type of `application/json` and will set the response `Content-type` headers automatically. This is an example of hapi making sensible assumptions for you.

1.4.4 *Registering a plugin*

Let's imagine now that I want to log details of every single request that is received by the server to the console. I can use the Good plugin for this. I need to register this plugin with the server using the `server.register()` method.

HAPI API `server.register(plugins, [options], [callback])` (http://hapijs.com/api#serverregisterplugins)

I also need to choose a *reporter* and specify which event types I want to log.

NPM PACKAGE `good` v6 (http://npmjs.com/package/good)

Good is a hapi plugin for monitoring and reporting on events that occur in your applications. There are several reporters available for Good, including console, HTTP, and UDP. You can also create your own reporters.

In this case, I will use the console reporter GoodConsole.

NPM PACKAGE `good-console` v5 (http://npmjs.com/package/good-console)

I only want to report on the `request` event type. My example will rely on both the `good` and the `good-console` npm packages, so I must install them first:

```
npm install --save good@6 good-console@5
```

Before a server can start listening for requests, you need to tell it to start. You do this with the `server.start()` method.

Listing 1.6 Registering a plugin and starting the server

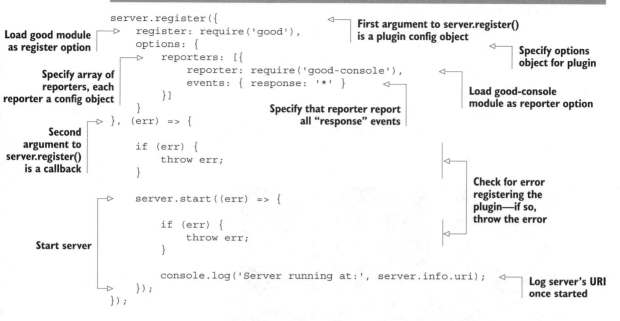

```
server.register({
    register: require('good'),
    options: {
        reporters: [{
            reporter: require('good-console'),
            events: { response: '*' }
        }]
    }
}, (err) => {

    if (err) {
        throw err;
    }

    server.start((err) => {

        if (err) {
            throw err;
        }

        console.log('Server running at:', server.info.uri);
    });
});
```

Load good module as register option

Specify array of reporters, each reporter a config object

Second argument to server.register() is a callback

Start server

First argument to server.register() is a plugin config object

Specify options object for plugin

Load good-console module as reporter option

Specify that reporter report all "response" events

Check for error registering the plugin—if so, throw the error

Log server's URI once started

Next, let's try to run this sample program to see what it does.

1.4.5 Taking it for a spin

You can start this application by running the index.js script with the Node program:

```
node index.js
```

Open a browser and view the page at http://localhost:4000/. You should see a response from hapi in your browser. Then load the page at http://localhost:4000/json.

Every time a request is made, you should also see a log in the console with some information about the request:

```
141226/162232.034, [response], http://localhost:4000: get / {} 200 (3ms)
141226/162235.019, [response], http://localhost:4000: get /json {} 200 (2ms)
```

You can stop the server by pressing Ctrl-C. In this very basic example, you've seen how to create a server, add routes, define simple handlers, and register and use plugins to extend functionality.

1.5 Getting help

This book tries to be as comprehensive as possible, but for the sake of keeping your interest and setting a good pace, it won't be examining in great detail every single feature of hapi.js. You're likely going to run into problems or have questions that aren't answered here. When this happens it's important that you know the right places to go for help.

1.5.1   *hapi.js website*

The hapi.js website (http://hapijs.com) should be your first port of call for documentation on hapi's features and APIs. It offers a number of basic tutorials along with full API documentation. If you want to know how a certain method works, or what parameters it should take, this is the place to look.

1.5.2   *Make Me hapi*

The hapi core contributors have created an interactive tutorial called Make Me hapi. This is a self-guided tour of hapi and it's a lot of fun to work through. Figure 1.7 shows its console interface.

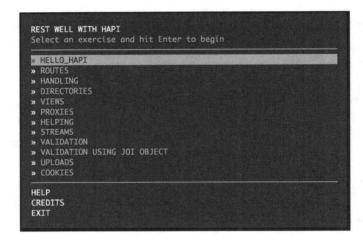

Figure 1.7   The console interface for Make Me hapi

I recommend every reader work through Make Me hapi at some point. To install, run `npm install -g makemehapi` in your terminal. Once downloaded, you can start it by running `makemehapi`.

1.5.3   *GitHub*

If you think you've found an issue or bug with hapi, you should place an issue on the GitHub project (https://github.com/hapijs/hapi/issues). You can also make issues on GitHub for questions you may have that aren't answered in its documentation.

1.5.4   *IRC*

hapi.js has an IRC room where you can direct support queries. The room name is #hapi on irc.freenode.net. If you're not familiar with IRC, it's a chat room where developers and users of software hang out and discuss the framework and help with support issues. A quick way to connect to the IRC room is by using a web interface. To join the hapi room, follow this link: http://webchat.freenode.net/?channels=hapi.

1.5.5 *Stack Overflow*

If you have a question that has a real answer and isn't opinion-based, you can post your question on Stack Overflow under the *hapijs* tag.

1.5.6 *Read the code!*

One of the benefits of using an open source framework is that all the code is available online for you to study yourself. If you're feeling brave, reading the actual source code can be the most useful and quickest way to get answers about how things really work in the framework.

Documentation can sometimes be vague or inexact, but the code never lies. The hapi.js modules are well written and composed from small, easy-to-understand parts, so they should be fairly easy to follow along with.

Some of the discussion in this chapter has been a little abstract, but in the next chapter you're going to build a small, real hapi application step-by-step.

1.6 Summary

- hapi.js is a web application framework that helps you build websites, APIs, or just about any kind of HTTP service.
- The main building blocks of hapi apps are servers, connections, routes, handlers, and plugins.
- hapi encourages you to build your apps in a modular way by making use of its powerful plugin system and npm.
- The hapi philosophy is configuration over code.

Building an API

You saw in chapter 1 that hapi apps are constructed by working with servers, routes, handlers, plugins, and your own business logic. In this chapter, you'll see how those pieces come together. First I introduce a fictional brief for an API project that I'm going to build. Next I figure out the technical requirements and plan the API endpoints. Then I move on to implementing this in hapi step-by-step.

I won't be diving too deeply into any single component of hapi yet. Instead, I'm going to take a more high-level approach, giving you the bigger picture of how apps in hapi are built.

2.1   Designing the API

This section introduces a fictional HTTP API project that will be the focus of this chapter. First I gather some requirements for the API. Once it's clear how the API should work, I design the endpoints through which clients can access the API.

2.1.1 Your mission, should you choose to accept it

Hey there, Developer. I've just gotten word that I've been hired to work on a new project. Our client Mrs. Bigbucks has an idea for a startup called DinDin. She says it's going to be the next Pinterest and wants us to build a prototype for the API. So far, all I've heard is the elevator pitch: DinDin is a social network for food. Users can create a profile and upload their own recipes. Users can also search for recipes that match their favorite ingredients. When a user likes a recipe they can award a star. Collect enough stars and amateur chefs can become mini-celebs!

2.1.2 Gathering requirements

My client has interesting ideas, but if I'm going to build a prototype, I need to collect more solid requirements. I've decided to use the method of writing user stories to define the functionality. User stories are short scenarios that take the following form:

As a/an _____ I want _____ so that _____.

After a few hours of brainstorming, my client and I produce the user stories shown in figure 2.1.

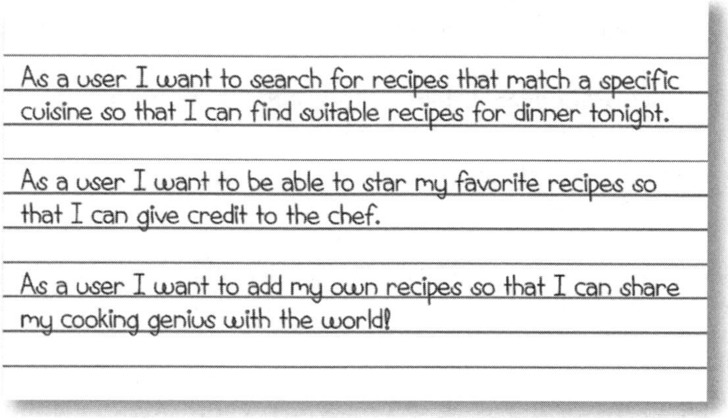

As a user I want to search for recipes that match a specific cuisine so that I can find suitable recipes for dinner tonight.

As a user I want to be able to star my favorite recipes so that I can give credit to the chef.

As a user I want to add my own recipes so that I can share my cooking genius with the world!

Figure 2.1   The user stories that I've collected from the customer. These are the requirements for the DinDin application.

Now that I have an idea of the requirements of the prototype, I need to design the API.

2.1.3 Designing the API endpoints

It's very common when developing any system to first design the public-facing interface that you will offer to users. When developing a website, this might be the visual

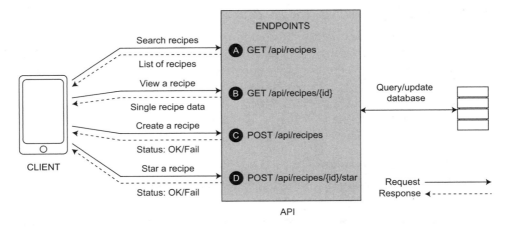

Figure 2.2   A high-level overview of the API

design of the UI. With an API, the interface is the HTTP endpoints that will be exposed—this is your contract with the consumer of the API, illustrated in figure 2.2. Each endpoint has a few important properties associated with it, namely the HTTP method used, the URI path, the parameters it can accept, and the structure of the response.

Based on the user stories, I decide that the four endpoints shown in figure 2.2 will suffice. I'll talk a bit more about each of these later. First I need to prepare my environment to start building the prototype.

2.2   Getting set up

Before I can write any code, I need to set up a couple of things. First I need a directory to contain the project.

2.2.1   A directory to work in

All code for the API will live within a project directory. There are no naming or location restrictions with hapi apps—you call your directory whatever you like and keep it anywhere you like. I'll be calling my project directory dindin, and my main file will be named index.js.

Because I'm going to be using npm to manage my dependencies, I also create a package.json file.

Listing 2.1   package.json

```
{
 "name": "dindin",
 "version": "1.0.0",
 "description": "A social network for food",
 "main": "index.js",
```

```
"author": "Matt Harrison",
"private": true,
"license": "BSD-3-Clause"
}
```

Now it's time to install hapi. To install hapi with npm, I run the following command in the root of the project:

```
npm install --save hapi@13
```

After also creating an index.js file, I have a directory structure that looks like the following:

```
dindin
├── index.js
├── node_modules
│   └── hapi
│       └── ...
└── package.json
```

When building an API it's useful to have sample data available that's as close as possible to the real thing. So before I write any code, I'm going to create a simple SQLite database with some sample data.

2.2.2 Preparing a database and sample data

There are modules on npm for working with practically every database system available. I expect many readers will be familiar with both SQLite and SQL. So to keep things simple, that's what I'll be using as a datastore for this project. Later chapters look at other databases and key-value stores and discuss how they can be used with hapi.

I've modeled the DinDin API around two database tables: recipes and users. The structure and relationship of the database tables are show in figure 2.3.

If you're following along, you can use the database bundled with the supplied code for this book on GitHub (http://mng.bz/193e). Place the database file called dindin.sqlite at the root of your project directory, beside the index.js file.

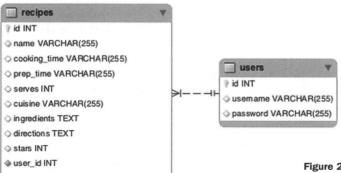

Figure 2.3   The entity relationship diagram for the dindin SQLite database

2.2.3 *The sqlite3 node module*

To work with the SQLite database, I'll be using the sqlite3 node module.

NPM PACKAGE   `sqlite3 v3 (http://npmjs.com/package/sqlite3)`

I can download and add sqlite3 to the app's dependencies in the same way I did with hapi:

```
npm install --save sqlite3@3
```

I can now load the sqlite3 module and connect to the database.

Listing 2.2   Creating a connection to SQLite using sqlite3

```
const Sqlite3 = require('sqlite3');
const db = new Sqlite3.Database('./dindin.sqlite');   ⟵  Pass the database filename
                                                          to the constructor
```

The database object returned by sqlite3 has a number of methods for querying and updating the SQLite database. I'll look at a couple of simple examples now.

The `db.all()` method, used for fetching multiple records, accepts two arguments: the SQL query you wish to run, as a string, and a callback to be executed once the query has finished. The callback will be called with two arguments: an error (or `null` if no error occurred) and an array of found records. This pattern of returning an error as the first parameter to a callback function is common in Node, and you'll see it come up many times in this book, so become familiar with it now.

The following listing contains a code sample that fetches all recipes from the recipes table and logs their name to the console.

Listing 2.3   Querying a database for all recipes and printing each recipe's name

```
db.all('SELECT * FROM recipes', (err, results) => {

    if (err) {
        throw err;                            If there was an error running the
    }                                         query, throw the error now.

    for (let i = 0; i < results.length; ++i) {
        console.log(results[i].name);         Loop through each result
    }                                         and log name of recipe
});
```

If I want to include data that has come from user input in the SQL query, I can't simply concatenate this with the query using the + operator. That would leave the API open to an SQL injection attack. `db.all()` takes an additional, optional middle argument, which is an array of values to be sanitized and interpolated into the query. A ? character is placed in the query to denote where these values should be placed in the final query. Here is an example that uses this approach to search for recipes matching a cuisine.

Listing 2.4 Using placeholders to safely include variables in a SQL query

```
db.all('SELECT * FROM recipes WHERE cuisine = ?',
    ['American'],
    (err, results) => {

    if (err) {
        throw err;
    }

    ...
```

← Include placeholder symbol in SQL query

← Include array of parameters to be bound to query

So, I've designed the API, I have a place to keep my project, a database, and some sample data. I can write a few simple SQL queries for SQLite too. I think it's time to start building this thing!

2.3 Retrieving and searching recipes

This section implements the first two endpoints identified in section 2.1: endpoint A for searching recipes and retrieving all recipes and endpoint B for retrieving a single recipe. To create an endpoint in hapi, you need to define a route using the `server.route()` method. Remember, in chapter 1 we said that hapi matches requests with a route and then runs a handler associated with the route.

2.3.1 Introducing server.route()

The `server.route()` method can take either an object to create a single route or an array of objects to create multiple routes.

> **HAPI API** `server.route(options)` (http://hapijs.com/api#serverrouteoptions)

The `options` object passed to `server.route()` is a configuration object, which is like a list of the various bits of information that hapi needs to know to set up the route. Simple examples are shown in figure 2.4.

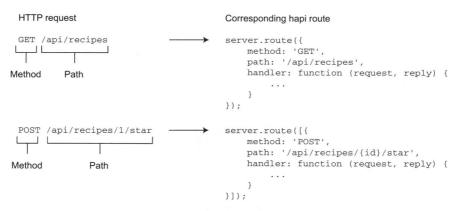

Figure 2.4 Simple HTTP requests and their corresponding hapi routes

There are three required options, method, path, and handler, that you'll need for every route you ever create. Many other options are also available, and they're often specific to one feature of hapi, such as documentation, validation, or authentication. You'll see many options used throughout the book. Table 2.1 shows a full list of all the options used in this chapter.

Table 2.1 Route configuration options used in this chapter

Option	Type	Purpose
method	string/array	HTTP verb(s) to match
path	string	URI path to match
handler	function/object	Defines what should happen for a matching route; for example, how to build a response
config	object	Further optional configuration for the route
config.auth	string	Authentication strategy to use on a matched request

The handler function is the way you tell hapi how it should behave when it receives a request that matches the route. Route handling is examined in detail in chapter 4, but it's such an important matter, it's worth a quick discussion before moving on.

2.3.2 *Route handlers*

A route handler can be a basic JavaScript function that has two parameters: request and reply:

```
function (request, reply) {}
```

If you've ever used the built-in http module in Node, you'll recognize this pattern. The request and reply objects in hapi are much more powerful than the req and res objects you'll see in plain Node.

THE REQUEST OBJECT

The request object is what you might imagine it to be—an object containing data about the HTTP request. Even though the request object does have some methods that you can call on it, in most routes, you'll only be reading data from it.

   HAPI API   request object (http://hapijs.com/api#request-object)

Table 2.2 shows common properties on request that you may use in your routes.

Table 2.2 Some of the properties available on request

Properties	Type	Purpose
server	object	The hapi server for this request
query	object	Parsed query string parameters

Table 2.2 Some of the properties available on request

Properties	Type	Purpose
headers	object	A key-value representation of all the request headers; for example `{'content-type': 'text/plain'}`
params	object	Parsed URI path `params`
auth	object	Information about the authentication method used in the request and the user's credentials

The request object contains all the headers sent by the client, information about any authentication method used, parsed query string parameters, and a lot more. Here's an example of a route that logs the value of the request's Host header on each request:

```
server.route({
    method: 'GET',
    path: '/log-host',
    handler: function (request, reply) {

        console.log(request.headers.host);
        reply();
    }
});
```

THE REPLY INTERFACE

The reply interface is used for responding to the client with some data. In its simplest form it can be used as a function, provided directly with the data to respond with.

> **HAPI API**   reply interface (http://hapijs.com/api#reply-interface)

hapi will figure out how to respond, depending on the type of data you provide. If you pass a string to reply(), hapi will respond with a content-type: text/html header and will send the string as the body of the response. If you pass a JavaScript object to reply(), hapi will respond with content-type: application/json. You'll see some other ways of using reply later in the book.

Here's an example of a route that responds with a JSON response:

```
server.route({
    method: 'GET',
    path: '/who',
    handler: function (request, reply) {

        reply({
            name: 'Matt',
            age: 30,
            human: true
        });
    }
});
```

2.3.3 *Endpoint A: retrieving all recipes*

To search recipes with the API, a user will call endpoint A, appending an optional search parameter to the query string. For example:

```
GET /api/recipes?cuisine=Irish
```

The API will respond with a JSON array of all found recipes that match the search query, as shown in figure 2.5.

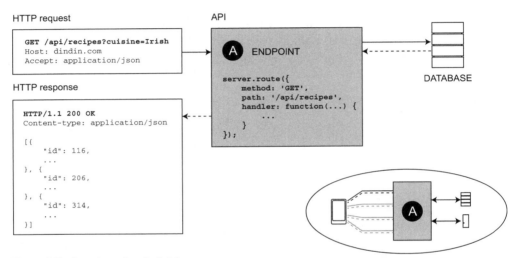

Figure 2.5   Overview of endpoint A

If endpoint A is called without any search parameters, the API simply returns all the recipes in the database. The following listing uses the `server.route()` method to implement this simple case first.

Listing 2.5   index.js: the route for endpoint A

```
'use strict';

const Hapi = require('hapi');                           ← Load the hapi module
const Sqlite3 = require('sqlite3');    ← Load the sqlite3 module

const db = new Sqlite3.Database('./dindin.sqlite');     ← Create database connection

const server = new Hapi.Server();
server.connection({ port: 4000 });    ← Create a hapi server bound to port 4000

server.route([{                        ← Call server.route() method to add new route to server
    method: 'GET',
    path: '/api/recipes',
    handler: function (request, reply) {   ← Respond to GET requests to /api/recipes
```

Send query
to database

```
db.all('SELECT * FROM recipes', (err, results) => {

    if (err) {
        throw err;
    }

    reply(results);
});
}
}]);
```

If error occurred,
throw the error

Respond with results
object as JSON

```
server.start(() => {

    console.log('Server listening at:', server.info.uri);
});
```

Start the server

The server can now be started by running the following command in the terminal:

```
node index.js
```

When I visit http://localhost:4000/api/recipes in a browser, I see the API is successfully responding with all recipes, as shown in figure 2.6.

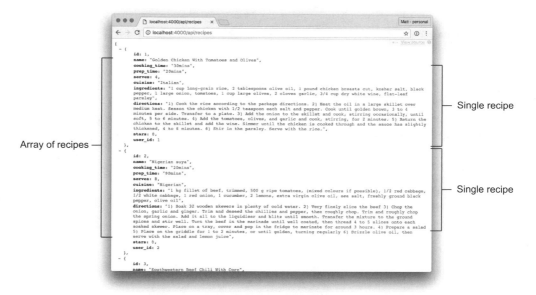

Array of recipes

Single recipe

Single recipe

Figure 2.6   Response to endpoint A with no search parameters

NOTE I recommend using a browser plugin that prettifies the output of JSON. In the screenshots in this book, I'm using the JSONView plugin for Google Chrome.

2.3.4   *Endpoint A: searching recipes*

I need to extend the route created previously to allow an optional query string parameter cuisine and then use that parameter's value to search for matching recipes.

hapi automatically parses the URI for query string parameters and converts the query string keys and values into a JavaScript object stored in request.query so they can be accessed easily inside handler functions, as shown in figure 2.7.

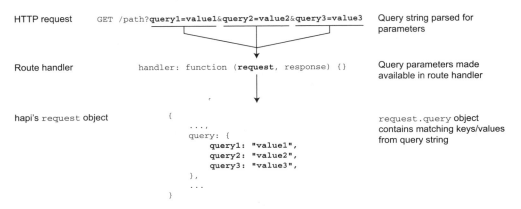

Figure 2.7   hapi parses query parameters into the request.query **object**

Using this knowledge, I can now extend the route for endpoint A to search recipes, when a cuisine parameter is present, for only recipes for that cuisine. For example, you could search for Italian recipes by requesting http://localhost:4000/api/recipes?cuisine=Italian.

Listing 2.6   index.js: the extended route for endpoint A

```
...

server.route([{
    method: 'GET',
    path: '/api/recipes',
    handler: function (request, reply) {

        let sql = 'SELECT * FROM recipes';          Create base
        const params = [];                          SQL string.
                                                    Define empty array
                                                    of SQL params.
        if (request.query.cuisine) {
            sql += ' WHERE cuisine = ?';            Extend SQL query with
            params.push(request.query.cuisine);     WHERE clause if cuisine
        }                                           query parameter is present.
Add value of cuisine
query parameter to
SQL params.
        db.all(sql, params, (err, results) => {
```

```
        if (err) {
            throw err;
        }

        reply(results);
    });
  }
}]);
```

2.3.5 *Endpoint B: retrieving a single recipe*

To retrieve a single recipe using the API, a user will call endpoint B, providing the ID of the recipe in the URI path. For example:

```
GET /api/recipes/2
```

The API will respond with a JSON object representation of that recipe, as shown in figure 2.8.

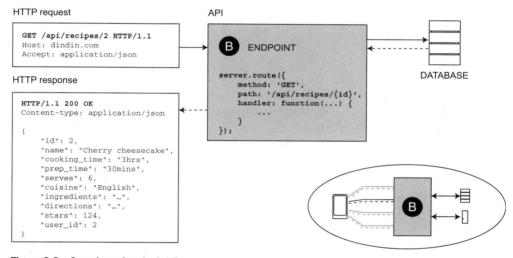

Figure 2.8 Overview of endpoint B

The segment of the URI path that contains the ID of the recipe varies between requests, so we need a way to tell hapi that this is a variable. You do that using named path parameters. To create a named path parameter, you wrap the variable segment name in curly braces. For example:

```
/api/recipes/{id}
```

hapi makes any named parameters available in the `request.params` object. I can now implement the route for endpoint B by parameterizing the path option to take a variable `id` parameter.

Listing 2.7   index.js: the new route for endpoint B

```
server.route([{
    ...
}, {
    method: 'GET',
    path: '/api/recipes/{id}',
    handler: function (request, reply) {

        db.get('SELECT * FROM recipes WHERE id = ?',
            [request.params.id],          ◁──┐  Bind value of request.params.id
            (err, result) => {                │  to SQL query

            if (err) {
                throw err;
            }

            if (typeof result !== 'undefined') {     │ If result undefined,
                return reply(result);                │ reply with result
            }

            return reply('Not found').code(404);  ◁──┐ Otherwise, send 404 response
        });                                          │ code and text "Not found"
    }
}]);
```

Why am I checking if `result` is undefined in the listing? The `db.get()` method differs slightly from `db.all()` in that the `result` parameter inside the callback is a single object representing a row in the database, rather than an array of rows. If there are zero matching rows for the query, the result will be undefined. When there's no result found for the request, the right thing to do is send a 404 response code to the client.

hapi will always send a response code, usually an implicit 200 OK code. To override this default, you can chain the `.code()` method to the `reply()` call, passing the integer code you want to send, as shown in listing 2.7.

2.4   *Writing maintainable code*

Writing code is an iterative process. Every now and then, you should take a step back and see how you can refactor your code to keep it clean and maintainable. This section shows you a few tips you can follow to keep your hapi apps in good shape.

2.4.1   *Modularizing routes*

If you keep all the code for your entire application within the index.js file, it can quickly become an ugly, unmaintainable mess. A common approach in hapi apps and Node apps in general is to split out chunks of related code into modules.

One way I can help clean things up is to place the routes in a separate module. To achieve this, I move the array of route objects from my index.js and place them inside a new file called route.js. I also make sure this array is the exported value of the module by assigning it to `module.exports`. The resulting routes.js file is shown in the following listing.

Listing 2.8   routes.js

```
'use strict';

module.exports = [{
    method: 'GET',
    path: '/api/recipes',
    handler: function (request, reply) {
        ...
    }
}, {
    method: 'GET',
    path: '/api/recipes/{id}',
    handler: function (request, reply) {
        ...
    }
}];
```

The index.js file can now simply use the return value of `require()` from this module as the argument to `server.route()`:

```
server.route(require('./routes'));
```

But wait! This no longer will work. The route handlers need the `db` object to be in scope so they can query the database. Because I placed the routes in a separate module, they've now lost access to the `db` object.

To fix this, I could move the SQLite connection code to the routes module, but what if another part of my application also needs access to the same connection elsewhere? I don't want to create the same connection in several modules. If only there were a way to make an object available throughout your hapi app. Luckily `server.bind()` lets you do exactly that.

2.4.2   Meet server.bind(): setting the context in handlers

hapi provides a method called `server.bind()`, which allows you to explicitly set the value of `this` to be used within all handler functions.

> **HAPI API**   server.bind(context) (http://hapijs.com/api#serverbindcontext)

> **NOTE**   server.bind() work if you use ES6 arrow functions to define your route handlers, and that's why I recommend that you never use arrow functions to define route handlers.

I can use `server.bind()` now to ensure that the database connection is available within my routes module at `this.db`. This listing shows the updated index.js.

Listing 2.9   index.js: using `server.bind()`

```
'use strict';

const Hapi = require('hapi');
const Sqlite3 = require('sqlite3');
```

```
const db = new Sqlite3.Database('./dindin.sqlite');

const server = new Hapi.Server();
server.connection({ port: 4000 });

server.bind({ db: db });                          ⟵  Bind db object
                                                      to the server

server.route(require('./routes'));                ⟵  Use loaded routes.js module as
                                                      argument to server.route()

server.start(() => {

    console.log('Server listening at:', server.info.uri);
});
```

The database connection object can now be accessed within handler methods at
`this.db`. The updated routes.js module is shown in the following listing.

Listing 2.10   routes.js: using `this.db` to access database object

```
'use strict';

module.exports = [{
    method: 'GET',
    path: '/api/recipes',
    handler: function (request, reply) {

        let sql = 'SELECT * FROM recipes';
        const params = [];

        if (request.query.cuisine) {
            sql += ' WHERE cuisine = ?';
            params.push(request.query.cuisine);
        }

        this.db.all(sql, params, (err, results) => {

            if (err) {
                throw err;
            }

            reply(results);
        });
    }
}, {
    method: 'GET',
    path: '/api/recipes/{id}',
    handler: function (request, reply) {

        this.db.get('SELECT * FROM recipes WHERE id = ?',
    [request.params.id], (err, result) => {

            if (err) {
                throw err;
            }
```

```
        if (typeof result !== 'undefined') {
            reply(result);
        }
        else {
            reply('Not found').code(404);
        }
    });
    }
}];
```

Using `server.bind()` can help you write significantly cleaner code. By placing
resources such as database connections inside the context of handler methods, you
can avoid repetition and the use of global variables.

2.4.3 *Modularizing handlers*

A further step I can take toward creating a clean and scalable application structure is to
modularize the handlers for each of my routes. Because there's no official way to organize your code in hapi, it's up to you how to do this. Some people like to place each handler in a new module, and that can be a good approach for very large applications.

I like to group related handlers into a single module. In the case of the DinDin
API, I only have one object that users work with: `recipes`. I place my handlers inside a
directory called handlers. Inside handlers, I will create a single file called recipes.js.
Here's the directory tree (excluding node_modules) of the project at this point:

```
├── handlers
│   └── recipes.js
├── index.js
├── package.json
└── routes.js
```

The recipes.js file will be the module where I keep my handlers for all the routes that
interact with recipes. Each handler is an exported function that is identical to the handler previously in my routes module.

Listing 2.11 handlers/recipes.js: route handlers as exported functions

```
'use strict';

exports.find = function (request, reply) {         ◁─┐ Create exported functions
                                                      │ for the route handlers
    let sql = 'SELECT * FROM recipes';
    const params = [];

    if (request.query.cuisine) {
        sql += ' WHERE cuisine = ?';
        params.push(request.query.cuisine);
    }

    this.db.all(sql, params, (err, results) => {
```

```
          if (err) {
              throw err;
          }

          reply(results);
      });
};

exports.findOne = function (request, reply) {          ◁─┐  Create exported functions
                                                            └─  for the route handlers
      this.db.get('SELECT * FROM recipes WHERE id = ?', [request.params.id],
      (err, result) => {

          if (err) {
              throw err;
          }

          if (typeof result !== 'undefined') {
              return reply(result);
          }

          return reply('Not found').code(404);
      });
};
```

The routes.js file can then reference the handlers loaded from the new handlers.

Listing 2.12   routes.js: using the new recipes handlers module

```
'use strict';

const Recipes = require('./handlers/recipes');      ◁─┐  Load the recipes
                                                         │  handler module
module.exports = [{
    method: 'GET',
    path: '/api/recipes',
    handler: Recipes.find
}, {                                                 ◁─┐
    method: 'GET',                                       │  Set route handlers to
    path: '/api/recipes/{id}',                           │  exported functions within
    handler: Recipes.findOne                             │  the recipes module
}];                                                  ◁─┘
```

Following the code organization approaches in this section will help to keep your applications more manageable as both the features and the number of people working on them grow.

Next I look at how I can improve the API further, by thinking about security and implementing a bit of authentication.

2.5   *Authentication*

So far I haven't considered security. All the existing endpoints of the API have been open to the world. Endpoints C (creating recipes) and D (starring recipes) have the requirement that users must be logged in to access them (so we know who created or starred the recipe!). It's about time I looked at the basics of how authentication works in hapi.

2.5.1 Schemes and strategies

hapi offers many ways to authenticate users, using passwords and tokens and other methods. Central to the way of thinking about authentication in hapi are the concepts of schemes and strategies.

SCHEMES

A *scheme* is a general type of authentication. HTTP Basic authentication and HTTP Digest authentication are different types of authentication, and in hapi each would be a different scheme. You can think of a scheme as a template for authentication. A scheme isn't used directly to authenticate users; instead you create a specific *strategy* from the scheme.

STRATEGIES

A *strategy* is a configured instance of a scheme with an assigned name. Strategies exist so you can use the same scheme several times, in a slightly different way. For instance, you may decide that you want to use HTTP Basic authentication in your app. But for some routes you might want to validate a user's passwords against a value in a database, and for some other routes you might want to check the password against a value stored in a file. In this case you can create two different strategies from the scheme. The scheme-to-strategies relationship is shown in figure 2.9.

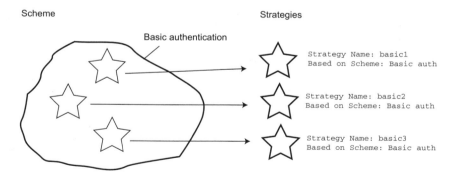

Figure 2.9   Cookie-cutter analogy of schemes and strategies

A strategy is created using the server.auth.strategy() method.

> **HAPI API** server.auth.strategy(name, scheme, [mode], [options])
> (http://hapijs.com/api#serverauthstrategyname-scheme-mode-options)

A commonly required option for strategies is validateFunc. This is a function you'll define to decide if a user should be authenticated. The next listing is an example of creating two different strategies from the same scheme.

Listing 2.13 Creating two different strategies from the same scheme

```
server.strategy('basic1','basic', {
    validateFunc: function (username, password, callback) {
        // Validation logic goes here
    }
});

server.strategy('basic2','basic', {
    validateFunc: function (username, password, callback) {
        // Different validation logic here
    }
});
```

2.5.2 *Implementing bearer token authentication*

Bearer token authentication is a very simple authentication scheme whereby a string, called the token, is included in all requests, usually in a header. To include the token in the header, you can place it in an Authorization header, like so:

```
GET /path
Host: site.example.com
Authorization: bearer tiebzfjwavdatersgyj3r4n
Accept: application/json
```

> **NOTE** Bearer tokens don't offer a great level of security. First, they must be used in production over SSL/TLS. Otherwise the token is sent unencrypted to the web server and can be captured by anybody who might be eavesdropping. Bearer tokens also lack means of expiry or integrity checking. There are better alternatives, JWT (JSON web tokens). For the sake of this example, I'll be using bearer token authentication because it's easy to understand and quick to implement. Chapter 9 examines alternative authentication schemes.

I've stored a random token for each user in the database. When a user attempts a request that requires authentication, the API goes through the steps in the following listing, in pseudocode.

Listing 2.14 Authentication routine in pseudocode

```
if(token exists in database) {
    authenticate user;
    load credentials;
    continue request;
} else {
    reply 401 Unauthorized;
}
```

I will use the hapi-auth-bearer-token plugin, which defines the authentication scheme. Because this module is a hapi plugin, it needs to be registered with the server using the `server.register()` method.

> **NPM PACKAGE** `hapi-auth-bearer-token` v4 (http://npmjs.com/package/hapi-auth-bearer-token)

Remember to install the package by running `npm install --save hapi-auth-bearer-token@4`. As shown in listing 2.15, `server.register()` takes a callback as its second parameter, which is called once the plugin has loaded. Inside this callback, you can then define a strategy. To define a strategy, I call the `server.auth.strategy()` method. I will give this strategy the name `api`.

Another change I need to make is to move the creation of the routes within the `plugin.register()` callback. That's because some of those routes will need to reference the new authentication strategy. It's therefore necessary that the routes be added after the plugin has loaded and after the new authentication strategy has been created.

Listing 2.15   index.js: registering and configuring hapi-auth-bearer-token

```
...

const validateFunc = function (token, callback) {        Load hapi-auth-bearer-
                                                         token plugin and register it
};                                                       with hapi server

server.register(require('hapi-auth-bearer-token'), (err) => {    ◄

    if (err) {                              If error registering the
        throw err;                          plugin, throw error
    }

    server.auth.strategy('api', 'bearer-access-token', {    ◄
        validateFunc: validateFunc                Define new strategy called api
    });                                           using bearer-access-token scheme

    server.route(require('./routes'));    Move routes and server start code into
                                          plugin registration callback—must
    server.start(() => {                  happen after plugin is registered

        console.log('Server started on', server.info.uri);
    });
});
```

Define validateFunc option

The `validateFunc` function is where I need to write the logic to check whether the token in the request is valid, which I defined earlier in pseudocode.

Listing 2.16   index.js: implementing the `validateFunc` function

```
...

const validateFunc = function (token, callback) {
```

```
db.get('SELECT * FROM users WHERE token = ?',          ◁─┐  Query users table
    [token],                                               │  for matching
    (err, result) => {

    if (err) {
        return callback(err, false);                            If error occurred with query,
    }                                                           don't authenticate user

    const user = result;

    if (typeof user === 'undefined') {
        return callback(null, false);                           If no user record found,
    }                                                           don't authenticate user

    callback(null, true, {
        id: user.id,                                            Otherwise, there must be
        username: user.username                                 matching record, so authenticate
    });                                                         user and set their credentials
    });
};
```

2.5.3   *Working with user credentials*

In listing 2.16 the `validateFunc` callback receives a third argument, which is an object containing user credentials:

```
callback(err, isValid, {
    id: user.id,
    username: user.username
});
```

After a user is authenticated, this credentials object is now available to use within route handlers, stored in the `request.auth.credentials` object. I'll be using this when implementing the next endpoint for the API.

2.6   *Creating and starring recipes*

When you're building a website, you'll probably have a browser window open during the process, refreshing every now and then to get feedback on your changes. Building APIs is a little different. Before I move on to implementing the remaining endpoints, I will discuss some tools that will be useful to you when testing out your own APIs.

2.6.1   *Test-driving your endpoints*

You can test GET requests in a browser and see visual feedback using a decent browser plugin to format JSON. When it comes to testing more complex endpoints that require a POST request or include custom headers, you need a better tool. There are a couple common options. One of those is cURL.

cURL

cURL is a cross-platform command-line tool for making HTTP requests. It's most basic use is making a GET request to a URL:

```
curl http://localhost:4000/endpoint
```

You can also use cURL to make a POST request or a request with any allowable HTTP verb with the -X option:

```
curl -X POST http://localhost:4000/endpoint
```

The -H option allows a custom header to be sent, and the -d option allows you to include data in the body of the request. For example:

```
curl -H "Content-type: application/json" -d "{"name": "My data"}" -X POST
    http://localhost:4000/endpoint
```

Read more about cURL or download it from http://curl.haxx.se. If the terminal isn't your thing, there are also some good apps that let you do similar things in a visual way.

POSTMAN

Postman is a Google Chrome app that can also be used as a standalone desktop app (see figure 2.10). With Postman, you can test HTTP endpoints visually.

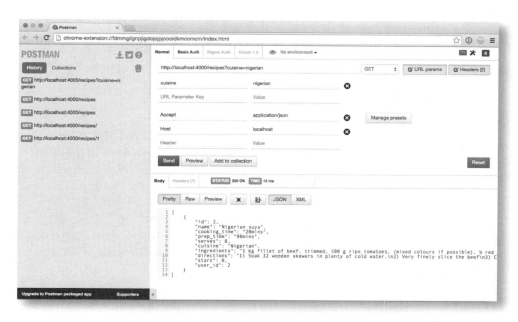

Figure 2.10   The Postman interface

Postman has lots of features, such as basic authentication, saving requests, and submitting form data, and can be a really great weapon in the arsenal of the API developer. Search for *Postman* in the Chrome Web Store to download it.

2.6.2   *Endpoint C: creating recipes*

To create a recipe using the DinDin API, a user sends a POST request to endpoint C, along with a JSON payload (see figure 2.11). For example:

```
POST /api/recipes
```

```
{"name":"My new recipe", "cooking_time": "1hr", ...}
```

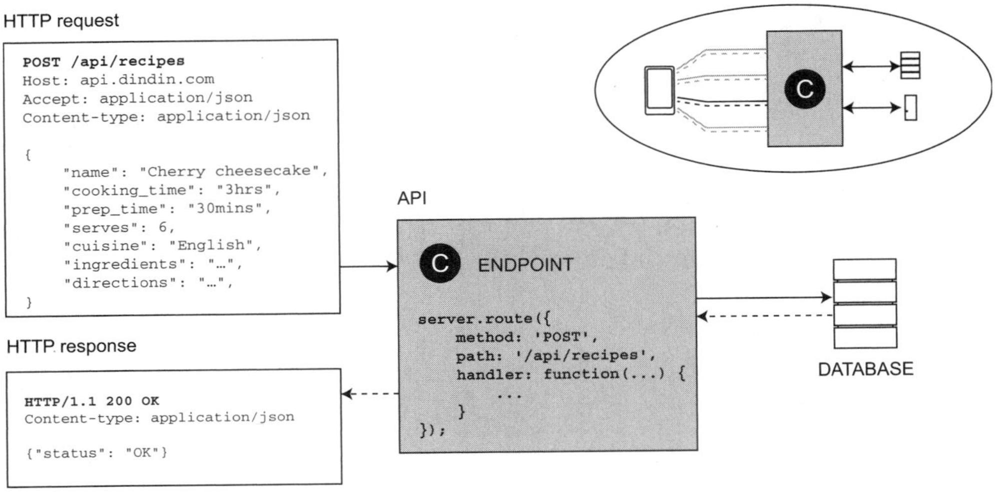

Figure 2.11   Overview of endpoint C

The API will respond with a JSON object with a single key status. If a recipe has been successfully created, the value of status will be "OK", as shown in figure 2.11.

This endpoint is different from those that have already been implemented in that it accepts a payload, or HTTP body. I need to use the data within the payload in my route handler to create the recipe. By default, hapi will automatically parse any incoming payloads based on the Content-type header of the request and place the parsed payload at request.payload. hapi is very configurable in terms of what it does with the payload, but in this case, the default is exactly what we want.

PUTTING IT ALL TOGETHER

I can now create a new route for endpoint C.

Listing 2.17   routes.js: updated for endpoint C

```javascript
const Recipes = require('./handlers/recipes');

module.exports = [{
    method: 'GET',
    path: '/api/recipes',
    handler: Recipes.find
}, {
```

```
        method: 'GET',
        path: '/api/recipes/{id}',
        handler: Recipes.findOne
}, {
        method: 'POST',
        path: '/api/recipes',
        config: {
            auth: 'api'
        },
        handler: Recipes.create
}];
```

> Configure this route to use the 'api' authentication strategy

The last step is to create the handler for the create recipe route. This is placed within recipes.js along with the other handlers.

Listing 2.18   handlers/recipes.js: the create recipe handler

```
exports.create = function (request, reply) {

    const sql = 'INSERT INTO recipes (name, cooking_time, prep_time, serves,
    cuisine, ingredients, directions, user_id) VALUES (?,?,?,?,?,?,?,?)';

    this.db.run(sql,
        [
            request.payload.name,
            request.payload.cooking_time,
            request.payload.prep_time,
            request.payload.serves,
            request.payload.cuisine,
            request.payload.ingredients,
            request.payload.directions,
            request.auth.credentials.id
        ],
        (err) => {

            if (err) {
                throw err;
            }

            reply({ status: 'ok' });
        });
};
```

> Bind payload parameters to SQL query

> Use authenticated user's id as user_id of new recipe

> If no SQLite error, respond with 'ok' status

If you're following along, you can now test the recipe creation endpoint with a cURL command. Remember, this is an authenticated route using bearer token authentication, so a token needs to be included in the request. The sample SQLite database provided contains a user record for a user with the username john. The token for this user is q8lrh5rzkrzdi4un8kfza5y3k1nn184xn. Try spinning up the app and issuing the following cURL command from a terminal to create a new recipe:

```
curl -X POST \
-H "Content-Type: application/json" \
-H "Authorization: Bearer q8lrh5rzkrzdi4un8kfza5y3k1nn184x" \
```

```
-d '{
    "name": "Test recipe",
    "cooking_time": "1hr",
    "prep_time": "1hr",
    "serves": 1,
    "cuisine": "Canadian",
    "ingredients": "a, b, c",
    "directions": "1, 2, 3"
}' http://localhost:4000/api/recipes
```

If all is well, you should see a {"status":"ok"} response. You can verify that the new recipe has been created. Do this by requesting the GET /recipes endpoint again, and you should now see your new recipe in the list.

> **EXERCISE** As an exercise, use the knowledge you've gained so far in this chapter to implement the route for endpoint D (starring recipes) yourself. When a user makes a request to endpoint D, the star field in the database for the corresponding recipe will be incremented, and a status message returned to the user. See figure 2.12 for a clue.

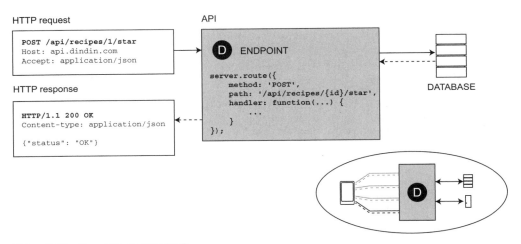

Figure 2.12 Overview of endpoint D

In the next chapter the focus shifts to the front end, and you'll see many of the features that hapi offers for building websites and single page applications, such as static file serving and HTML template rendering. Onward!

2.7 *Summary*

- You use server.route() to add routes to a server.
- Routes have a method (such as GET) and a path (such as /users).
- You tell hapi what to do with a request by writing a route handler.

- Handlers can have several input types, such as query parameters, path parameters, and payloads.
- You can add authentication to routes by creating an authentication strategy from a pre-existing authentication scheme.
- You can use `server.bind()` to specify a context for your route handlers.
- You can keep your code clean and maintainable by splitting it out into Node modules.
- You can use tools like cURL and Postman to test drive your API endpoints.

Building a website

This chapter follows the building of a simple website to show off some of the front-end features in hapi.js. The website we'll be creating builds on top of the API project from the previous chapter. It will retrieve data from the API and create dynamic web pages using this data.

Don't worry if you haven't followed along with the API project in chapter 2. The finished API has been released as an npm package called `dindin-api`, which we'll use as a dependency in this chapter.

NPM PACKAGE `dindin-api` (http://npmjs.com/package/dindin-api)

We'll be looking at how you can use hapi's powerful plugin system to modularize your own applications in this way in chapter 5.

3.1 The DinDin website

Hey, and welcome back! If you've just joined us, we're working for a client called Mrs. Bigbucks, a tech entrepreneur. We're building a prototype for her latest venture, a food-oriented social network called DinDin. The idea is that people can post their own recipes online, and other people can search and star their favorites.

The DinDin API prototype from chapter 2 was a big success. Mrs. Bigbucks was happy with the result and is already talking to potential investors. What she wants now is something visual to show off in presentations. We've got all the mechanics of the back end figured out now, so it's time to work on the presentation a bit. We've agreed to build a simple website that showcases some of the features in the API.

3.1.1 What it looks like

The website we'll be building consists of four pages, shown in a simple sitemap in figure 3.1.

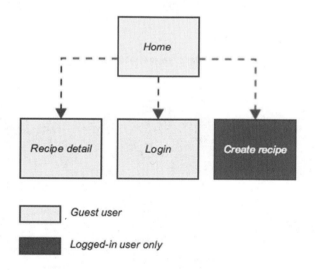

Figure 3.1   Sitemap of the DinDin website

The visual design and functionality of the website is shown in figure 3.2.

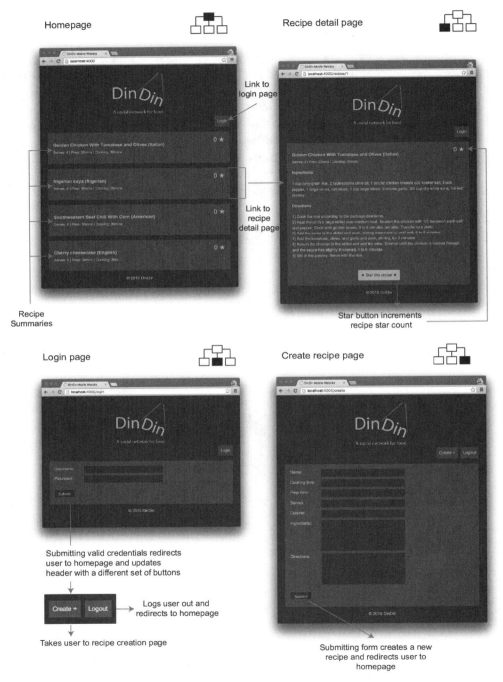

Homepage

Recipe detail page

Link to login page

Link to recipe detail page

Recipe Summaries

Star button increments recipe star count

Login page

Create recipe page

Submitting valid credentials redirects user to homepage and updates header with a different set of buttons

Logs user out and redirects to homepage

Takes user to recipe creation page

Submitting form creates a new recipe and redirects user to homepage

Figure 3.2   The visual design and functionality of the website

3.1.2 How it works

Each page and action on the website will have a corresponding hapi route. For instance, the home page will have a route that matches GET requests to /. In response, hapi will send back the HTML that represents the page, and the browser will then render the page, also downloading any additional assets like Cascading Style Sheets (CSS) styles or images. This works similarly to how we built an API with hapi, except rather than using JSON, we're now responding with HTML and static files.

We'll see other new things in this chapter, such as how to maintain state between requests with cookies and sessions, perform redirects, and work with form data. Nevertheless, the core principles are the same: We create and configure a server, set up routes, and define handlers to manage requests.

WORKING WITH THE API

The front end web server for the website won't store data or query the database directly. Rather it will act as a client for the API produced in chapter 2. This API has been published as an npm package, complete with an embedded SQLite.

Each request made from the browser will be matched to a route and a handler that will in turn make an HTTP request to the API. The response from the API will then be used to construct an HTML document, which is sent back to the browser. You can see an example of this entire transaction in figure 3.3.

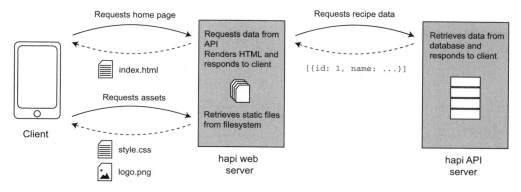

Figure 3.3 Overview of how the whole application will work together to serve clients

3.1.3   *Getting set up*

Before I begin building the website, I need to prepare a project environment. I will use the same structure that I used in the previous chapter to organize my hapi application. This basic structure is shown here:

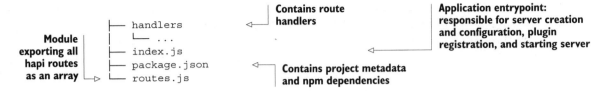

Our application has four dependencies: hapi, the dindin-api module, which is a hapi plugin, and the Invert and Vision plugins, which we'll discuss later in the chapter. For now, add the package.json file shown in the next listing. After creating package.json, you can install all the dependencies by running npm install in the project's directory.

Listing 3.1   package.json

```
{
  "name": "dindin-web",
  "version": "1.0.0",
  "description": "A social network for food",
  "dependencies": {
    "dindin-api": "2.x.x",
    "hapi": "13.x.x",
    "inert": "3.x.x",
    "vision": "4.x.x"
  }
}
```

There are no routes yet, so the route.js module exports an empty array.

Listing 3.2   routes.js

```
'use strict';

module.exports = [];          ⟵┐ Export an
                                └ empty array
```

In the application's index.js file, a hapi server is created and connected to port 4000. The dindin-api, Inert, and Vision plugins are loaded, the routes are loaded and applied, and the server is started.

Listing 3.3   index.js

```
'use strict';

const Hapi = require('hapi');   ⟵┐ Load hapi
                                 └ module
```

Create hapi server →
```
const server = new Hapi.Server();
server.connection({ port: 4000 });
```
Make connection to port 4000 ←

```
server.bind({
    apiBaseUrl: 'http://localhost:4000/api',
    webBaseUrl: 'http://localhost:4000'
});
```
Bind useful URLs so they can be accessed in handlers

```
server.register([
    require('dindin-api'),
    require('inert')
], (err) => {
```
Register plugins

```
    if (err) {
        throw err;
    }
```
If error occurred registering the plugin, throw it

Add routes from routes module →
```
server.route(require('./routes'));

server.start(() => {

    console.log('Started server at', server.info.uri);
});
});
```
Start server

This bare-bones project, although it doesn't seem to do much, is a perfectly functioning hapi application. You can start the server by typing this into a terminal:

```
node index
```

Even though you've not yet written any logic for the application, you can open http://localhost:4000/api/recipes in a browser and see that the API is running from inside the loaded dindin-api plugin.

So now that the basic project skeleton is all set up, it's time to move on to writing code to serve the first web pages.

3.2 Serving web pages and static content

This section looks at how you can configure hapi for static file serving and creating dynamic HTML documents. These tasks are the bread and butter of web applications. First I show you how to create routes that respond with a single static file, and then take a look at serving an entire directory of assets. I'll also introduce you to hapi's powerful view-rendering functionality. I put these building blocks together to construct the home page of the DinDin website.

3.2.1 Serving a static file

So far, all the hapi routes you've seen in this book respond to requests by calling the reply() function with a simple data type, such as a String or an Object. But reply() is capable of much more.

Imagine we want to respond to a request with the contents of a file instead. We could do this in hapi by first reading the contents of the file into a Buffer object, determining the content type from the file extension, and then responding with the `Buffer` object and setting the correct content-type header in the response. This would be a tedious volume of code to write every time we wanted to send a file. Thankfully we don't have to bother.

The Inert plugin that we loaded earlier saves you from all that work. When loaded, Inert decorates the `reply` interface with `reply.file()`. `reply.file()` takes a string, which is a relative or absolute path to a file in the filesystem and does all the work for you to serve the file (see figure 3.4).

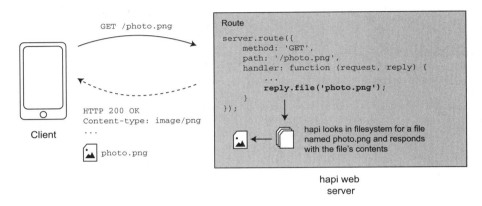

Figure 3.4   A request and response cycle with `reply.file()`

Sample HTML for the DinDin home page is shown next. The linked CSS and the logo image can be found in the book's source code on GitHub (https://github.com/mtharrison/hapi.js-in-action). The files are stored under the chapter subsection number—for example, CH03 - Building a Website/3.2/3.2.3.

Listing 3.4   index.html: the HTML document for the DinDin home page

```html
<!DOCTYPE html>

<html lang="en">
<head>
    <meta charset="UTF-8">
    <title>DinDin Mobile Website</title>
    <link href="/css/style.css" rel="stylesheet">
</head>

<body>
    <header>
        <a href="/" id="logo"><img src="/images/logo.png"></a>
        <a class="header-button" href="/login">Login</a>
    </header>
```

Website header

Example recipe summary

```
    <a class="recipe-summary" href="/recipes/1">
        <h3 class="recipe-summary-name">Golden Chicken With Tomatoes and
    Olives (Italian)</h3>
        <span class="stars">6 ★ </span>
        <p class="recipe-info">Serves: 4 | Prep: 20mins | Cooking: 30mins</p>
    </a>
    <footer><p>&copy; 2015 DinDin</p></footer>
</body>
</html>
```

Website footer

First I'll create a module to contain all the handlers that I'll be writing to serve up the various pages that make up the website. I'll add the first handler, which uses `reply.file()` to send the index.html file to the user, as shown here.

Listing 3.5   handlers/pages.js: the home page handler

```
'use strict';

exports.home = function (request, reply) {

    reply.file('./index.html');
};
```

Respond with index.html file

I'll then create the route for the home page, which uses the `home` handler. The updated routes module is shown in this listing.

Listing 3.6   routes.js: the home page route

```
'use strict';

const Pages = require('./handlers/pages');

module.exports = [{
    method: 'GET',
    path: '/',
    handler: Pages.home
}];
```

If I start the server and open http://localhost:4000 in a browser, there's a slight problem, as shown in figure 3.5.

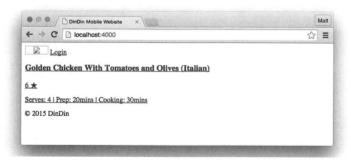

Figure 3.5   The unstyled home page. We need to fix this by making some assets available.

Things aren't working quite right, as you can probably see. There are no styles, and the logo is missing. That's because the browser will try to download the linked CSS file and the logo image, but we haven't created routes for them yet.

3.2.2 *Serving an entire directory*

For the home page to work properly, I need to be able to serve more files to the browser. Creating a separate route for each and every new file I want to serve isn't a scalable solution. Luckily, hapi has a way to serve an entire directory of files. In the index.html file in listing 3.4, there are two files that need to be served to the browser: the CSS file (/css/style.css) and the logo image (/images/logo.png).

I'm going to place all the static files I want to serve into a single directory that I will call public. I will move the index.html file into here so it can be served statically too. I will also create a new module in `handlers` to contain handlers for routes that serve assets, called assets.js. Here's what my directory tree looks like now:

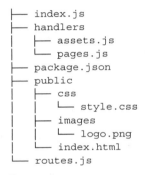

```
├── index.js
├── handlers
│   ├── assets.js
│   └── pages.js
├── package.json
├── public
│   ├── css
│   │   └── style.css
│   ├── images
│   │   └── logo.png
│   └── index.html
└── routes.js
```

THE DIRECTORY HANDLER

The `directory` handler, which is also added by the Inert plugin, is different from all the handlers I've used so far. The `directory` handler isn't defined as a function. The handler property of the route is instead assigned an object with a `directory` property, as can be seen in the following two listings.

Listing 3.7 handlers/assets.js: Statically serving a directory of assets

```
'use strict';

exports.servePublicDirectory = {
    directory: {
        path: 'public'
    }
};
```

Listing 3.8   routes.js: Statically serving a directory of assets

```
'use strict';

const Pages = require('./handlers/pages');
const Assets = require('./handlers/assets');

module.exports = [{
    method: 'GET',
    path: '/{param*}',
    handler: Assets.servePublicDirectory
}];
```

The path I've used in listing 3.8 (/{param*}) might look a little confusing at first. To understand what this does, let's look at how hapi chooses a route.

HOW HAPI MATCHES A ROUTE TO A REQUEST

When hapi receives a new request, it tries to match one of your routes based on method and path properties. Once a route is successfully matched, hapi will execute the associated handler.

If hapi encounters conflicting routes that match an incoming request, it will pick the more specific one, as illustrated in figure 3.6. The /{param*} path is a special path in hapi. It's somewhat a catch-all route, meaning it will match any path that doesn't have a more specific route defined. I explain the * part more in chapter 4. The choice of the word param is totally arbitrary here and could as easily be /{lasagna*}, if that's more your thing.

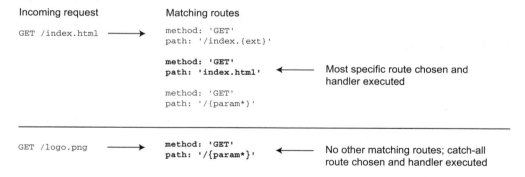

Figure 3.6   hapi always chooses the most specific matching route for a request.

When a request comes into hapi for the logo image with a path of /images/logo.png, hapi will try to find a route that matches the path specifically. If one isn't found, hapi will match the catch-all route shown in listing 3.6. hapi will then search in the specified directory (public) for a file with the path ./images/logo.png. As this file exists, hapi will serve it in response.

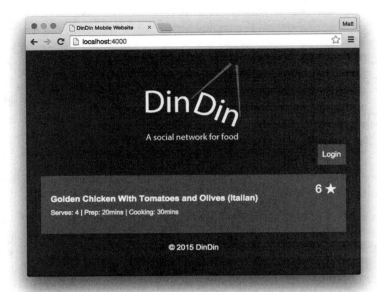

Figure 3.7   The working
home page

Starting the server and opening http://localhost:4000 in a browser shows the home
page is now working correctly, with all the assets loaded, as you can see in figure 3.7.
Exciting times—we're finally getting somewhere!

Now it's time to start looking at how to generate these views dynamically, populat-
ing them with data stored on the server.

3.2.3   *server.views(): dynamic view rendering with Handlebars*

Thankfully, it's no longer 1995, and websites aren't merely a collection of linked static
HTML documents. What we want is to be able to dynamically generate HTML documents from data structures in our applications.

Any serious web programming language has its way of doing this. In PHP, you'd
stick `<?= $variable ?>` tags in your HTML to print out this dynamic data. Ruby has
.erb templates for the same purpose. In JavaScript we use templates too. The libraries
that we work with to convert templates to HTML are called templating engines.

TEMPLATING ENGINES

HTML *templating engines* are pieces of software that typically take two inputs: the template itself and a collection of data, often referred to as the *context*. Using these inputs,
templating engines then produce HTML, as illustrated in figure 3.8.

As with everything in the JS world, there are *many* options available to developers,
and it's often a matter of taste which you choose. Two very popular JavaScript templating engines are Jade and Handlebars. Either can be used with hapi.

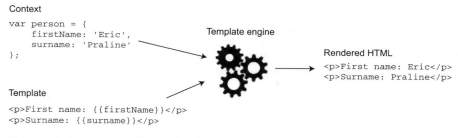

Context
```
var person = {
    firstName: 'Eric',
    surname: 'Praline'
};
```

Template
```
<p>First name: {{firstName}}</p>
<p>Surname: {{surname}}</p>
```

Template engine

Rendered HTML
```
<p>First name: Eric</p>
<p>Surname: Praline</p>
```

Figure 3.8 What a templating engine does

In this chapter I'll be using Handlebars, but the same principles will apply to Jade and probably to other templating engines too.

CONFIGURING HAPI FOR HANDLEBARS
The first step is to add Handlebars as a dependency of the project and install it with npm. You can do this by running `npm install --save handlebars@4`.

NPM PACKAGE handlebars v4 (http://npmjs.com/package/handlebars)

We also need to load the hapi Vision plugin. Vision adds view rendering (a.k.a. template rendering) capabilities to hapi. One of the methods it adds is `server.views()`, which is used for configuring hapi for view rendering. In the next listing, which shows an example configuration that I'll be using in this chapter, the annotations explain each property. We must remember to call `server.views()` *after* the Vision plugin has loaded.

Listing 3.9   index.js: configuring hapi for handlebars

```
...

server.register([
    require('dindin-api'),
    require('inert'),
    require('vision')                        ◁── Load Vision
], (err) => {                                        plugin

    if (err) {
        throw err;
    }

    server.views({
        engines: {
            hbs: require('handlebars')       ◁── Use Handlebars engine to render
        },                                         views with .hbs extension
        relativeTo: __dirname,
        path: './views',                     ◁── Look here
        isCached: false                            for views
    });
    ...
```

All other paths are relative to this.

Don't cache views—instead reload them each time they're used (only recommended for development).

NOTE   In Node scripts, __dirname is a globally available variable that holds the absolute path to the directory that the currently executing file is stored within. This is useful because in a node script, paths are typically relative to the directory where you run a script (commonly called the current working directory or CWD). By using __dirname to specify a relative root, you can confidently start your scripts from any directory and be sure they properly resolve paths.

CREATING A DYNAMIC HOME PAGE

The home page I created earlier was a static HTML file, but now I'm going to use a Handlebars template to dynamically render the list of recipes, as shown in figure 3.9.

Figure 3.9   The home page dynamically populated with recipes

First I need to create a Handlebars template. Because Handlebars templates are like HTML with special expressions embedded within, I can reuse my existing index.html file. To create the index.hbs file, all I need to do is rename my index.html file to index.hbs and move it inside the views folder in my project. I'm going to create this views directory at /views relative to the root of the project.

The part of the template I want to make dynamic first is the `<a>` block with the recipe-summary class. I want to have one of these elements for each recipe in my context. Handlebars has a special `{{#each}}` tag for iterating through an array. Using this, I can loop through each recipe object in the array and print out a recipe-summary block.

Listing 3.10   Dynamically outputting an array of recipes

```
{{#each recipes}}
    <a class="recipe-summary" href="/recipes/{{id}}">
        <h3 class="recipe-summary-name">{{name}} ({{cuisine}})</h3>
        <span class="stars">{{stars}} ★ </span>
        <p class="recipe-info">Serves: {{serves}} | Prep: {{prep_time}} |
    Cooking: {{cooking_time}}</p>
    </a>
{{/each}}
```

The Vision plugin for hapi adds a new method to the `reply()` interface: `reply.view()`, which tells hapi to render the view with the name given as the first argument and the context given as the optional second argument. For example:

```
reply.view('person', {
    firstName: 'Eric',
    surname: 'Praline'
});
```

I need to define a context to use when rendering the template. Later I will be retrieving this data dynamically from the API, but for now I can define a simple JavaScript array containing two recipe objects. This listing shows the route for the new dynamic home page.

Listing 3.11   routes.js: the route for the dynamic home page

```
const Pages = require('./handlers/pages');

module.exports = [{
    method: 'GET',
    path: '/',
    handler: Pages.home
},{
    ...
}];
```

This listing shows the implementation of the `Pages.home` handler.

Listing 3.12   handlers/pages.js: the home handler for the dynamic home page

```
exports.home = function (request, reply) {

    const recipes = [{
        id: 1,
        name: 'Silicate soup',
        cuisine: 'Martian',
        stars: 100,
        serves: 1,
        prep_time: '2 hours',
        cooking_time: '12 minutes'
    }, {
        id: 2,
        name: 'Methane trifle',
        cuisine: 'Neptunian',
        stars: 200,
        serves: 1,
        prep_time: '1 hours',
        cooking_time: '24 minutes'
    }];

    reply.view('index', {
        recipes: recipes
    });
};
```

Define sample data to include in template context

Respond with rendered view using index template and the given context

Restarting the server and visiting http://localhost:4000/ shows that the home page now contains a dynamically generated section featuring the sample recipes (figure 3.10).

Figure 3.10   The dynamically rendered block with sample data

3.2.4   *DRY views: layouts and partials*

Don't repeat yourself, more commonly referred to as DRY, is an oft-repeated mantra in software development. This principle applies as equally to front end code as it does to server-side code. Websites are often composed of many pages with common layouts or reused blocks or widgets.

Most templating engines provide a way for you to compose views from common or repeating elements. These elements are normally called *layouts* and *partials* and by using them, you can avoid repeating code.

Layouts provide a common wrapper around the content of your views. Typically, layouts contain headers and footers of pages, with the view content sandwiched in the middle. The layout is usually markup that doesn't change between different child views, so it's convenient to keep this in a common place.

Partials are smaller, self-contained blocks. They may be used for repeating elements in a list, or for blocks that appear on many different views, such as ads or widgets.

I can refactor the home page view created in the previous section to make use of layouts and partials. Figure 3.11 shows how the home page view can be deconstructed into a single layout and multiple partials.

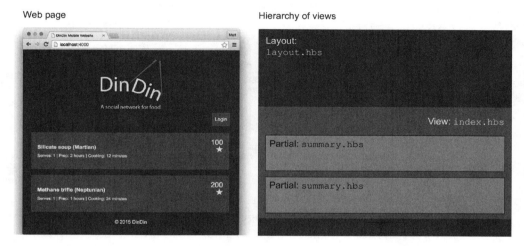

Figure 3.11   Deconstructing the home page into a layout, view, and partials

CONFIGURING HAPI

Before you can use layouts and partials, you need to tell hapi where it should look for these templates.

Listing 3.13   index.js: views configuration updated with layout and partials options

```
server.views({
    engines: {
        hbs: require('handlebars')
    },
    relativeTo: __dirname,
    path: './views',
    layoutPath: './views/layout',        Look here
    layout: true,                         for layouts
    isCached: false,
    partialsPath: './views/partials'     Look here
});                                       for partials
```

Use a layout when rendering a view → layout: true,

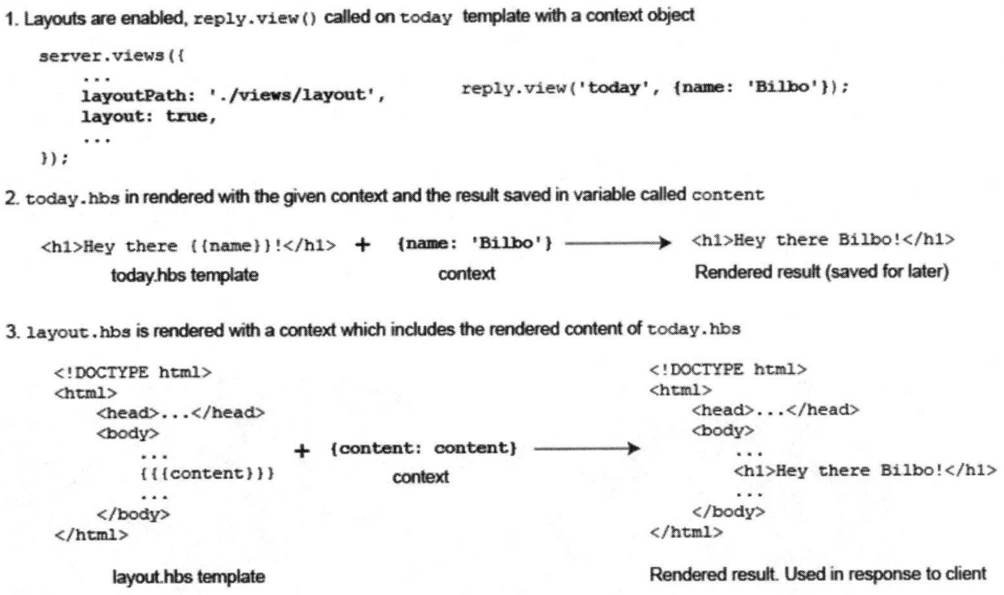

1. Layouts are enabled, `reply.view()` called on `today` template with a context object

```
server.views({
    ...
    layoutPath: './views/layout',        reply.view('today', {name: 'Bilbo'});
    layout: true,
    ...
});
```

2. `today.hbs` in rendered with the given context and the result saved in variable called `content`

`<h1>Hey there {{name}}!</h1>` **+** `{name: 'Bilbo'}` ⟶ `<h1>Hey there Bilbo!</h1>`

today.hbs template   context   Rendered result (saved for later)

3. `layout.hbs` is rendered with a context which includes the rendered content of `today.hbs`

```
<!DOCTYPE html>                                              <!DOCTYPE html>
<html>                                                       <html>
    <head>...</head>                                             <head>...</head>
    <body>                  +  {content: content}  ⟶            <body>
        ...                         context                          ...
        {{{content}}}                                                <h1>Hey there Bilbo!</h1>
        ...                                                          ...
    </body>                                                      </body>
</html>                                                      </html>
```

layout.hbs template   Rendered result. Used in response to client

Figure 3.12   The process that hapi uses to render a view using a layout

When the `layout` option is set to `true` and you use the `reply.view()` method, hapi will go through the steps shown in figure 3.12.

In your layouts, you must include a Handlebars expression for outputting the content variable. This contains the rendered content of your view. Handlebars has two different expressions for outputting variables. One is the double curly bracket form which looks like {{var}}. The other is the {{{var}}} form. The {{{var}}} form is humorously called the *triple-stash*, because curly brackets look somewhat like moustaches.

When using the double form, Handlebars will escape any HTML inside the string before outputting it—this is for security purposes. When you trust the source of the HTML, though, you can use the triple-stash form. But don't use this unless you absolutely need it. The best practice is to always stick with the double form. The content variable in layouts is one such example of trusted HTML because it only contains the HTML that you've written yourself in the view. The `layout.hbs` for the DinDin home page is shown next.

Listing 3.14   views/layout/layout.hbs: handlebars layout

```
<!DOCTYPE html>

<html lang="en">
<head>
    <meta charset="UTF-8">
    <title>DinDin Mobile Website</title>
```

```
    <link href="/css/style.css" rel="stylesheet">
</head>

<body>
    <header>
        <a href="/" id="logo"><img alt="DinDin" src="/images/logo.png"></a>
        <a class="header-button" href="/login">Login</a>
    </header>

    {{{content}}}                        ⟵┐ Output trusted content using
                                            triple-stash expression
    <footer><p>&copy; 2015 DinDin</p></footer>
</body>
</html>
```

The repeating recipe summary block from the index view can be placed into a partial template called `summary.hbs`, the content of which is shown in the next listing.

Listing 3.15   views/partials/summary.hbs: the recipe summary partial

```
<a class="recipe-summary" href="/recipes/{{id}}">
    <h3 class="recipe-summary-name">{{name}} ({{cuisine}})</h3>
    <span class="stars">{{stars}} ★ </span>
    <p class="recipe-info">Serves: {{serves}} | Prep: {{prep_time}} | Cook-
    ing: {{cooking_time}}</p>
</a>
```

The index view now contains only the repeating recipe summary partial. To output a partial, the expression used is `{{> partialName}}`. The stripped down index.hbs view is shown here.

Listing 3.16   views/index.hbs

```
{{#each recipes}}
  {{> summary}}
{{/each}}
```

Layouts and partials are invaluable elements in building DRY views. They help keep your templates small and focused and they increase reusability and improve the maintainability of your web applications.

Next, I'm going to start to integrate the website with the API and get real data into this application.

3.3   *Working with an external API*

In this section I'll be removing the reliance on the sample data I've been using and will start working with the DinDin API to retrieve and update real data. First I'll introduce Wreck, a Node module and utility for making requests to HTTP services. Then I'll show how Wreck can be used in the example project to make requests to the DinDin API. I'll be using the data fetched by Wreck to render the web pages based on the real content stored by the API.

3.3.1   *Using Wreck: consuming APIs with hapi*

During the life of a request, it's common for your application to need to communicate with other external HTTP services. For example, if you're building a travel API that aggregates the prices of flights, similar to Expedia, you might need to contact several airlines' APIs to get the latest prices before you can send a response to a user.

The hapi contributors have built a Node module called Wreck for this purpose. Wreck is an HTTP client for Node. We'll be using Wreck v7.

NPM PACKAGE   wreck v7 (http://npmjs.com/package/wreck)

At its heart, Wreck is a wrapper around Node's built-in HTTP client functionality in the http module, with some of the complexity abstracted away for ease of use. It's particularly useful for consuming JSON APIs. Wreck can be installed into your project the same way as any other Node module:

```
npm install --save wreck@7
```

Probably the most basic use of Wreck is to make a GET request to a JSON API. The following listing shows an example of requesting the recipe with an id of 1 from the Din-Din API.

Listing 3.17   Performing a GET request with Wreck

```
const Wreck = require('wreck');

Wreck.get('http://localhost:4000/api/recipes/1', (err, res, payload) => {

    if (err) {
        throw err;
    }

    const recipe = JSON.parse(payload.toString());
});
```

Wreck will call the callback provided once all the response payload has been buffered into memory. The payload by default is of type `Buffer`. For this reason we have to convert it to a string using the `Buffer.prototype.toString()` method and then use `JSON.parse()` to get the recipe as a JavaScript object. Wreck is highly configurable, though, and one of the ways we can save ourselves work is by providing `Wreck.get` with a `json` option.

Listing 3.18   Specifying the `json` option with Wreck

```
Wreck.get('http://localhost:4000/api/recipes/1', {
    json: true
}, (err, res, payload) => {

    if (err) {
        throw err;
```

```
    }

    const recipe = payload;
});
```

When you set the json option, Wreck will parse the payload for you, so you don't need to. Wreck can also perform POST requests with an optional payload to send. The payload can be a string or a buffer.

Listing 3.19   Using Wreck to send a POST request with a payload

```
const recipe = {
    name: 'My new recipe',
    ...
};

Wreck.post('http://localhost:4000/api/recipes', {
    json: true,
    payload: JSON.stringify(recipe)
}, (err, res, payload) => {

    if (err) {
        throw err;
    }
    ...
});
```

Check out the readme for Wreck on GitHub for a full list of available methods and options. You'll be seeing Wreck used throughout this chapter (and indeed the entire book) to communicate with the DinDin API.

3.3.2   *The dynamic home page*

The first attempt at creating the home page involved using some sample recipe data when rendering the view. In this listing I'll be using Wreck to pull the real data from the API.

Listing 3.20   handlers/pages.js: home handler updated to use Wreck

```
'use strict';

const Wreck = require('wreck');          ◁——— Load the
                                               Wreck module
exports.home = function (request, reply) {

    const apiUrl = this.apiBaseUrl + '/recipes';   ▷ Define URL for this API request using URL bound earlier with server.bind()

    Wreck.get(apiUrl, { json: true }, (err, res, payload) => {   ◁——— Request JSON from API

        if (err) {
            throw err;          ◁——— If error occurred with API request, throw that error
        }
```

```
        reply.view('index', {
            recipes: payload
        });
    });
};
```

| Render index view, passing in payload recipe data as part of context

3.3.3   *The recipe detail page*

Now I'm going to build the recipe detail page. Figure 3.13 serves as a reminder of how this page looks.

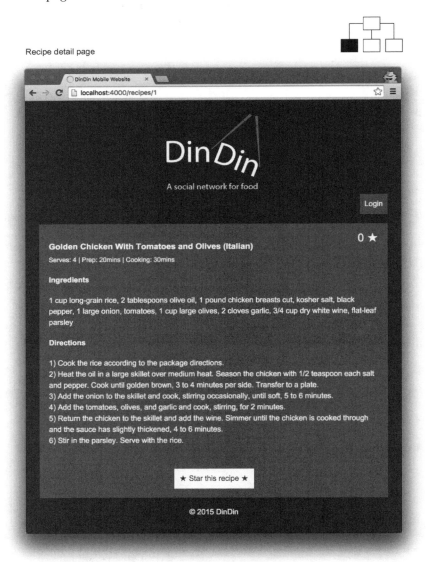

Recipe detail page

Figure 3.13   The recipe detail page

The recipe detail page shows an extended view of a single recipe. Creating this page is a case of following the same process I've used to create the home page. First I will create a view file called recipe.hbs containing my Handlebars template for this page.

```
<div class="recipe-detail">
    <h3 class="recipe-summary-name">{{recipe.name}} ({{recipe.cuisine}})</h3>

    <span class="stars">{{recipe.stars}} ★ </span>
    <p class="recipe-info">Serves: {{recipe.serves}} | Prep: {{rec
ipe.prep_time}} | Cooking: {{recipe.cooking_time}}</p>
    <h4>Ingredients</h4>
    <p>{{recipe.ingredients}}</p>
    <h4>Directions</h4>
    <p>{{recipe.directions}}</p>

    <a class="star-button" href="/recipes/{{recipe.id}}/star"> ★ Star this
    recipe ★ </a>
</div>
```

Now I need to add a new route for the recipe detail page. Nothing too special here—as you can see in the following listing, we follow the same pattern as before.

```
module.exports = [{
    ...
}, {
    method: 'GET',
    path: '/recipes/{id}',
    handler: Pages.viewRecipe
}, {
    ...
}];
```

The handler for this route will work similarly to the handler for the home page, except this time I will pass the id parameter present in the request into the API request to retrieve the correct recipe.

```
exports.viewRecipe = function (request, reply) {

    const apiUrl = this.apiBaseUrl + '/recipes/' + request.params.id;

    Wreck.get(apiUrl, { json: true }, (err, res, payload) => {

        if (err) {
            throw err;
        }
```

Use the id parameter to construct the API request URL

```
        reply.view('recipe', {
            recipe: payload
        });
    });
};
```

Each recipe given out by the API has an `ingredients` and a `directions` property, which are strings. These strings may contain newline (\n) characters if they've been written in an HTML form or within an app, but newline characters in HTML are ignored by browsers. This means that when you view the recipe detail page, the output might not be what you were expecting, as shown in figure 3.14.

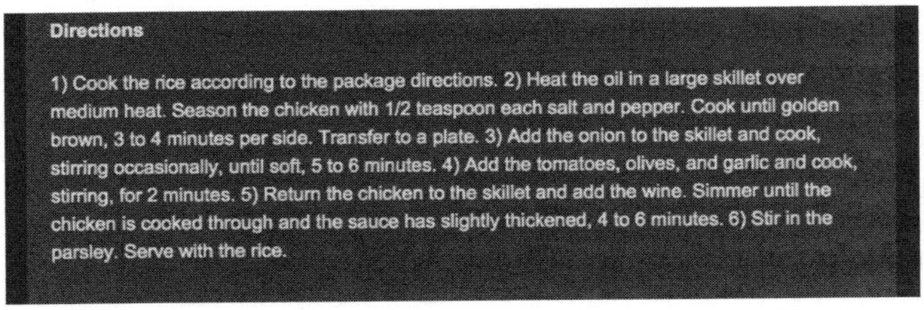

Figure 3.14   The recipe's directions with newline ignored

What I'd like is for every newline character to be converted into an HTML `<br>` tag. This kind of inline transformation of text is something that view helpers are useful for.

3.3.4   *View helpers*

Handlebars has a feature called *helpers*, which are like reusable functions that you can use inside your view templates. A helper transforms the context or data it's given into another form for output.

View helpers are defined in hapi by placing each helper into a module in a common directory. The directory is defined within the `server.views()` method. We're going to want to update our index.js file with the following configuration:

```
server.views({
    ...
    helpersPath: './views/helpers',
    ...
});
```

If I wanted to write a JavaScript function that accepted a string and replaced each newline with `<br>`, I would write something like this:

```
const breaklines = function (text) {
    text = text.replace(/(\r\n|\n|\r)/gm, '<br>');
};
```

To create a Handlebars helper that does the same thing, I can create a JavaScript file with the name I want to call the helper—for example, views/helpers/breaklines.js. A helper in hapi is defined as a Node module that exports a single function. Here is my first attempt.

Listing 3.24 views/helpers/breaklines.js: an unsecure handlebars helper for hapi

```
module.exports = function (text) {

    text = text.replace(/(\r\n|\n|\r)/gm, '<br>');
    return text;
};
```

Before I can put this into action, though, I'll need to consider a matter of security. The text passed to the helper may have come from user input and therefore shouldn't be trusted as a safe string to insert into HTML. Handlebars has a utility method for escaping strings, called `Handlebars.Utils.escapeExpression()`.

> **DEFINITION** *Escaping* a string means to replace characters or substrings that have special significance in a language with other substrings that don't. You escape strings produced by user input before inserting them into HTML, removing any HTML tags, to avoid unintended or malicious behavior. For example, the string `<script>alert('pwned')</script>` would be escaped to `&lt;script&gt;alert(&#x27;pwned&#x27;)&lt;/script&gt;` to prevent our page from executing the script.

Once the text has been escaped and the newlines changed, it can be returned from the helper as a *safe string*, which tells Handlebars that you've taken care of escaping the string yourself and it's now safe to insert into HTML. The finished helper is shown in the following listing.

Listing 3.25 views/helpers/breaklines.js: a secure Handlebars helper for hapi

```
const Handlebars = require('handlebars');          ⟵ Load Handlebars module

module.exports = function (text) {
                                                        Escape any HTML in text string
    text = Handlebars.Utils.escapeExpression(text);  ⟵
    text = text.replace(/(\r\n|\n|\r)/gm, '<br>');
    return new Handlebars.SafeString(text);          ⟵ Return new string as Handlebars safe string
};
```
Replace all newlines with HTML <br> tags

Note that without that last step, you'd get `<br>` appearing as text in your web page rather than an HTML `<br>` tag.

To use a helper in your template, you prefix the variable to output with the name of the helper, as in this listing.

Listing 3.26 views/recipe.hbs

```
<div class="recipe-detail">
    <h3 class="recipe-summary-name">{{recipe.name}} ({{recipe.cuisine}})</h3>
```

```
   <span class="stars">{{recipe.stars}} ★ </span>
   <p class="recipe-info">Serves: {{recipe.serves}} | Prep: {{rec-
ipe.prep_time}} | Cooking: {{recipe.cooking_time}}</p>
   <h4>Ingredients</h4>
   <p>{{breaklines recipe.ingredients}}</p>
   <h4>Directions</h4>
   <p>{{breaklines recipe.directions}}</p>

   <a class="star-button" href="/recipes/{{recipe.id}}/star"> ★ Star this
   recipe ★ </a>
</div>
```

The recipe directions will now be neatly split into lines at each newline character, as shown in figure 3.15.

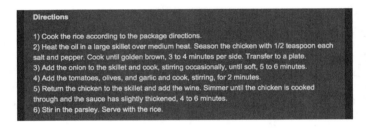

Figure 3.15 The recipe's directions with added line breaks

You should now be comfortable using Wreck to pull in data from external APIs and writing view helpers to create even more flexible views. For some more advanced options, be sure to check out the readme for Wreck on GitHub (https://github.com/hapijs/wreck).

Next up I'll be looking at how to implement sessions and store user state between requests.

3.4 *Managing logins and user sessions*

HTTP is described as a *stateless protocol* which is a technical way of saying it has a terrible memory. In the movie *Memento*, the main character, Leonard Shelby, has a condition called anterograde amnesia. That means he can't form new memories. Every time he meets someone, it's as if it's the first time he's ever met them. That's similar to how HTTP works. Every new request is as anonymous as the last.

This sounds unhelpful for a protocol that powers websites, where users expect to be remembered as they go from page to page. The way Leonard deals with his amnesia is that he keeps lots of artifacts from his meetings—written notes, photographs, and even tattoos. He only needs a name and he can bring his relationship with the person back to life, using his notes.

This is analogous to how sessions work in web applications. A request comes to a web application with a cookie, and using the cookie, the server can look up information about the user, either from the cookie itself or from server-side storage. It can then forget all about them for a while until the next request, and the same process continues for every request.

This section introduces hapi-auth-cookie, which is an authentication plugin for hapi.

> **NPM PACKAGE** `hapi-auth-cookie` v6 (http://npmjs.com/package/hapi-auth-cookie)

Using hapi-auth-cookie, you can also store session data for a user. I'll be showing you how to configure hapi-auth-cookie and start working with sessions in your hapi apps. I'll then talk about forms before going on to show how to combine this new knowledge to implement login in the DinDin website.

3.4.1 *hapi-auth-cookie plugin*

hapi-auth-cookie (https://github.com/hapijs/hapi-auth-cookie) is a simple-but-powerful plug working with cookie-based authentication and sessions. You can install it and save it to your project's dependencies with npm:

```
npm install --save hapi-auth-cookie@6
```

Because hapi-auth-cookie is a hapi plugin, it must be registered with a hapi server before you can use it. I'm going to include hapi-auth-cookie in the `server.register()` call of the DinDin website I've been building.

> **Listing 3.27   index.js: registering and configuring hapi-auth-cookie**

```
server.register([
    require('dindin-api'),
    require('inert'),
    require('vision'),
    require('hapi-auth-cookie')          ◁——  Load
], (err) => {                                 hapi-auth-cookie

    if (err) {
        throw err;
    }
                                                            Create authentication
    server.auth.strategy('session', 'cookie', 'try', {  ◁——  strategy (see chapter 9)
        password: 'password-that-is-at-least-32-chars',
        isSecure: false                      ◁——  Let insecure connections
    });                                            receive cookie

    server.route(require('./routes'));

    server.start(() => {

        console.log('Started server at', server.info.uri);
    });
});
```

Set cookie password used to encrypt cookie →

By default, hapi-auth-cookie will only allow the cookie to be transferred over a secure TLS/SSL connection. This may not be convenient during development, so you can set the `isSecure` option to `false`, meaning hapi will set the cookie regardless of whether or not the connection is over TLS/SSL. In a production application you should always use TLS and set isSecure to true to avoid exposing private credentials over an unsecure network.

STORING AND RETRIEVING SESSION DATA

After hapi-auth-cookie is installed and registered with a server, you can use it to set and retrieve session data for a user during requests. Inside a handler, you can use the request.cookieAuth.set() function to set session data in the cookie, as shown in the this listing.

Listing 3.28   Using `request.cookieAuth.set()` to set session data

```
server.route({
    method: 'GET',
    path: '/setName/{name}'
    handler: function (request, reply) {

        request.cookieAuth.set({
            name: encodeURIComponent(request.params.name)
        });

        reply('Name set!');
    }
});
```

When a user requests a route, you can access their decoded session information at request.auth.credentials, shown here.

Listing 3.29   Using request.auth.credentials to retrieve some session data

```
server.route({
    method: 'GET',
    path: '/getName'
    handler: function (request, reply) {

        const name = request.auth.credentials.name;
        reply('Hello there ' + name);
    }
});
```

3.4.2   *Forms*

Forms are an essential part of almost any website and working with forms in hapi is simple, as shown in the examples that follow. Here's an example of a search form that uses the GET method to send its data:

```
<form action="/search" method="GET">
    <input name="search1" type="text">
      <input name="search2" type="text">
    <input type="submit" value="Submit">
</form>
```

Forms that use the GET method send the data as part of the query string, like so:

```
GET /search?search1=yourQuery&search2=yourOtherQuery
```

This data can be accessed in hapi's `request.query`.

Listing 3.30 Accessing form data from GET method forms

```
server.route({
    method: 'GET',
    path: '/search',
    handler: function (request, response) {

        doSearch(request.query.search1, request.query.search2,
            (err, results) => {

            if (err) {
                throw err;
            }

            reply(results);
        });
    }
});
```

The same form can be modified to use the POST method:

```
<form action="/search" method="POST">
    <input name="search1" type="text">
    <input name="search2" type="text">
    <input type="submit" value="Submit">
</form>
```

Forms with the POST method will send the data as part of the HTTP request body, a.k.a. the payload. Data will be form-encoded, like so:

```
POST /search
```

```
search1=yourQuery&search2=yourOtherQuery
```

When any data is sent in the request payload that's useful to your application, you must configure the hapi route to deal with the payload accordingly. We saw this in chapter 2, when POSTing JSON to an API.

The payload configuration when working with JSON or form data is exactly the same. hapi's smart enough to know what encoding the payload is in before attempting to parse it by checking the Content-type header of the request. The route for dealing with the preceding POST request would look like this.

Listing 3.31 Accessing form data from POST method forms

```
server.route({
    method: 'POST',
    config: {
```

```
        payload: {
            output: 'data'
        }
    },
    path: '/search',
    handler: function (request, response) {

        doSearch(request.payload.search1, request.payload.search2,
            (err, results) => {

            if (err) {
                throw err;
            }

            reply(results);
        });
    }
});
```

NOTE Adding forms to your website can lead to a security vunerability known as Cross-Site Request Forgery (CSRF/XSRF), which can be dangerous unless you take proper measures. I haven't covered it in this section, to keep things brief, but chapter 9 looks into mitigation strategies for CSRF.

3.4.3   *Implementing login*

In this section we build the login feature of the DinDin website. Users must log in via a form, shown in figure 3.16, before they can create their own recipes.

Login page

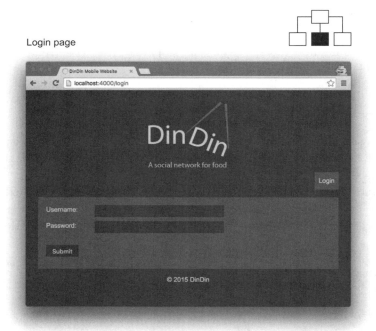

Figure 3.16   The login page with username and password form

Before implementing login, I think it's a good idea to define what being *logged in* means.

Here's a recap of how authentication works with the DinDin API. Only authenticated users are allowed to create recipes. The authentication scheme used with the API is bearer token authentication. When the API receives a request that uses this authentication strategy, the authorization header is checked for presence of a token. If a token is present, it's looked up in the database. If a matching token is found, the user is authenticated.

Because tokens are usually long, random strings, we can't expect users to remember them. In reality, they should be expired after a set period to limit the amount of time an attacker could use a stolen token.

The DinDin API we produced in chapter 2 has been extended slightly in the dindin-api module with an extra route for login. This route has a path of `/api/login` and a method of POST. A payload containing a `username` and `password` should be sent to the login route. If a matching `username` is found and the `password` is correct, the response will contain the user's current `token`.

Once a token has been gained, it can be stored in the user's session and will be available until the session has expired. A logged-in user is defined as a user with a valid API token stored in their session.

CREATING THE LOGIN FORM

When a user of the website clicks the login button, they are taken to the login page, the template for which is shown here.

Listing 3.32   views/login.hbs: the login form view

```
<div id="login-form">
    <form action="/login" method='POST'>
        <div class="form-control">
            <label for="username">Username:</label>
            <input type="text" id="username" name="username">
        </div>
        <div class="form-control">
            <label for="password">Password:</label>
            <input type="password" id="password" name="password">
        </div>
        <div class="form-control">
            <input type="submit" value="Submit">
        </div>
    </form>
</div>
```

The login button in the website header is hyperlinked to /login. The matching handler and route for this are shown in the next two listings.

Listing 3.33   handlers/pages.js: the login form handler

```
exports.login = function (request, reply) {

    reply.view('login');
};
```

Listing 3.34   routes.js: the login form route

```
'use strict';

const Pages = require('./handlers/pages');
const Assets = require('./handlers/assets');
const Actions = require('./handlers/actions');

module.exports = [{
    ...
}, {
    method: 'GET',
    path: '/login',
    handler: Pages.login
}, {
    ...
}];
```

You can restart the server and point your browser to http://localhost:4000/login to view the login page.

Next, I need to create the route that handles the posted username and password from the form and retrieves the token from the API.

LOGGING IN USERS

When a user submits the login form with their credentials, the credentials should then be forwarded to the API. If those credentials are correct, a token will be given and this can then be stored in the user's session for all future requests. After a successful login, the user will be redirected to the home page.

> **NOTE**   The SQLite database provided in chapter 2 has been preseeded with two users to allow you to test logging in. The usernames are john and jane, and the password for both users is secret.

If a login attempt is unsuccessful, the API will return a non-200 response code. You can check for this and redirect the user to the login form.

Listing 3.35 routes.js: the login form route

```
'use strict';

const Pages = require('./handlers/pages');
const Assets = require('./handlers/assets');
const Actions = require('./handlers/actions');

module.exports = [{
    ...
}, {
    method: 'POST',
    path: '/login',
    config: {
        payload: {
            output: 'data'
        }
    },
    handler: Actions.login
}, {
    ...
}];
```

The corresponding handler for processing the submitted login form is shown in this listing.

Listing 3.36 handlers/actions.js: the login form handler

```
const Wreck = require('wreck');

exports.login = function (request, reply) {

    const apiUrl = this.apiBaseUrl + '/login';

    Wreck.post(apiUrl, {
        payload: JSON.stringify(request.payload),
        json: true
    }, (err, res, payload) => {

        if (err) {
            throw err;
        }

        if (res.statusCode !== 200) {
            return reply.redirect(this.webBaseUrl + '/login');
        }

        request.cookieAuth.set({
            token: payload.token
        });
        reply.redirect(this.webBaseUrl);
    });
};
```

Include payload from login form in POST request to API

Tell Wreck to expect JSON response from API and parse it automatically

If API responded with non-200 code, redirect user to login page

... otherwise, add token to user's session

Redirect user to home page

After a user has been logged in, the session data in the cookie is available in every subsequent route for the user. I can use this to conditionally update the buttons in the header.

UPDATING THE WEBSITE HEADER

The login button in the header should only display for users who aren't logged in. Once a user has logged in, it should be replaced with two different buttons. One for creating a recipe and one for logging out, as shown in figure 3.17.

Figure 3.17   The header buttons before and after logging in

I can update the layout template with a conditional block to display one of the two sets of buttons, depending on whether the user is logged in.

Listing 3.37   views/layout/layout.hbs: rendering header buttons based on login state

```
. . .

{{#if user}}
    <a class="header-button" href="/logout">Logout</a>
    <a class="header-button" href="/create">Create +</a>
{{else}}
    <a class="header-button" href="/login">Login</a>
{{/if}}

. . .
```

To ensure that the user variable is available in the template context, I must update all reply.view() calls to include the user session data in the view context.

Listing 3.38   handlers/pages.js: rendering views with the user session data in context

```
. . .

reply.view('index', {                          Set user property of
    recipes: payload,                          template's context to
    user: request.auth.credentials   ◁─────────  user's credentials
});

. . .
```

You can use this pattern of rendering views conditionally, based on some user session data to powerful effect, creating a personal experience for each user.

3.4.4 Creating recipes

To create recipes, users will visit the recipe creation page in their browser at http://localhost:4000/create or click the Create + button in the header. Figure 3.18 shows how the create recipe page will look.

Create recipe page

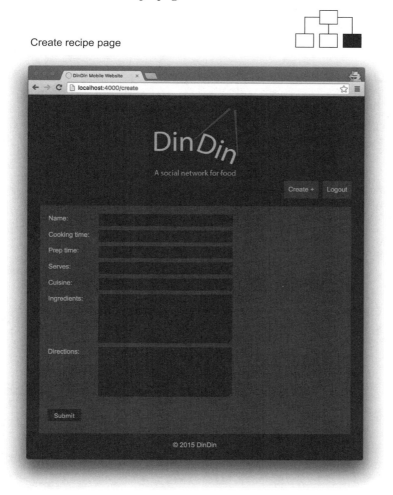

Figure 3.18 The Create recipe page

This listing shows the view template for this page, named create.hbs.

Listing 3.39 views/create.hbs: view template for the recipe creation page

```
<div id="login-form">
    <form action="/create" method='POST'>
        <div class="form-control">
```

```
            <label for="name">Name:</label>
            <input type="text" id="name" name="name">
        </div>
        <div class="form-control">
            <label for="cooking_time">Cooking time:</label>
            <input type="text" id="cooking_time" name="cooking_time">
        </div>
        <div class="form-control">
            <label for="prep_time">Prep time:</label>
            <input type="text" id ="prep_time" name="prep_time">
        </div>
        <div class="form-control">
            <label for="serves">Serves:</label>
            <input type="text" id ="serves" name="serves">
        </div>
        <div class="form-control">
            <label for="cuisine">Cuisine:</label>
            <input type="text" id ="cuisine" name="cuisine">
        </div>
        <div class="form-control">
            <label for="ingredients">Ingredients:</label>
            <textarea id ="ingredients" name="ingredients"></textarea>
        </div>
        <div class="form-control">
            <label for="directions">Directions:</label>
            <textarea id ="directions" name="directions"></textarea>
        </div>
        <div class="form-control">
            <input type="submit" value="Submit">
        </div>
    </form>
</div>
```

The handler and route for the page are shown in the next two listings.

Listing 3.40   handlers/pages.js: recipe creation route

```
exports.createRecipe = function (request, reply) {

    reply.view('create', {
        user: request.auth.credentials
    });
};
```

Listing 3.41   routes.js: create recipe page route

```
...

module.exports = [{
    ...
}, {
    method: 'GET',
    path: '/create',
    handler: Pages.createRecipe,
```

```
    config: {
        auth: {
            mode: 'required'
        }
    }
}, {
    ...
}];
```

> Make authentication
> non-optional
> for this route

When the form is submitted, a POST request is sent to hapi.

Listing 3.42   routes.js: recipe creation action route

```
...

module.exports = [{
    ...
}, {
    method: 'POST',
    path: '/create',
    config: {
        auth: {
            mode: 'required'
        }
    },
    handler: Actions.createRecipe
}, {
    ...
}];
```

> Make authentication non-
> optional for this route

When the form data is received by hapi, it can be forwarded to the API to create the recipe. But first, I must set the authentication header so the API knows who the user is. To do that, I need to include an authorization header.

Additional headers can be set with Wreck by including a `headers` object in the options. The value of the authorization header should be `Bearer [token]`. I can retrieve the token value from the user's session as shown here.

Listing 3.43   handlers/actions.js: createRecipe handler

```
...

exports.createRecipe = function (request, reply) {

    const apiUrl = this.apiBaseUrl + '/recipes';
    const token = request.auth.credentials.token;

    Wreck.post(apiUrl, {
        payload: JSON.stringify(request.payload),
        headers: {
            'Authorization': 'Bearer ' + token
        }
    }, (err, res, payload) => {
```

> Retrieve user's API token
> from session data

> Stringify form data for
> forwarding to API

> Set Authorization
> header for API request

```
        if (err) {
            throw err;
        }

        reply.redirect(this.webBaseUrl);        ◁──┐  Redirect user
    });                                              │  to home page
};
```

The form data will be passed on to the API to create the recipe.

If a recipe has been successfully created via the API, the user's browser will be told to redirect to the home page. hapi's `reply()` interface has a method `reply.redirect(url)`. When used, the request will be responded to with a 302 response code, and the browser will navigate to the URL defined in the `url` argument.

3.4.5   *Implementing logout*

If you allow a user to log in to your website, it's important that you also allow them to log out. A user may leave a machine unattended, and you don't want the next person who sits down to be able to use the original user's session.

When a user is logged in to the DinDin website, the Login button in the header is replaced with a Logout button. To log out a user, I need to ensure that their session has been destroyed.

CLEARING A SESSION

hapi-auth-cookie provides the method `request.cookieAuth.clear()` to let you clear a user's session. When a user has successfully logged out of a website, a common action is to redirect that user to a page, often the home page. I can put this all together now to build the logout route, as shown in the following two listings.

Listing 3.44   routes.js: The logout action route

```
module.exports = [{
    ...
}, {
    method: 'GET',
    path: '/logout',
    handler: Actions.logout
}, {
    ...
}];
```

Listing 3.45   handlers/actions.js: the logout handler

```
exports.logout = function (request, reply) {
                                                       ┌─  Clear user's
    request.cookieAuth.clear();                  ◁────┘    session data
    reply.redirect(this.webBaseUrl);      ◁──┐  Redirect user
};                                            │  to home page
```

The last two chapters have been a whirlwind tour of hapi, constructing an application composed of two parts with many features. In the next chapter we're going to ease up on the pace somewhat and take a more thorough look at one aspect of hapi: handling requests.

3.5 Summary

- We can use the Inert hapi plugin to serve static content. We can serve single files or entire directories using the file and directory handlers that Inert gives us.
- We can render dynamic HTML content by using the Vision plugin and a template engine such as Handlebars.
- We can organize our views into smaller, reusable chunks by making use of layouts and partials.
- Wreck is a utility for making HTTP requests to other services.
- hapi-auth-cookie is a hapi plugin for managing cookie-based authentication and session for storing state between requests.

Part 2

Expanding your toolbox

By now you should have a pretty good idea of what hapi.js is all about and how all the parts fit together. The five chapters in this part of *hapi.js in Action* build on that knowledge, covering some in-depth topics and giving you more superpowers.

In chapter 4, you'll master routes and handlers. In chapter 5, you'll learn how hapi handles requests using the request lifecycle. You'll also learn how useful extension points are for customizing hapi to do whatever you need.

In chapter 6, you'll meet Joi, an incredibly powerful library for validating data, which can help make your applications extremely reliable and predictable.

In chapter 7, you'll dive into plugin development, and you'll be blown away at the level of modularity and flexibility that hapi offers in the way that you and your team piece together applications from small chunks of functionality.

In chapter 8, you'll look at boosting the performance of your application by making the best use of both server- and client-side caching.

Routes and handlers in-depth

4

This chapter covers

- More routing techniques
- Server methods and prerequisites
- Creating custom handlers
- Uploading files

In this chapter we'll take an in-depth look at two of the most important concepts in hapi: routes and handlers. Routes are how you tell hapi what kind of requests you're interested in. Handlers are how you choose to respond to those routes. Having a mastery of these two will greatly broaden the types of applications you can create with hapi.

4.1 Routing in-depth

You should be familiar now with what routes are in hapi and how to create them (using `server.route()`). If you've been following along with the example projects in earlier chapters, you will have even made quite a few routes yourself. This section attempts to shore up that understanding with a more in-depth examination of routing, including routing features and approaches you haven't seen yet.

4.1.1   *The hapi router: ordering and conflicting routes*

In some frameworks, such as Express, the order in which routes are added is significant. In such a framework, if you added two routes in an order contrary to what you intended, you might be left befuddled when things don't work how you expected.

Routes should be independent of one another in an application because they're separate concerns. If you make a shopping list before you go to the grocery store, it shouldn't matter whether you put bananas at the top of the list or the bottom—you should be arriving home with bananas either way.

hapi's router works differently than Express's. It doesn't care about the order in which you add routes. Rather than matching routes on a first-come, first-served basis, hapi's router will categorize each new route and add it to a data structure called the *routing table*. No matter which order you add your routes, the same routing table will be constructed.

This deterministic routing system gives you more freedom in the way you structure your application. You can have lots of developers working on separate chunks of your application without worrying about how their routes might be affecting someone else's.

Another notable difference from some other frameworks is that hapi won't allow you to create conflicting routes. hapi considers conflicting routes to be routes that look equivalent to its routing algorithm. An example could be two routes with the same path and method. Let's run an application with conflicting routes and see what happens.

> **Listing 4.1   Application with conflicting routes**

```
const Hapi = require('hapi');

const server = new Hapi.Server();
server.connection({ port: 4000 });

server.route([
    {
        method: 'GET',
        path: '/',
        handler: function (request, reply) {}
    }, {
        method: 'GET',
        path: '/',
        handler: function (request, reply) {}
    }
]);

server.start(() => {

    console.log('Server started!');
});
```

These two routes will conflict because they have the same path and method.

You should be prevented from running this application. hapi will abort the program and output an error containing the message:

```
Error: New route / conflicts with existing /
```

This might seem trivial in such a simple example (how often would you do that?), but when you're working with a large application with dozens of routes, this feature could save you a lot of painful debugging. That fact will become even more apparent when we look deeper into plugins later in the book.

4.1.2 Route methods

HTTP requests always contain a method. The method is the *GET* part of a GET request, as in the following:

```
GET /pictures/cats
Host: example.com
```

When we make a route in hapi, we specify which method we want to associate the route with by setting the option `method`:

```
server.route({
    method: 'GET'
    ...
});
```

Technically, you can add a route with any custom method name you like, but please don't! The commonly used methods all have well-defined semantics on the web. All of the methods you will probably ever care about when creating routes are listed in table 4.1.

Table 4.1 Commonly used HTTP request methods

Method	Meaning/Use	Example
GET	Used to retrieve a resource or a collection of resources, such as a record from an API or webpage	Fetch/search all books or a single book in a bookstore
POST	Used to create a resource; for example, to create a user account or to send a new form submission	Add a new book to the bookstore
PUT	Used to update a whole resource	Change a book's info
PATCH	Used to update part of a resource	Change a single field of a book
DELETE	Used to delete a resource	Permanently delete a book

If you want to use the same route configuration and handler for multiple actions, you can create a route with an array of methods.

Listing 4.2 A route with multiple methods

```
server.route({
    method: ['GET', 'POST'],          ◁── Match GET and
    path: '/',                              POST requests
    handler: function (request, reply) {

        const method = request.method;                              ◁──
        reply('Handler was called for a ' + method + ' request');
    }
});                                   Method used for this request is stored
                                      in request.method (always lowercased).
```

This might be convenient if the behavior of your handler is similar across different HTTP methods, and you don't want to create a whole new route for each method. As is often the case with pages containing forms, the GET and the POST requests might render the same form again if the form data posted was invalid.

4.1.3 *Parameterized paths*

In chapters 2 and 3, you saw examples of creating routes with parameterized paths. Probably the most obvious use for parameterized paths is when you're creating a route that retrieves a single resource by using an identifier. Such a route, where id is the identifier, might look like this:

```
server.route({
    path: '/pastries/{id}/ingredients'
    ...
});
```

PARTIAL SEGMENT PARAMETERS

One feature we haven't yet looked at is the ability to parameterize a partial path segment. A *path segment* is a single unit of a path separated from neighboring segments by a slash (/). In the path /mary/had/a/little/lamb, the segments are mary, had, a, little, and lamb.

Sometimes the part of the path you want to parameterize might not be a complete segment. If you're building an API for a stock photography website, for example, you might want to add the ability for a user to specify both the image and the format to download as a single path segment. The following URLs would fetch the same image in different image formats:

```
/nature/flowers/orchids/cymbidium.png
/nature/flowers/orchids/cymbidium.tiff
/nature/flowers/orchids/cymbidium.jpg
```

To create a single route to serve these requests, we can parameterize the final segment into two parts, as this listing does.

Listing 4.3   Route with partial segment path parameters

```
server.route({
    method: 'GET',
    path: '/nature/flowers/orchids/{image}.{ext}',        ◁── Final segment of path
    handler: function (request, reply) {                          has two parameters:
                                                                 {image} and {ext}.
        const image = request.params.image;
        const ext = request.params.ext;

        reply('You requested ' + image + '.' + ext);
    }
});
```

NOTE If you use multiple parameters within a single segment, as in the preceding example, you must separate them with at least one valid character that isn't a parameter. If you had a path such as /download/{file}{ext}, hapi wouldn't know where to break the final segment into the file and the ext parameters, because there's no separator.

MULTIPLE PARAMETERS

In the URL example, the first three segments (/nature/flowers/orchids) of the path are related. Together they form the category hierarchy of the image to be downloaded. Our route from listing 4.3 isn't very flexible, because it has this category hierarchy hard-coded into the route path. If our API were going to contain images from lots of different categories and subcategories, we would need to generalize this path by using more parameters. An obvious approach might be something like this:

```
server.route({
    method: 'GET',
    path: '/images/{category}/{subcat1}/{subcat2}/{image}.{ext}',
    ...
});
```

If we make a request to /images/nature/flowers/roses/dog-rose.jpg, the value of request.params will be:

```
{
  "category": "nature",
  "subcat1": "flowers",
  "subcat2": "roses",
  "image": "dog-rose",
  "ext": "jpg"
}
```

We can make this path even more succinct, though, grouping the category into a single variable by using a multiple parameter:

```
server.route({
    method: 'GET',
    path: '/images/{category*3}/{image}.{ext}',
    ...
});
```

If we request the same URL again, the value of request.params will now be:

```
{
  "category": "nature/flowers/roses",
  "image": "dog-rose",
  "ext": "jpg"
}
```

As you can see, the segments that make up the category are now treated as a single parameter.

OPTIONAL PARAMETERS

It's also possible to include optional parameters in route paths. If you're building a "Meet the Team" page for your company's website, you might have a page to show the whole team and a page for each team member. The URLs might look something like this:

```
/team
/team/josh
/team/anita
```

You can match all those URLs by making the name an optional parameter in the path.

Listing 4.4 Route with an optional path parameters

```
server.route({
    method: 'GET',
    path: '/team/{name?}',                          {name?} parameter is
    handler: function (request, reply) {            an optional parameter.

        if (request.params.name) {
            return reply('Showing ' + request.params.name + '\'s page')
        }

        return reply('Showing the whole team page!');   ... otherwise
    }                                                    execute this
});
```

Execute this if optional name parameter is present ...

In general, you can use optional parameters any time you want to have a single route to fetch a single resource or collection of resources. You might also use an optional parameter to include an optional flag, which takes a default value, assigned in your handler, when the flag is not present.

WILDCARD PARAMETERS

The final kind of parameter we'll look at is a wildcard parameter. This is a named parameter where the name is followed by an asterisk; for example, {path*}. Wildcard parameters are useful when you don't know exactly how deeply nested (how many segments it has) a path is going to be, but you still want to match all possibilities with a single route.

You used a wildcard parameter in chapter 3 when serving static content with the directory handler. Let's have another look at that route:

```
server.route({
    method: 'GET',
    path: '/{path*}',
    ...
});
```

This route will match *any* GET request to the server, making the entire path available in request.params.path. This kind of route is called a *catch-all route* because it catches all requests that aren't routed to another, more-specific route. Catch-all routes are also useful for implementing custom 404 pages.

Earlier in this section I discussed conflicting routes, and you may be wondering now how it's possible to create a route that matches all requests (catch-all) and yet still be able to create other routes. Shouldn't any other route then be in conflict? The answer is no. The catch-all route doesn't conflict with all other routes. It's all down to the way hapi's router stores and categorizes routes. To understand why this is, let's peek inside the router.

4.1.4 How hapi picks a route

All of the routes that you add using `server.route()` get added internally to something called the *routing table*. Each server connection has its own copy of the routing table, illustrated in figure 4.1.

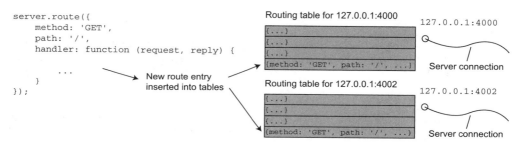

Figure 4.1 Each server connection has a copy of the routing table.

Remember, a *connection*, in hapi terms, is something that associates a hapi server with a physical port and network interface on your computer. We create connections using `server.connection()`. If you add a route to a server with `server.route()`, hapi will add an entry into the routing table for all the server's associated connections.

ADDING A ROUTE

When you add a new route, the router will split the route's path into segments and analyze each one. Each segment will be categorized. Here are some example paths and their categorization—these are all valid and non-conflicting routes within the same routing table:

```
Path: /document            Segments: document
                                     ^ literal
Path: /document/{id}       Segments: document, {id}
                                     ^ literal ^ param
Path: /document/{id}.xml   Segments: document, {id}.xml
                                     ^ literal ^ mixed
Path: /document/{path*}    Segments: document, {path*}
                                     ^ literal ^ wildcard
```

`literal`, `param`, `mixed`, and `wildcard` are all types of segments. This segment-by-segment analysis of each path is stored in the routing table and used when matching an incoming request to a route.

NOTE   The following is a simplification of how hapi's router works. The order of events and details differ from the real implementation, but the concepts are the same.

MATCHING A REQUEST TO A ROUTE

When a request is received, the path of the incoming request is split again. As each segment is examined, the router will narrow down the list of possible routes for the request, as shown in figure 4.2. Based on the example of the routes already discussed, let's say we have received a request for /document/mydoc.xml.

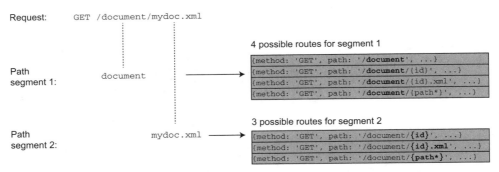

Figure 4.2   Matching routes are narrowed down with each segment of the request path.

After looking at the path, it should be quite easy to see that three of the routes match this request:

```
/document/{id}         (with id === 'mydoc.xml')
/document/{id}.xml     (with id === 'mydoc')
/document/{path*}      (with path === 'mydoc.xml')
```

In this case, it looks like we have three matching routes for a given request. How does hapi decide which one to choose? It will always choose the route that is *most specific*. The way it decides that is by ranking different segment types. The segment types in table 4.2 are listed most-to-least specific in terms of ranking.

Table 4.2   Route path segment types in order specificness

	Segment type	Example(s)
Most specific	Literal segment	/something
	Mixed segment	/some{thing} /{some}-{thing}
	Param segment	/{something} /{something?}
Least specific	Wildcard segment	/{something*}

From the three possible routes found when requesting /document/mydoc.xml, it should be clear that the second one is the winner. The final segment in number two is a mixed parameter, so it trumps the first (param segment) and the third (wildcard segment).

The reason there's no conflict between those routes is that they all have a different ranking in terms of specificity. There's always a clear winner for any possible request path. When hapi complains that you've created a route conflict, it means there's a possibility that a request could be received and it wouldn't be able to make a definitive decision about which route to select. If you remember this simple rule on the order of segment specificity, you should be able to easily reason through all of the routes that you create.

4.2 Building custom handlers

Handlers are where you declare what should happen when a request matches one of your routes. The basic handler is a JavaScript function with the signature:

```
function (request, reply) {...}
```

There are also a number of configuration-driven handlers that you can use to define complex behavior through configuration. The following listing shows an example of one of these—the directory handler, added by Inert, for serving static content, which you saw in chapter 3.

Listing 4.5 Directory handler added by the Inert plugin

```
server.route({
    method: 'GET',
    path: '/assets/{path*}',
    handler: {
        directory: {
            path: Path.join(__dirname, 'assets')    ⟵  Behavior of the route is
        }                                               defined in configuration
    }                                                   using directory handler.
});
```

Remember in chapter 1, I discussed that one of the central philosophies of hapi is that configuration is favorable over code. Configuration is usually easier to write, easier to read, and easier to modify and understand than the equivalent code.

If you find yourself repeating a common set of tasks or behaviors in your handlers, you could consider extracting a new custom handler type. Without further ado, let's see an example.

4.2.1 The internationalization (i18n) example

In this example we're building a (very) small website. The website will cater to an international audience, so we want to include support for multiple languages from the start. Internationalization, also known as i18n, isn't a feature that's built into hapi, so you're going to create it yourself. In this section you're going to see how you can write a custom handler to wrap up the complexity of this task into a simple-to-use handler.

You should prepare your environment in the usual way: create a directory to hold the project and add a package.json (either manually or by using npm init). Add any dependencies, as you need them, by running npm install --save [package name].

The website, which is in its early stages of development, currently only has one page—the home page. This listing shows we have created a Handlebars template for that.

Listing 4.6   templates/index.hbs

```
<h1>Hello!</h1>
```

Okay, so when I called it a *website* I was probably overstating things. It's a single line of HTML that says Hello!—but it has potential!

As the following listing shows, we currently have a simple skeleton hapi application to serve this view.

Listing 4.7   index.js: the basic website application

```
const Hapi = require('hapi');
const Path = require('path');

const server = new Hapi.Server();
server.connection({ port: 4000 });

server.register(require('vision'), (err) => {        ◁──┐  Load vision
                                                        │  module
    if (err) {
        throw err;
    }

    server.views({
        engines: {
            hbs: require('handlebars')                    Configure
        },                                                view engine
        path: Path.join(__dirname, 'templates')
    });

    server.route([
        {
            method: 'GET',
            path: '/',
            handler: {                        Use view handler to
                view: 'index'                 render index template
            }
        }
    ]);

    server.start(() => {
```

```
        console.log('Server started!');
    });
});
```

We've decided to send our Handlebars templates to translators. So we send them to a French and a Chinese translator. We also come up with a new naming scheme, suffixing the template name with the ISO 639-1 two-letter language code. We now have three templates, named as follows:

```
templates/index_en.hbs        ◄─── English template
templates/index_fr.hbs        ◄─── French template
templates/index_zh.hbs        ◄─── Chinese template
```

4.2.2 Parsing the Accept-Language header

Our application needs to look at an incoming request and decide which language-specific template it should serve, as illustrated in figure 4.3.

Figure 4.3   The application should determine which template to use.

The Accept-Language header, when present, specifies the user's preferred languages, each with a weighting or priority (called a *quality factor* in the HTTP spec, denoted by q). Here's an example of an Accept-Language header:

```
Accept-Language: da, en-gb;q=0.8, en;q=0.7
```

This can be translated conversationally:

> *I would like this resource in Danish. If you don't have Danish, I would like British English. If you don't have British English, I will settle for any kind of English.*

We can use a Node.js package, appropriately named accept, to help parse those headers into a more usable form.

NPM PACKAGE accept v2 (http://npmjs.com/package/accept)

To see what kind of thing the accept module gives us back, you can run this one-liner (after npm install --save accept@2 in our project) in your terminal:

```
node -e "console.log(require('accept').languages('da, en-gb;q=0.8, en;q=0.7'))"
```

The output should be:

```
['da', 'en-gb', 'en']
```

The array returned by `Accept.languages()` is ordered by user language preference, with most preferred first.

4.2.3 *First implementation*

We can use our language-specific templates and knowledge of the Accept-Language header to build a naïve implementation of our i18n-enabled hapi-powered website.

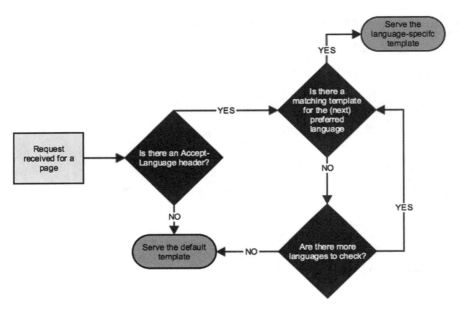

Figure 4.4   The process we will use to find a suitable template for a request

When a request is received, we want to check if we have a matching template for any of the languages in the Accept-Language header. If there's no header present, or there are no matching templates, we will fall back to rendering the default language template. This process is shown in figure 4.4. The implementation of this for a single route is shown here.

Listing 4.8   index.js: I18n-enabled route serving language-specific templates

```
'use strict';

const Accept = require('accept');

server.route([
    {
        method: 'GET',
        path: '/',
        handler: function (request, reply) {
```

Define some
settings

```
const supportedLanguages = ['en', 'fr', 'zh'];
const defaultLanguage = 'en';
const templateBasename = 'index';
```

Parse Accept-
Language header

```
const langs = Accept.languages(request.headers['accept-language']);
```

Loop through each
preferred language. If
current one is supported,
render the view ...

```
for (let i = 0; i < langs.length; ++i) {
    if (supportedLanguages.indexOf(langs[i]) !== -1) {
        return reply.view(templateBasename + '_' + langs[i]);
    }
}

reply.view(templateBasename + '_' + defaultLanguage);
        }
    }
]);
```

... otherwise, render
default language's view.

You can test this trying different Accept-Language headers by sending some requests with cURL:

```
$ curl localhost:4000/ -H "Accept-language: en"
<h1>Hello!</h1>

$ curl localhost:4000/ -H "Accept-language: zh"
<h1>你好!</h1>

$ curl localhost:4000/ -H "Accept-language: fr"
<h1>Bonjour!</h1>

$ curl localhost:4000/ -H "Accept-language: de"
<h1>Hello!</h1>
```

4.2.4 *Making things simple again*

Although our first implementation works for sure, it's pretty ugly and involves a lot of boilerplate code that needs to be copied into each of our handlers for any new routes we add. Do you remember how easy it was to use the basic view handler from Vision? That was a simpler time—we want to get back to that:

```
server.route([
    {
        method: 'GET',
        path: '/',
        handler: {
            view: 'index'
        }
    }
]);
```

What we need to do then is to build a custom handler that can be used like the preceding code sample and take care of all the messy business behind the scenes for us. You create new custom handlers using the server.handler() method.

HAPI API `server.handler(name, method)` (http://hapijs.com/api# serverhandlername-method)

Your custom handler function will accept the route and the options given to it as parameters and should return a handler with the usual function signature.

Listing 4.9   index.js: creating the custom `i18n-view` handler

```
server.handler('i18n-view', (route, options) => {

    const view = options.view;                                          View name passed in
                                                                        through options
    return function (request, reply) {

        const settings = {
            supportedLangs: ['en', 'fr', 'zh'],                         Define some settings
            defaultLang: 'en'
        };

        const langs = Accept.languages(request.headers['accept-language']);

        for (let i = 0; i < langs.length; ++i) {
            if (settings.supportedLangs.indexOf(langs[i]) !== -1) {
                return reply.view(view + '_' + langs[i]);
            }
        }

        reply.view(view + '_' + settings.defaultLang);                  ... otherwise, render
    };                                                                  default language's view.
});
```

Parse Accept-Language header →

Loop through each preferred language. If current one is supported, render the view ...

One improvement I would like to add to this is to remove the `settings` object from the handler. Having these explicit values in the code tightly binds the custom handler to our usage. It's a good idea to keep configuration like this in a central location.

When creating a hapi server you can supply an app object with any custom configuration you would like. These values are then accessible inside `server.settings.app`. The following listing moves the i18n configuration there.

Listing 4.10   index.js: storing app config in `server.settings.app`

```
const server = new Hapi.Server({
    app: {
        i18n: {
            supportedLangs: ['en', 'fr', 'zh'],                         Store application
            defaultLang: 'en'                                           config when
        }                                                               creating server
    }
});

...
```

```
server.handler('i18n-view', (route, options) => {
    const view = options.view;
    return function (request, reply) {
        const settings = server.settings.app.i18n;
```

> Access the same config later in server.settings.app

```
...
```

Now using our shiny new custom handler is as simple as supplying an object with an i18n-view key and setting the template name.

Listing 4.11 index.js: using the custom `i18n-handler` handler

```
server.route([
    {
        method: 'GET',
        path: '/',
        handler: {
            'i18n-view': {
                view: 'index'
            }
        }
    }
]);
```

We can reuse this handler now throughout our codebase without any ugly boilerplate code.

EXERCISE Vision's `view` handler allows you to pass a `context` object, which will be used as the context when rendering the view.

Can you modify the `i18n-view` handler to also accept a context object? You should test this by making a new view that outputs a variable supplied in the context:

```
server.route({
    method: 'GET',
    path: '/sayHello',
    handler: {
        'i18n-view': {
            view: 'index',
            context: { name: 'steven' }
        }
    }
});
```

4.3 *Server methods*

Server methods are functions that are attached to a hapi server object. They can then be accessed and called from wherever the server object is in scope. Server methods are intended to be called from within route handlers.

Okay, so they are another way to access shared functions—probably doesn't sound impressive at this point, right? To be honest, my opinion of server methods was fairly low when I first encountered them too. They seem to be solving a problem that doesn't exist on the face of it (that's what modules are for!). But I was won over after seeing some of the powerful functionality you can get for free when opting to use them.

Probably the biggest advantage to using server methods is the simple caching model they provide. Chapter 8 looks at this in-depth.

First things first. Let's see what server methods look like and how to create and use them.

Assume that we're building a service that does all kinds of number crunching for consumers. One of the endpoints might be a simple averaging service, which accepts a bunch of numbers and returns the mean value.

The following listing shows a route that we might create to handle this. An array of numbers is posted to the route. The handler then finds the mean value and responds with it.

Listing 4.12   Route that calculates the mean value from a payload of numbers

```
'use strict';

server.route({
    method: 'POST',
    path: '/avg',
    handler: function (request, reply) {

        const values = request.payload.values;        ⟵ Expects payload to contain
        const sum = values.reduce((a, b) => a + b);        array of numbers, such as
                                                           {"values": [1,2,3,4,5]}
        reply({ mean: sum / values.length });

    }
});
```

We can test this route using a cURL command, for example:

```
curl -H "Content-Type: application/json" -X POST -d '{"values": [1,2,3,4,5]}'
    http://localhost:4000/avg
```

It may turn out that I want to reuse this `mean` functionality in another handler somewhere in my application. It makes sense to extract it as a function, or in this case, as a server method.

> **HAPI API** `server.method(name, method, [options])` (http://hapijs.com/api#servermethodname-method-options)

Server methods are created by calling `server.method()`. This method has three required arguments, a `name` for the server method, the function, and an `options` object. The server method is then usable inside route handlers by calling `server.methods.name()`, where `name` is the name you gave to the method. Figure 4.5 shows this pattern.

Creating a server method

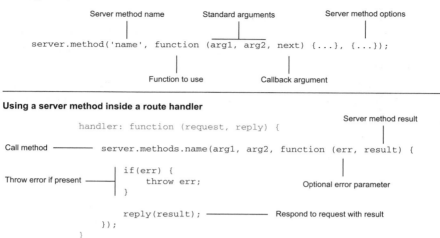

Using a server method inside a route handler

Figure 4.5 Creating and using a server method

Rather than returning the end result, notice that server methods *always* call the next callback with the result. Doing so allows for any asynchronous behavior that you may want to include in the server method, such as making an HTTP request or reading from the filesystem.

The following listing shows the example from listing 4.12 rewritten, using a server method to calculate the mean value of the array.

Listing 4.13 Creating and using the mean server method

```
const mean = function (values, next) {                      Defines JavaScript
                                                            function to be used
    const sum = values.reduce((a, b) => a + b);             as server method
    return next(null, sum / values.length);
};

server.method('mean', mean, {});                Creates new server
                                                method called mean
server.route({
    method: 'POST',
    path: '/avg',
    handler: function (request, reply) {

        server.methods.mean(request.payload.values, (err, mean) => {

            if (err) {
                throw err;
            }
            return reply({ mean: mean });
        });
    }
});
```

Uses mean server method in handler to calculate mean value of payload

You should now understand what server methods are and how to create and use them.

AN ALTERNATE SYNTAX FOR CREATING SERVER METHODS

There is another, more configuration-oriented approach for creating server methods. If you find yourself working on a hapi application written by someone else, it's possible you'll see either form in use, so it's good to know how to deal with both.

Rather than supply the server method name, function, and options as an argument list, you can create a server method by passing a configuration option to `server.method()`. Here's the `mean` server method from earlier created this way:

```
server.method({
    name: 'mean',
    method: mean,
    options: {}
});
```

Both syntaxes are equal. They will create the same server method under the hood. Personally, I prefer the configuration object approach because it feels more like doing things the "hapi" way, and is similar to the API we've used before for `server.route()`. You can also supply an array of these objects to `server.method()` to create multiple server methods at once:

```
const methods = [
    {
        name: 'method',
        method: method1,
        options: {}
    },{
        name: 'method2',
        method: method2,
        options: {}
    }
];

server.method(methods);
```

There are several features in hapi, including server-side caching and route prerequisites, that become extremely simple and convenient to use in conjunction with server methods. Hold tight—if you're still a server method skeptic. I promise to win you over eventually!

4.4   *Route prerequisites*

We use callbacks in Node when working with asynchronous operations. The callback pattern can become cumbersome, though, when we need to manage workflows composed of multiple steps, especially when some of those steps are allowed to take place concurrently. hapi offers a feature called *route prerequisites*, which help to simplify request processing workflows involving multiple steps that must execute sequentially or in parallel.

4.4.1 The problem with concurrency in asynchronous JavaScript

Let's look at an example of a program for cooking an omelette. The algorithm is composed of three steps:

1. Crack the eggs (crack)
2. Whisk the eggs (whisk)
3. Fry the omelette (fry)

Each step happens in series. That is, one step can't begin until the previous step has finished. The flow of execution is shown in figure 4.6.

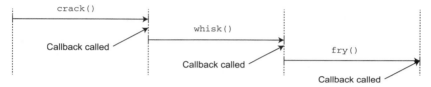

Figure 4.6 Execution flow for the simple omelette program

If each task is performed by calling an asynchronous JavaScript function with a callback argument, we can write the program as the following listing.

Listing 4.14 Making an omelette in three steps

```
crack(() => {
    console.log('Eggs are cracked');
    whisk(() => {
        console.log('Eggs are whisked');
        fry(() => {
            console.log('Omelette is ready');
        });
    });
});
```

This code is already less than ideal. It has several levels of indentation, making it difficult to read and understand. But to make things worse, let's add another step: chopping some vegetables, shown in figure 4.7.

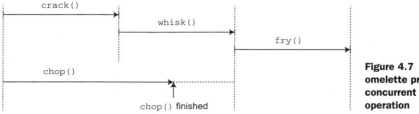

Figure 4.7 More complex omelette program with a concurrent chop() operation

The chopping of the vegetables isn't dependent on the eggs being cracked or whisked, so this step can be started immediately and run concurrently to the eggs being prepared. The omelette should only be fried after the eggs and the vegetables are ready:

```
let eggsReady = false;
let vegetablesReady = false;

crack(() => {

    whisk(() => {

        eggsReady = true;                         The eggs are
                                                  ready now.

        if (vegetablesReady) {
            fry(() => {
                                                  If vegetables are also
                console.log('Omelette is ready'); ready, fry omelette.
            });
        }
    });
});

chopVegetables(() => {
                                                  The vegetables
    vegetablesReady = true;                       are ready now.

    if (eggsReady) {
        fry(() => {
                                                  If eggs are also ready,
            console.log('Omelette is ready');     fry omelette.
        });
    }
});
```

Although the program works, the code is ugly. It's hard to read, and the true intentions are somewhat obscured by the wrestling that has to be done with the callbacks and the extra variables to record the state of the operations.

It will be difficult for any developer to look at this code and understand what it does a few months down the line. And this is a workflow made of four steps. How about one composed of 10? Clearly this isn't a scalable solution. These are the kinds of problems that you can get into when working with callbacks.

hapi offers a feature called *prerequisites*, which are an elegant and simple solution to this kind of spaghetti code.

4.4.2 *Specifying a route prerequisite*

A *route prerequisite*, or *pre*, is an asynchronous function that's run immediately before the handler for a route is executed. They're useful for performing tasks prior to your handler logic executing, such as fetching data from a file or a database. Pres are specified in the pre option when a route is created with server.route(). Here is a simple example of a single pre function that reads the contents of a file called poem.txt.

Listing 4.15   Using a pre function to read a file from the filesystem

```
const Hapi = require('hapi');
const Fs = require('fs');

const server = new Hapi.Server();
server.connection({ port: 4000 });

server.route({
    config: {
        pre: [{
            assign: 'poem',                                    Assign result of this pre
            method: function (request, reply) {                to request.pre.poem

                Fs.readFile('./poem.txt', (err, data) => {

                    if (err) {
                        throw err;
                    }
                    reply(data.toString());
                });
            }
        }]
    },
    method: 'GET',
    path: '/',
    handler: function (request, reply) {
                                                               Use result of pre as
        reply(request.pre.poem);                               response to request
    }
});

server.start((err) => {

    if (err) {
        throw err;
    }
    console.log('Server started!');
});
```

Pre function to read a file from filesystem

The handler for a route isn't executed until the pre function(s) have finished, as illustrated in figure 4.8.

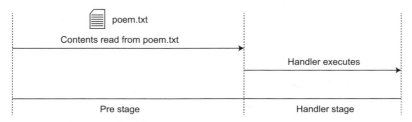

Figure 4.8   Route handlers run only once the pre stage is complete.

The function signature for a pre is exactly the same as a route handler:

```
function (request, reply) { ... }
```

The `request` and `reply` parameters are much the same too. The only difference is that calling `reply()` with a value won't send a response to the client as it does in a handler. Inside a pre, calling `reply()` will assign the given value to a property in the `request.pre` object. The property of pre that the value is assigned to is set by the `assign` option in the pre configuration.

The assign name `poem` is used in the example in listing 4.15, meaning the value passed to `reply()` inside the pre function is available in the handler at `request.pre.poem`.

4.4.3   *Using server methods with prerequisites*

Prerequisites are also designed to work with server methods. This means you can also get the benefit of caching if you combine the two features. We'll see more on caching with server methods in chapter 8. The following listing rewrites the example in listing 4.15 to use a server method instead.

> #### Listing 4.16   Using a server method as a prerequisite

```
server.method('poem', (request, reply) => {

    Fs.readFile('./poem.txt', (err, data) => {        Create a poem
                                                        server method
        if (err) {
            return reply(err);
        }
        reply(data.toString());
    });
});

server.route({
    config: {
        pre: [
            'poem'                       Use server method
        ]                                name to define the pre
    },
    method: 'GET',
    path: '/',
    handler: function (request, reply) {
                                              Use result of pre as
        reply(request.pre.poem);              response to the request
    }
});
```

4.4.4   *Multiple serial prerequisites*

You've seen how you can use a route prerequisite to run code and prepare a value before a route handler is executed. But so far, it's nothing groundbreaking. The real power of pre functions becomes apparent when you combine them into sequences of serial and parallel groups. By serial, I mean things that run in order, one by one, and by parallel, I mean things that run all together at the same time.

This section shows an example of combining multiple pre functions into a serial sequence that executes before the handler. You normally use a serial sequence when each step in the process requires access to the value acquired in the previous step.

For this example, we need to develop a fictional system that logs incoming one-way transmissions from secret agents out in the field. The secret agents will post a routine status update message to an API. The meaning of the message itself will be obscured. For instance, a message meaning "I have infiltrated the base" might be "The cat door is open." As an additional layer of security, each message will be encrypted with a symmetric-key algorithm, as illustrated in figure 4.9.

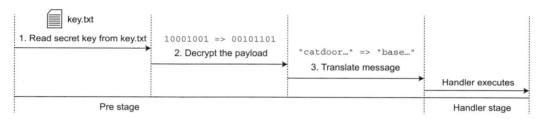

Figure 4.9 The steps in the pre phase of the secret agent app

The API needs to process each received message as follows:

1. Receive the message in the payload to a hapi route.
2. Read a secret key from a file in the filesystem.
3. Decrypt the message using the key.
4. Convert the message to its true meaning.
5. Log the message to the console.
6. Respond with an OK message so the agent knows we got the message.

This listing shows this set of steps in code, making use of route prerequisites.

Listing 4.17 Decrypting secret message using three prerequisites

```
const Crypto = require('crypto');
const Hapi = require('hapi');
const Path = require('path');
const Fs = require('fs');

const server = new Hapi.Server();
server.connection({ port: 4000 });

server.method('readKey', (request, reply) => {
```

Server method to read key from filesystem (and remove whitespace around key)

```
        Fs.readFile(Path.join(__dirname, 'key.txt'), 'utf8', (err, data) => {

            if (err) {
                throw err;
            }
            reply(data.trim());
        });
    });

    server.method('decryptMessage', (request, reply) => {
```

Server method to decrypt received message using key

```
        const decipher = Crypto.createDecipher('aes-256-cbc', request.pre.readKey);
        let cleartext = decipher.update(request.payload.message, 'hex', 'utf8');
        cleartext += decipher.final('utf8');

        reply(cleartext);
    });
```

Server method to look up and return real meaning of decrypted message

```
    server.method('convertMessage', (request, reply) => {

        const messages = {
            'Catflap is open': 'I have infiltrated the base',
            'Ink is dry': 'I have the blueprints',
            'Bird has flown': 'I am making my escape'
        };

        reply(messages[request.pre.decryptMessage]);
    });

    server.route({
        config: {
            pre: [
                'readKey',
                'decryptMessage',
                'convertMessage'
            ]
        },
```

These pre functions will execute serially (one after another).

```
        method: 'POST',
        path: '/',
        handler: function (request, reply) {

            console.log(new Date() + ': Incoming payload');
```

Log original received message and result of steps 2 and 3 in the process

```
            console.log('Encrypted message: ' + request.payload.message);
            console.log('Decrypted message: ' + request.pre.decryptMessage);
            console.log('Converted message: ' + request.pre.convertMessage);

            reply('ok');
        }
    });

    server.start(() => {

        console.log('Server started!');
    });
```

To test that this application works as expected, you can rely on your old friend cURL. First place the following key inside the file key.txt:

```
zAxjyjKuAvGdxmgCNyrjpbg
```

Start up the app by running `node index` and try the following cURL command:

```
curl -X POST -H "Content-type: application/json" -d '{"message":
    "65e11a21872da5477187bcdbfa1ef25f"}' http://localhost:4000
```

You should see something similar to the following output in the terminal running the application:

```
Fri May 08 2015 11:05:37 GMT+0800 (CST): Incoming payload
Encrypted message: 65e11a21872da5477187bcdbfa1ef25f
Decrypted message: Ink is dry
Converted message: I have the blueprints
```

Here are some other encrypted messages that you can try out too:

```
0dd31dde3980c1b7ecee12e0c52d85a5
ef2de8d315317333f7930901287fa768
```

4.4.5 *Parallel prerequisites: running tasks concurrently*

Sometimes you might have a set of prerequisite functions that you require to execute before your handler, but you don't care about the order in which they execute (the vegetable-chopping phase in the omelette example) or which finishes first. hapi allows this by specifying a set of *prerequisite functions*, or server method names in an array. The pre functions will all start executing at the same time, but the handler for the route won't execute until all the pre functions have finished.

To illustrate this, I will modify the example from the previous section. This time the key will be split in half, into two different files, key1.txt (containing `zAxjyjKuAvGd`) and key2.txt (containing `xmgCNyrjpbg`). This is a good example of when you might use parallel prerequisites, because here we only care that both halves of the key have been read before moving to the next step in the process—we don't care which order the keys are read in. This is shown in figure 4.10.

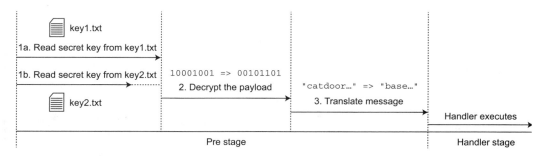

Figure 4.10   Step 1 is now composed of two concurrent tasks

First we need to modify the route configuration.

Listing 4.18   Splitting the first step into two parallel prerequisite tasks

```
server.route({
    ...
    config: {
        pre: [
            [
                'readKey1',
                'readKey2'
            ],
            'decryptMessage',
            'convertMessage'
        ]
    }
});
```

Will execute in series with adjacent elements in the array

Will execute concurrently with adjacent elements in the array

Then we can create the two new server methods readKey1 and readKey2. Each server method will read half of the key from separate files. The halves will then be combined at a later stage.

Listing 4.19   Creating the server methods `readKey1` and `readKey2`

```
server.method('readKey1', (request, reply) => {

    Fs.readFile('key1.txt', 'utf8', (err, data) => {

        if (err) {
            throw err;
        }
        reply(data.trim());
    });
});

server.method('readKey2', (request, reply) => {

    Fs.readFile('key2.txt', 'utf8', (err, data) => {

        if (err) {
            throw err;
        }
        reply(data.trim());
    });
});
```

The only other change that needs to be made is to combine the key halves in the decryptMessage server method.

Listing 4.20   Combining the halves of the key from `readKey1` and `readKey2`

```
server.method('decryptMessage', (request, reply) => {

    const key = request.pre.readKey1 + request.pre.readKey2;
```

```
        const decipher = Crypto.createDecipher('aes-256-cbc', key);
        ...
});
```

The application will now behave exactly like the one from chapter 3, with the exception that the two halves of the key will be read simultaneously from two different files. Remember, you can do anything inside a prerequisite function—read from the disk, make a network request, or process data.

> **EXERCISE**   Here are more ideas of where you could apply route prerequisites. Why not try building some yourself to help improve your skills with pres?
>
> 1   Fetch tweets using the Twitter API in a pre, then render these in a list inside the handler.
> 2   Geolocate a user inside a pre using their IP address with https://freegeoip.net and log this in the handler.
> 3   Create a workflow that combines the previous two examples to show the user a list of tweets about their current location.
> 4   Extend your solution to exercise 3 by also logging the user's IP address and location to a file. Note that this step can run in parallel to fetching the tweets.

4.5   *Managing file uploads to hapi applications*

As you saw in chapter 3, hapi will, by default, attempt to parse the payload from an incoming request based upon the existence and value of the request's Content-Type header. So far, you've seen examples in this book of payloads with application/x-www-form-urlencoded (from HTML forms) and application/json content types.

When we want to upload files from an HTML form, we use a different content type, multipart/form-data. This is specified in HTML by setting the enctype attribute on a <form> tag:

```
<form enctype="multipart/form-data" action="/upload" method="post">
    <input type="file" name="image" />
</form>
```

We can use the payload option in the route configuration to instruct hapi how to handle our payloads. The next listing shows an example route with the default values explicitly set. Note this is the same as not specifying options at all for payload.

> **Listing 4.21   POST route for uploading files with the default `payload` configuration**

```
server.route({
    method: 'POST',
    path: '/upload',
    handler: function (request, reply) {

        ...
    },
    config: {
```

```
        payload: {
            output: 'data',
            parse: true
        }
    }
});
```

hapi will parse `multipart/form-data` requests by default. But the way you work with the data from the files varies, depending on the value of the `payload.output` option in the configuration for the route. We'll look now at the available options using the HTML form in the following listing as an example for each option.

Listing 4.22   HTML page with a file upload form

```
<!DOCTYPE html>
<html lang="en">
<head>
    <meta charset="UTF-8">
    <title>Form</title>
</head>
<body>
    <form action="/upload" method="post" enctype="multipart/form-data">
        <input type="file" name="upload">
        <input type="submit">
    </form>
</body>
</html>
```

4.5.1   *Using data output: read the file contents into memory*

When using the `data` option with a multipart request, hapi will wait until the entire payload has been received over the network and read into memory and will attempt to parse each of the parts of the form into `request.payload`. Any text fields from the form will be available as strings. The contents of any uploaded files will be available as either strings (for files with a text mime type such as `text/plain`) or Node `Buffer` objects (for all other file mime types).

The next listing shows an example of a route that accepts a submitted multipart form and saves the uploaded files to the filesystem using the built-in Node `fs` module.

Listing 4.23   Receiving uploaded files as data and then saving to disk

```
...

server.route({
    config: {
        payload: {
            parse: true,          ◄──┐ Attempt to parse
            output: 'data'           │ payload into an object
        }                         ◄── Read full payload into memory
    },                               before calling handler (uploaded file
    method: 'POST',                  contents are strings or buffers)
```

```
     path: '/upload',
     handler: function (request, reply) {

         const upload = request.payload.upload;          ◁─┐  The file
                                                            │  we uploaded
         Fs.writeFile('uploadedFile', upload, (err) => {  ◁─┐  Save file contents into
             if (err) {                                      │  a file on filesystem
                 throw err;
             }
             reply('ok');                              ◁─┐  Respond to request
         });                                              │  with an "OK" message
     }
});
```

Notice in the previous listing that we save the file `uploadedFile`. When using the data option, hapi doesn't provide the content-type or the name of the file that has been uploaded. Therefore the data option is only useful when you're solely interested in the contents of the uploaded file. The stream option has greater flexibility.

4.5.2 *Using stream output: get the files as streams*

When using the `stream` option, hapi will parse all text fields into strings in `request.payload`. All file uploads will be node.js `Stream` objects. The `Stream` objects will have an additional property, `hapi`, which is added by the framework. `hapi .filename` will be equal to the filename of the uploaded file. The content type of the uploaded file is available at `hapi.headers['content-type']`. Let's try the example from listing 4.23 again, but this time save the file with the proper filename. Because the file upload is a stream, we can use the function `Fs.createWriteStream()`.

Listing 4.24   Receiving uploaded files as streams and saving to a file

```
...

server.route({
    config: {
        payload: {
            parse: true,              ◁─┐  Attempt to parse payload
            output: 'stream'             │  into an object
        }                                     ◁─┐  Present uploaded
    },                                           │  files as streams
    method: 'POST',
    path: '/upload',
    handler: function (request, reply) {       ◁─┐  Uploaded file as
        const upload = request.payload.upload;    │  a readable stream
        const uploadName = Path.basename(request.payload.upload.hapi.filename);
        const destination = Path.join(__dirname, 'uploads', uploadName);

        upload.pipe(Fs.createWriteStream(destination));  ◁─┐  Pipe uploaded file
        reply('ok');                                        │  stream into file
    }                                                       │  on filesystem
});
```

Filename of uploaded file

Create destination path on local filesystem to save file

NOTE The examples in listings 4.23 and 4.24 use `Path.basename()` to get only the last portion of the path specified in the filename. This is for security reasons, to prevent people from uploading files to arbitrary locations in the filesystem.

Saving the stream to disk is one of the many options available. The power of node.js streams lies in the simplicity of the interface and the composability available with hundreds of other components. Because saving uploads to disk is such a common requirement, there's another option available for the `payload.output` setting.

4.5.3   *Using file output: save the files to disk*

When using the `file` option, hapi will save any files uploaded through a multipart form directly to the filesystem as temporary files and provide some information, including the file path, inside the `request.payload` object. Once again, any text fields will be available as strings, as with the other options discussed earlier.

The files will be saved inside the directory specified by the `payload.uploads` route configuration option. This defaults to the value of `Os.tmpDir()`, which is usually `\\temp` on Windows machines and `/tmp` on all other platforms that Node supports.

Each saved file inside `request.payload` will be an object with the following properties available:

- `filename`–The filename of the original file uploaded through the form
- `path`–The path to the temporary file saved by hapi
- `headers`–Headers for the file, including `content-type`
- `bytes`–The size of the uploaded file in bytes

The typical pattern is to move this temporary file to its intended, final location inside your route handler. The following listing shows the example from earlier, adapted for the `file` option.

> **Listing 4.25   Using the `file` payload option to write uploads to temporary files**

```
...

server.route({
    config: {
        payload: {
            parse: true,                          Attempt to parse payload
            output: 'file'                        into an object
        }
    },                                            Save uploaded files
                                                  to temporary files
    method: 'POST',
    path: '/upload',                              Path to saved
    handler: function (request, reply) {          temporary file
        const uploadName = Path.basename(request.payload.upload.filename);
        const uploadPath = request.payload.upload.path;
```

Uploaded file's filename

Destination path on
local filesystem to
move uploaded file to ⊳

```
const destination = Path.join(__dirname, 'uploads', uploadName);

Fs.rename(uploadPath, destination, (err) => {

    if (err) {
        throw err;
    }

    reply('ok');
    });
    }
});
```

Move (rename) file
from temp location
into uploads directory

4.5.4 *Additional payload settings*

Aside from the parse and output settings you're already familiar with, there are some default settings that will affect file uploads, which you may want to tweak:

- *maxBytes*—The total payload size allowable. If the incoming payload exceeds this amount, a 400 Bad Request error will be sent to the client and handler activity will be terminated. Defaults to 1048576 bytes (1 MB).
- *timeout*—The maximum time, in milliseconds, allowed for receiving the full payload from the client. If the time exceeds this, a 408 Request Timeout error will be sent to the client and all handler activity will be terminated. Defaults to 10,000 (10 seconds).

These settings exist to ensure the reliability and security of your applications. If there's no upper limit on the size of an accepted payload, a user could technically exhaust all the memory on your server by uploading a huge file. You should tweak this setting, depending on what you're expecting to be uploaded for each route. A route for uploading video files needs different configuration than a route for text file uploads.

The timeout will also be affected by the size of the payload. A larger payload will take longer to upload, and you should factor this in when you change the maxBytes setting. If you're expecting clients with slow upload speeds, such as mobile clients using cellular data, you might also want to increase timeout to allow for these slower clients.

In the next chapter we'll be taking a deeper look into requests and responses.

4.6 *Summary*

- Parameterized paths make our routes more flexible. We can include wildcards, multiple and optional parameters.
- We looked at how hapi's router matches up a route with an incoming request. Understanding this will help you to devise routing strategies that make sense for your app.
- You can use route prerequisites to break up and simplify complex handler workflows, involving multiple parallel and sequential asyncronous tasks.

- You can build custom handlers to encapsulate complex behavior into a simple-to-use, configuration-oriented API.
- Server methods help you to share functionality across different parts of your application.
- You can easily manage file uploads in several ways, using the built-in payload output options.

Understanding requests and responses

I hope by now you've gotten a decent feel for hapi.js. You should have picked up useful, practical skills that you can apply in building your own applications. You also should have a good grasp of the language and terms we use in hapi—things like routes, handlers, requests, responses, and so on.

It should be clear that hapi has a lot going on under the surface. How things work and fit together internally is probably still rather unclear to you. We've only scratched the outer surface of the framework, superficially picking and choosing a small subset of the features without seeking a profound understanding of the framework. This has been an intentional decision on my part, and I'm hoping it has been a satisfying experience, and you're hungry for more. Now it's time to dig a little deeper.

What are requests, really? How are they processed by hapi? In what order do things happen? What and how does your code—and the building blocks we've used up until now—fit into that? These are some of the questions we'll be finding answers to in this chapter.

5.1   *The request object and lifecycle*

Requests are at the heart of everything in hapi. In this section we'll be looking at exactly what the `request` object is and the journey that each request takes when it turns up at your door.

5.1.1   *What is the request object?*

A hapi application's purpose in life is to serve HTTP requests. At a high level, you take a request and process it, make decisions based on the information in the request, and ultimately build an appropriate response to send back to the client. That's it. And with any luck, your application keeps on doing that over and over without stopping.

Requests look different depending on your point of view. In terms of the HTTP protocol, they look like messages in text format travelling on a TCP connection. On the physical layer, they're voltages in a wire or light signals in a fiber. The `request` that we work with in hapi is an abstract representation of an HTTP request, as a JavaScript object. We refer to this as the *request object*.

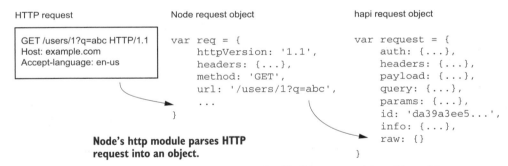

Figure 5.1   The HTTP request is parsed first by Node.js and then later by hapi into the `request` object that we know in our hapi applications.

When hapi receives an HTTP request, it builds this `request` object for us, as shown in figure 5.1. Everything we know about the request gets stored inside this single object and then it's this object that gets passed around our application. It's this same object that we've seen in our route handlers:

```
server.route({
    method: 'GET',
```

hapi adds a unique id property to every request.

```
path: '/',
handler: function (request, reply) {

    console.log('Got a new request with id: ' + request.id);
    reply('Hello World!');
  }
});
```

The `request` object comes laden with useful properties that we can access, such as the request's payload, query parameters, HTTP method, and cookies, all nicely parsed for us by hapi.

Aside from handlers, we've also seen the `request` object appearing in other places throughout this book so far, including when writing route prerequisites and server methods and when dealing with validation. The request is the thread that ties parts of your app together, progressing more and more through various levels until a response emerges. What might be confusing to you when you're new to hapi is how all these bits fit together—in what order do they run and how do they influence each other? Some of this might all seem a bit chaotic right now with so many different places to respond to a request available.

What if I told you there was a single concept that, if you understood it, would make all this confusion go away, give you a deep understanding of the framework, and allow you to bend hapi to your wildest intentions? Ready to take the red pill?

5.1.2 *The request lifecycle*

Every time a hapi application receives a new request, a journey is started. The `request` object passes through a predefined set of stages. This sequence of steps is called the *request lifecycle.* It's called a lifecycle because it starts with the birth of the `request` object and finishes with the end of its life, when a response is finally sent to the client. This concept is shown in figure 5.2.

The request lifecycle is made from 15 individual steps, which we'll see in full later. At

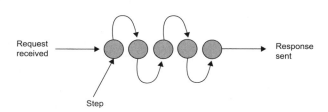

Figure 5.2 The request lifecycle is a series of steps.

a high level the steps in the request lifecycle can roughly be broken down into the half dozen groups or stages shown in figure 5.3.

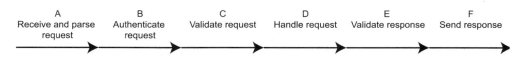

Figure 5.3 The six stages in the request lifecycle

The stages that will run for a given request may vary depending on both your application's configuration and runtime consequences. For instance, if you didn't set any validation rules for a route (configuration), then stage C will be skipped. If an incoming request fails authentication (runtime consequences), then steps C, D, and E will be skipped, as illustrated in figure 5.4, because there's not much point in validating or handling an unauthenticated request. This would be a waste of CPU time as the request is going to be discarded anyway.

Figure 5.4   An unauthenticated request won't be handled or validated.

Stages A and F will always run for every request, because there's always a response to send, even if it's one generated by hapi itself (a 500 response due to a payload parsing error, for example). These six stages can then be further subdivided into 15 individual steps that execute in series, one starting as soon as the previous has finished.

There's a lot of information following, and I don't expect you to memorize it or even take it all in at once. You need to get a gist of what's happening here and start to understand how the code and configuration that you write fit into this flow.

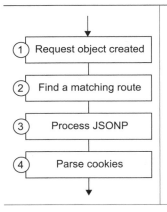

STAGE A: RECEIVE AND PARSE REQUEST

1 hapi server receives an HTTP request on one of its connections and creates an instance of the hapi `request` object. It's this object that will be passed along the request lifecycle. It's not complete yet, though. Things like `request.path` and `request.headers` are set here, but a route is not yet matched.

2 hapi looks at the request path and HTTP method and checks if there's a matching route in the routing table for the connection. If a route is found, it is placed at `request.route`.

3 hapi checks the `request` query string for a JSONP parameter.

4 hapi parses the Cookie header, if present, into an object and places it at `request.state`.

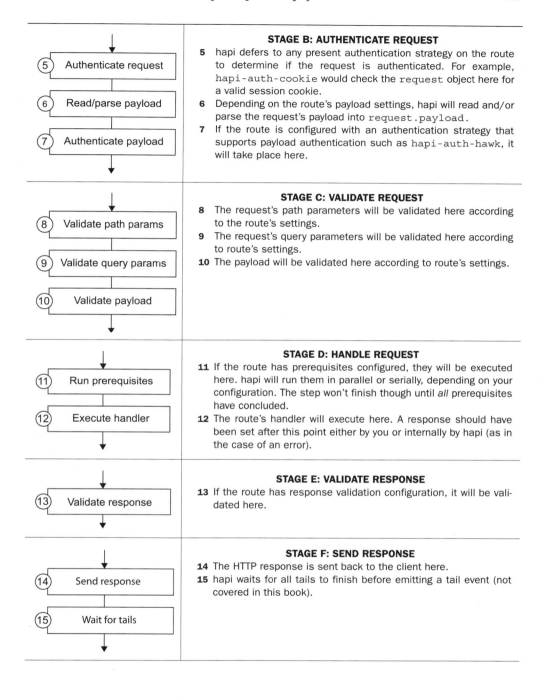

STAGE B: AUTHENTICATE REQUEST

5   hapi defers to any present authentication strategy on the route to determine if the request is authenticated. For example, `hapi-auth-cookie` would check the `request` object here for a valid session cookie.

6   Depending on the route's payload settings, hapi will read and/or parse the request's payload into `request.payload`.

7   If the route is configured with an authentication strategy that supports payload authentication such as `hapi-auth-hawk`, it will take place here.

STAGE C: VALIDATE REQUEST

8   The request's path parameters will be validated here according to the route's settings.

9   The request's query parameters will be validated here according to route's settings.

10   The payload will be validated here according to route's settings.

STAGE D: HANDLE REQUEST

11   If the route has prerequisites configured, they will be executed here. hapi will run them in parallel or serially, depending on your configuration. The step won't finish though until *all* prerequisites have concluded.

12   The route's handler will execute here. A response should have been set after this point either by you or internally by hapi (as in the case of an error).

STAGE E: VALIDATE RESPONSE

13   If the route has response validation configuration, it will be validated here.

STAGE F: SEND RESPONSE

14   The HTTP response is sent back to the client here.

15   hapi waits for all tails to finish before emitting a tail event (not covered in this book).

It's helpful to see the full picture too. Figure 5.5 shows the complete request lifecycle with extra details that we'll get to a little later.

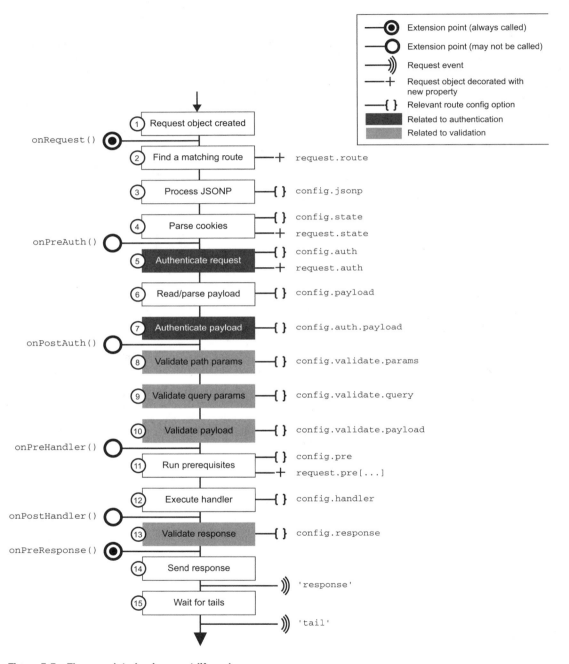

Figure 5.5   The complete hapi request lifecycle

The request lifecycle diagram is a map that every request in your application will navigate. Unknowingly, you've been working with the request lifecycle throughout this book. One thing that might be new to you altogether in the diagram is the notion of extension points, something I'll cover soon.

Whenever you define a route handler, you're controlling what happens at step 12. When we set up authentication for a route in chapter 2, we were influencing step 5. When we set some configuration for payloads when looking at file uploading in chapter 4, that was modifying the behavior at step 6. Pretty much all we're doing when we're writing code or configuration for hapi is molding exactly what happens during the request lifecycle.

WHAT'S THE POINT IN HAVING A REQUEST LIFECYCLE?

If you're familiar with Express or some other Node HTTP frameworks, you might wonder what the point in this grandiose-seeming request lifecycle is in hapi. It seems like just another detail to remember, right? What does being aware of it buy us?

When you're working with Express, there's a lifecycle of sorts, even if it's not something you're conscious of. The server receives requests, and responses are sent. The difference is that you can do anything at any point in between, including end the lifecycle altogether and send a response.

In hapi some of the control is shifted away from you and toward the framework. You no longer have free rein over the lifecycle of a request. You put your behavior inside predetermined configuration, handler functions, prerequisites, and extension points, and hapi determines where these things will happen based on the request lifecycle.

This approach gives you some assurances that you don't have with Express. In Express it would be possible to write a plugin (middleware function) that attempts to read session data before the request cookies have been parsed. You would never make this same mistake in hapi because the point at which cookies will have been parsed is explicitly advertised in the request lifecycle.

Also note that you don't send the response yourself in the hapi request lifecycle—rather, you request that hapi sends one later (at step 14). Because of this, you always have the chance to inspect or modify all responses before they're sent. There's no such facility in Express because a response could be sent at any point.

5.1.3   *Extension points*

Although hapi provides a rich set of configuration options to influence the request lifecycle, sometimes we might find one of our needs is missing. For instance, we may decide that we want our server to block all requests from IP addresses on a blacklist. There's no built-in configuration option or step in the request lifecycle for this. But hope doesn't end there. There are six *extension points* provided, where you can insert your own custom behavior into the lifecycle, in the form of an extension function, shown in figure 5.6.

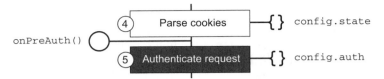

Figure 5.6   The `onPreAuth` extension point is found between steps 4 and 5.

To attach a function to an extension point, we use the `server.ext()` method. The signature of the `method` argument is the same as a route handler.

HAPI API `server.ext(event, method, [options])` (http://hapijs.com/api#serverextevent-method-options)

Your extension function interrupts the normal flow of the request cycle. It's your job to tell hapi when you've finished and hand control back to the framework so it can continue running through the remaining steps in the lifecycle. We do this using the `reply` interface. Inside every extension point you have a choice. You can either allow the request lifecycle to continue on its normal path by calling `reply.continue()` or you can choose to set a response there and then by calling `reply(value)`.

NOTE   Always conclude an extension function with one of those two uses of the `reply` interface. Not doing so will mean the request hangs until it ultimately times out.

AN EXAMPLE

We'll use an extension point now to implement the IP address-blocking functionality I gave as an example earlier. We'll want to block unwanted requests as soon as possible, so the `onRequest` extension point looks like a good fit for this purpose because it's the first extension point available.

Adding extension functions is like inserting your own new box into the lifecycle diagram. Every request received will then pass through that step. Figure 5.7 shows what we're trying to achieve in this example.

Let's assume we have a list of bad IP subnets that we want to block. Anytime we get a request from a client, we should compare the IP address to check if it's in one of these subnets, and if it is we'll respond with a 403 Forbidden response, as shown in the following listing. We can use the npm package `netmask` to check if a given IP address is within a subnet.

NPM PACKAGE   netmask v1 (https://npmjs.com/package/netmask)

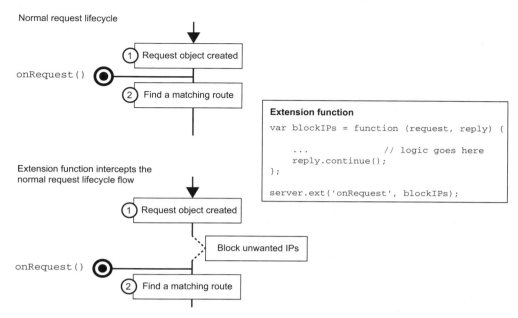

Normal request lifecycle

Extension function
```
var blockIPs = function (request, reply) {

    ...                  // logic goes here
    reply.continue();
};

server.ext('onRequest', blockIPs);
```

Extension function intercepts the normal request lifecycle flow

Figure 5.7   Adding an extension function is like inserting a new box in the request lifecycle diagram.

Listing 5.1   Implementing an IP blacklist using an `onRequest` extension function

```
'use strict';

const Boom = require('boom');
const Hapi = require('hapi');
const Netmask = require('netmask').Netmask;

const blacklist = [
    '12.166.96.32/27',
    '41.58.0.0/16',
    '41.66.192.0/18'
];

const server = new Hapi.Server();
server.connection({ port: 4000 });

const blockIPs = function (request, reply) {

    const ip = request.info.remoteAddress;

    for (let i = 0; i < blacklist.length; ++i) {
        const block = new Netmask(blacklist[i]);

        if (block.contains(ip)) {
            console.log('Blocking request from ' + ip + '.
            ➥ Within blocked subnet ' + blacklist[i]);
```

List of blocked subnets

Define extension function

Get client's IP

Check each subnet in blacklist

Check if client IP is within blocked subnet

If client IP is blocked, log message to console

```
                            return reply(Boom.forbidden());
            }
        }
        reply.continue();
};
server.ext('onRequest', blockIPs);

server.route({
    method: 'GET',
    path: '/',
    handler: function (request, reply) {

        reply('Greeting, you were allowed in.');
    }
});

server.start((err) => {

    if (err) {
        throw err;
    }

    console.log('Started server');
});
```

Set response to Boom.forbidden() (403) error, hand control back to hapi

If client IP doesn't match any blocked subnet, hand control back to hapi and proceed as normal.

Attach blockIPs function to the onRequest extension point

Listing 5.1 uses a package called Boom to create a 403 error response. We'll be looking a lot more at what Boom is later in the chapter.

> **NPM PACKAGE**   boom v3 (https://npmjs.com/package/boom)

If you install the required dependencies (boom@3, hapi@13, and netmask@1.0.5) and run this example, you should find that you can access the route at http://localhost:4000 and get the message "You were allowed in." Try adding a subnet that includes your local address to the blacklist:

```
const blacklist = [
    ...
    '127.0.0.0/8'
];
```

If you attempt to access the server again, you should be blocked and see a message logged to the console:

```
Blocking request from 127.0.0.1. Within blocked subnet 127.0.0.0/8
```

This example has shown how you can insert your own logic into the request lifecycle with extension points to implement new functionality that isn't offered by hapi itself.

5.1.4   *Which extension point should I use?*

Once you've decided to use an extension point, you need to decide *which* extension point fits your needs. The request object that is passed to an extension function is the same object you see in a route handler, but depending on which extension point you're attaching to, it might not have all the full set of properties populated that you expect. When looking at the request lifecycle diagram in figure 5.5, for instance, you can see that the onRequest extension point comes before payload reading and parsing occurs (step 6). So, at that point request.payload is still null, even though there may indeed be an incoming payload. These are the kinds of things to be aware of when picking an extension point.

You should choose at which point to add an extension function based on what you're trying to achieve. If you want access to the request payload in your extension function, you need to use onPostAuth or a later extension point. But if you're writing an extension function that modifies the URL of the incoming request to affect how the request is routed (step two), you need to use onRequest.

Another important factor when adding an extension point is whether you can be sure that it will be called for a given request. The onRequest and onPreResponse are the only extension points that hapi guarantees will always be called for every request.

Next up, we'll look at the reply interface under the microscope.

5.2 The reply interface and the response object

We took a deeper look into the request object in the previous section, but how about its close friend and neighbor the reply interface? We've used that plenty of times throughout the book so far, in almost every example, in fact. But we've never talked about what it is. Let's fix that now.

5.2.1 What is the reply interface?

The reply interface has a couple of different roles to play to hapi:

- Setting a response to a request
- Acting as a callback to give control back to hapi in user-defined functions such as handlers, prerequisites, and extension functions

HAPI API   reply interface (http://hapijs.com/api#reply-interface)

The first role is pretty clear. We've seen loads of examples of using reply(value) to set a response:

```
server.route({
    method: 'GET',
    path: '/',
    handler: function (request, reply) {

        reply('Well hello there!');
    }
});
```

reply() sets the string 'Well hello there!' as a response

```
server.ext('onRequest', function (request, reply) {      server.ext('onRequest', function (request, reply) {

    ...                                                       ...
    reply.continue();                                         reply('Stopping here!');
});                                                       });
```

Return control to hapi without setting a response

Set response and return control to hapi

Figure 5.8   Extension functions may or may not set a response.

Inside an extension function we can use the `reply` interface to either set a response or to hand control back to hapi and continue the request lifecycle, depending on whether we call `reply()` or `reply.continue()`, as shown in figure 5.8.

Things are different yet again inside route prerequisites. Calling `reply(value)` sets that value as the result of the `pre` (it puts it inside `request.pre[assignName]`).

If you want to set a response inside a `pre`, you have to call `reply().takeover(value)`. Is your head spinning yet? For me, this is a slightly confusing area in hapi's API. Table 5.1 lists the semantics of the `reply` interface in these different contexts.

Table 5.1   `reply` interface semantics

Context	`reply(...)`	`reply.continue()`	`reply(...).takeover()`
Handlers	Sets a response to send back to the client	Sets empty response and 200 OK status code	Same as `reply()`, takeover has no effect
Prerequisites	Sets the result of the pre under `request.pre`	Assign `pre` a null result in request.pre	Sets a response to send back to client, handler is never called
Extension functions	Sets a response to send back to client	Returns control back to framework	Same as `reply()`, takeover has no effect

The grey cells in the table show combinations that you would never normally use. For instance, you would never normally call `reply.continue()` in a handler, or `reply().takeover()` in an extension function. Why include them in the list?

WHY IS IT SO COMPLICATED?

There's a good reason for the API inconsistency with the `reply` interface and the fact that methods are supported in cases you wouldn't normally use them. The reason is code reusability. I'll explain this in the following listing. Let's say we wrote a route handler that fetches data from an API and responds with it.

Listing 5.2   Listing 5.2 Using a function as a handler

```
const getInfo = function (request, reply) {

    Wreck.get('http://myapi/info', (err, res, payload) => {
```

Fetch data from API

```
        reply(payload);
    });
};
```
◁─┐ **Set response to request**
  │ **with data from API**

```
server.route({
    method: 'GET',
    path: '/info',
    handler: getInfo
});
```

Because getInfo is a handler here, we want it to set a response to the client when we call reply() in this case. Now let's say we end up writing more routes later, which require this same data. We may decide that we'd like to reuse the same getInfo function as a route prerequisite.

Listing 5.3   Reusing the same function as a prerequisite

```
server.route({
    config: {
        pre: [
            { method: getInfo, assign: 'info' }    ◁─┐ Use getInfo
        ]                                             │ as a pre
    },
    method: 'GET',
    path: '/otherInfo',
    handler: function (request, reply) {

        ...                    ◁─┐ Do something with
    }                            │ request.pre.info
});
```

In this case, we don't want reply() in the getInfo function to set a response to the client. We want it to set the result value of the pre in request.pre.info. This is the whole reason behind the slightly different reply() semantics—it allows us to reuse the same functions interchangeably as handlers or pres and have them behave how we'd expect in both instances.

5.2.2 Valid arguments to reply()

When we call the reply interface to set a response to the client, we can pass reply() a variety of different data types. We've already seen many examples of calling reply() with strings and with objects. Other values can be set as responses too. There's a full list in table 5.2, along with the corresponding behavior by hapi.

Table 5.2   Valid argument types/values to reply() and the corresponding response behavior

Type/Value	Content-type	Status code	Notes
string	text/html	200	
number	application/json	200	Responds with JSON number

Table 5.2 Valid argument types/values to `reply()` and the corresponding response behavior

Type/Value	Content-type	Status code	Notes
boolean	application/json	200	Responds with JSON `true` or `false`
Error	application/json	500	Wraps `Error` object with `Boom` object and responds with JSON payload— see section 5.4.3 for more info
Buffer	application/octet-stream	200	For sending arbitrary binary data
Stream	Must set manually	200	
Promise	Depends on promises resolved/rejected value	Depends on promises resolved/ rejected value	
Boom `Object`	application/json	Depends on `Boom` type	See section 5.4.3
Plain `Object` or `Array`	application/json	200	Stringified JSON response
null	None	200ᵃ	Empty payload
undefined	None	200	Empty payload

ᵃ Technically, an empty payload should probably be a 204 code according to the HTTP spec (RFC 7231), but hapi sends a 200 because there's more chance every client will understand that is a successful request. If you want, you can override it with .code(204).

5.2.3 *The response object*

For experienced Noders, a common misconception when first using hapi is that the `reply` argument in a handler is the same thing as the `res` argument used when working with Express or Node's built-in http module:

```
app.get('/', (req, res) => {

    res.send('Hi from Express');
});
```
Express starts sending the response to client immediately here.

In the case of Express, `res` represents the response sent to a client. When you call `res.send(value)`, Express starts sending that data to the client straight away. Your chance to control the response after this moment is gone. Things are different in the hapi world: *the* `reply` *interface isn't a response object* but instead returns a `response` object to you.

The HTTP response isn't sent to the client until later in the request lifecycle (see step 14 from figure 5.5). Think of calling `reply()` in hapi as expressing your intention for hapi to send a response, rather than sending one yourself:

```
server.route({
    method: 'GET',
    path: '/',
    handler: function (request, reply) {
```

```
        const response = reply('Hello');
    }
});
```

◁─── **Reply interface returns response object when reply() called with valid response value**

Because calling `reply()` doesn't send our response, we can still modify the response that it gives us before our handler function returns. There are several methods available on the `response` object for this, such as `response.type()`, `response.code()`, and `response.header()`.

> **HAPI API** `response` object (http://hapijs.com/api#response-object)

Listing 5.4 Modifying a response via methods on the `response` object

```
server.route({
    method: 'GET',
    path: '/',
    handler: function (request, reply) {

        const response = reply('Hello');
        response.type('text/plain');
        response.code(202);
        response.header('x-powered-by', 'hapi');
    }
});
```

The `response` object methods are chainable, so for convenience you can write the same thing as is done in this listing.

Listing 5.5 Chaining `response` object method calls

```
server.route({
    method: 'GET',
    path: '/',
    handler: function (request, reply) {

        reply('Hello')
            .type('text/plain')
            .code(202)
            .header('x-powered-by', 'hapi');
    }
});
```

RETRIEVING THE RESPONSE OBJECT IN EXTENSION POINTS

After a response has been set, hapi will store the `response` object inside the request object at `request.response`. This makes it easy to retrieve later, for example inside an `onPreResponse` extension function, as shown next.

Listing 5.6 Inspecting set response in an `onPreResponse` extension function

```
server.route({
    method: 'GET',
    path: '/',
    handler: function (request, reply) {
```

```
            reply('Hello')
                .type('text/plain')
                .code(202)
                .header('x-powered-by', 'hapi');
    }
});

server.ext('onPreResponse', (request, reply) => {

    const response = request.response;
    console.log(response.statusCode);
    console.log(response.headers);
    reply.continue();
});
```

Logs: 202

Logs: { 'content-type': 'text/plain', 'x-powered-by': 'hapi' }

We'll use this method of inspecting a response before it is sent in section 5.3 when trapping errors in the lifecycle to create HTML error pages.

5.2.4   *Responding with streams*

Streams are a powerful feature in Node. If you haven't used them before, you're missing out. Streams are somewhat of like pipes that can be connected, and chunks of data flow down the connected pipeline.

Streams are useful when you're moving or processing a large resource. You can start processing the chunks of the resource immediately rather than waiting for the whole resource to be available.

As an example, there are two distinct ways to copy a file using Node. One is by using `Fs.readFile()` and `Fs.writeFile()`

Listing 5.7   Copying a file with `Fs.readFile` and `Fs.writeFile`

```
const Fs = require('fs');
const Path = require('path');

const src = Path.join(__dirname, 'file.txt');
const dst = Path.join(__dirname, 'file (copy).txt');

Fs.readFile(src, (err, data) => {

    if (err) {
        throw err;
    }

    Fs.writeFile(dst, data, (err) => {

        if (err) {
            throw err;
        }
    });
});
```

In this example, we read the entire contents of the file into memory first and then write that `Buffer` into another file.

Another way to go about this is by using `Fs.createReadStream()` and `Fs.create-WriteStream()`.

Listing 5.8   Copying a file with `Fs.createReadStream` and `Fs.createWriteStream`

```
const Fs = require('fs');
const Path = require('path');

const src = Path.join(__dirname, 'file.txt');
const dst = Path.join(__dirname, 'file (copy).txt');

Fs.createReadStream(src).pipe(Fs.createWriteStream(dst));
```

Aside from being much more succinct, the second method is also much more efficient in memory use—and it's faster. There is little buffering involved. As soon as a chunk of data is read from a file, it's passed to the write stream and written to the file. If you're copying big files, the second method is much more efficient with resources because you're not waiting for the entire file to be read before doing anything with the data.

Jumping into streams

Streams can be a tricky concept to grasp at first, so don't feel bad if you have trouble. They seem almost magical in the way that you can combine different inputs and outputs and they work.

Once you get the hang of streams, you'll appreciate the power and potential they offer for simplifying interfaces between different parts of your code.

There are great free resources out there for learning more about streams. I would advise all readers to devote time to each of the following:

- John Resig's Stream Playground: http://ejohn.org/blog/node-js-stream-playground/
- Substack's Stream Handbook: https://github.com/substack/stream-handbook
- Substack's Stream Adventure: https://github.com/substack/stream-adventure

Streams are first-class citizens to hapi's `reply` interface. When you call `reply()` with a `Stream` object, chunks of data will be sent to the client as part of the response payload as soon as they can be read from the stream. To see an example of this in action, the following listing downloads a large video file using Wreck and streams this to the browser as it's being downloaded.

Listing 5.9   Downloading and streaming a video in response to a request

```
'use strict';

const Hapi = require('hapi');
const Wreck = require('wreck');
const server = new Hapi.Server();
```

```
server.connection({ port: 4000 });

server.route({
    method: 'GET',
    path: '/video',
    handler: function (request, reply) {
```
Initiate request for "A for Atom" video from archive.org server using Wreck (any mp4 will do)
```
        Wreck.request('GET',
        'https://archive.org/download/isforAto1953/isforAto1953_512kb.mp4',
        { redirects: 3 },
        (err, response) => {

            if (err) {
                throw err;
            }

            const resp = reply(response);
```
Call reply() interface with Wreck response stream
```
            let sent = 0;
            resp.on('peek', (chunk) => {
```
Listen to response peek events and log number of bytes sent to client
```
                sent += chunk.length;
                process.stdout.write(sent + ' bytes written to response \r');
            });
        });
    }
});

server.start((err) => {

    if (err) {
        throw err;
    }
    console.log('Server running at:', server.info.uri);
});
```

In listing 5.9, when the server receives a request for GET /video, we start a request for a video from the archive.org server, and as we receive chunks of the response, they're immediately passed onto the client.

The `response` object we get from the `reply` interface emits peek events as each chunk is flushed to the client. We listen on those events and measure the length of each chunk. If you run this example and open http://localhost:4000/video in your browser, you'll notice that you can start watching the video as bytes are still being written. You'll see in your console the progress of the file downloading at the same time that you're watching it in your browser.

To recap, in this section you've learned:

- The `reply` interface is a way of generating responses.
- The `reply` interface is also a callback mechanism.
- The `reply` interface works differently in different contexts such as handlers, pres, and extension points.
- When a reply is called with a non-error value, such as an object or `Buffer`, it returns a `response` object that can still be modified before the handler has returned.

The `reply` interface behaves a little differently when `reply()` is called with a Java-Script `Error` argument. The next section is devoted entirely to responding in error situations.

5.3 Dealing with errors

Wouldn't it be great if we could blissfully pretend our applications were going to work perfectly all the time, and there was no need to think about or plan for errors? Unfortunately, that's not the world we're living in. Unexpected things happen all the time. But rather than give up and leave to chance what happens to our applications when an error occurs, we can handle such cases maturely, making sure we always handle all error cases and communicate them to users in a useful way so they can react.

5.3.1 Programmer errors vs. operational errors

Errors in programs should be distinguished into two different types: *programmer errors* and *operational errors*. Programmer errors are things that occur from writing code with invalid syntax, referencing a variable that doesn't exist, or performing an operation on the wrong type. These three lines all contain programmer errors:

```
const x = 1,,,                          Uncaught SyntaxError:
console.log(undefinedVar);              unexpected token
"Hello".join('.');                      Uncaught ReferenceError:
                    Uncaught TypeError: undefinedVar isn't defined
                    "Hello".join isn't a function
```

We can avoid programmer errors by writing our code correctly. We can use tools like code linters to help us to ensure we don't release code containing programmer errors.

This section is going to focus on the other type: operational errors. Operational errors are those that occur during the runtime of our program due to factors often beyond our control. In a real-world web application, there are a lot of opportunities for operational errors, including:

- A user requested a resource that didn't exist.
- A user didn't have permission to view the resource they requested.
- An upstream service that we're dependent on doesn't respond or times out when we're reading a response from it.
- Our OS kernel reports too many files open when trying to read a file.

When performing an asynchronous operation in Node, the convention is for a callback to receive an `err` parameter as the first argument. Take, for example, the built-in function `Fs.readFile()`:

```
Fs.readFile('/file.txt', (err, contents) => {

    if (err) {
        throw err;
    }
    console.log(contents);
});
```

If an operational error occurs, such as the kernel refusing to open the file due to too many files being open, the `err` parameter will be an instance of a JavaScript `Error` object. It's important that you *always* check for the presence of such errors in all code that you write.

Upon encountering an operational error, it's likely that you'd want to log it. Chapter 11 looks at logging in detail. In a web application, you'll also need to alert the client that something has gone wrong. The standard way to communicate HTTP request status to a client is using status codes.

5.3.2   *HTTP status codes*

Every HTTP response has a *status code* associated with it. It's in the first line of text, which is called the status line:

```
HTTP/1.1 200 OK                          Status line of a
Content-type: application/json           200 OK response
Content-length: 5000
...
```

There are many different status codes available to communicate all kinds of scenarios to a client. You can find a full list at https://en.wikipedia.org/wiki/List_of_HTTP _status_codes.

CLIENT (4XX) VS. SERVER (5XX) STATUS CODES

HTTP status codes between 400 and 499 indicate a client error. Some examples are:

- 400 Bad request
- 403 Forbidden
- 404 Not found
- 429 Too many requests

HTTP status codes between 500 and 599 indicate a server error. Some examples are:

- 500 Internal server error
- 501 Not implemented
- 503 Service unavailable

hapi does a pretty good job of returning the correct status code to a client. If you call `reply()` with a value in your handler such as a string, object, or `Buffer`, hapi will assume everything is okay and send back a 200 OK response.

You can also override the default status code when creating a response by calling the `code()` method on the response object:

```
server.route({
    method: 'GET',
    path: '/error',
    handler: function (request, reply) {

        reply('Internal server error').code(500);
    }
});
```

In this case, hapi will respond to requests for GET /error with a 500 status code and the text "Internal server error" as the response payload:

```
HTTP/1.1 500 Internal Server Error
content-type: text/html; charset=utf-8
cache-control: no-cache
content-length: 21
Date: Mon, 03 Aug 2015 09:05:49 GMT
Connection: keep-alive

Internal server error
```

But there is another way to communicate errors to the client from a handler.

CALLING REPLY() WITH A JAVASCRIPT ERROR

It's possible to call reply(), passing a JavaScript Error object:

```
server.route({
    method: 'GET',
    path: '/error',
    handler: function (request, reply) {

        const err = new Error('Oh no, it didn\'t work!');
        reply(err);
    }
});
```

hapi will understand that an error has occurred in the handler, and the response in this case will also be a 500 Internal Server Error response:

```
HTTP/1.1 500 Internal Server Error
content-type: application/json; charset=utf-8
cache-control: no-cache
content-length: 96
Date: Mon, 03 Aug 2015 09:00:43 GMT
Connection: keep-alive

{"statusCode":500,"error":"Internal Server Error","message":"An internal
    server error occurred"}
```

Our response in this case, though, contains a JSON payload with additional information about the error. This kind of response for an error is more useful to clients than a plaintext response. They can parse the JSON and make decisions based on the details of the error. Whenever you pass a plain JavaScript Error object to reply(), hapi will respond in the same way—with a 500 internal server error response and a JSON payload.

What if we want to send a different status code, like a 501 Not Implemented, and still use this JSON error response pattern? Inside the hapi ecosystem lives a package, appropriately called Boom, for creating exactly these kinds of expressive HTTP errors.

5.3.3 *Introducing Boom: creating HTTP-friendly errors*

Boom is a Node package for creating "HTTP-friendly" errors. You can create a Boom error object by calling one of the exported functions in the package, such as Boom.notImplemented([message], [data]):

```
const err = Boom.notImplemented('Still working on this', { apiVersion: '4' });
```

A Boom object is a JavaScript Error object with additional properties added by Boom. What makes Boom objects so useful is that they're first-class objects as far as hapi's reply interface is concerned. It knows when it has been given a Boom object and sends a specially crafted HTTP response. Let's try it out.

Listing 5.10   Setting a Boom object as a response

```
const Boom = require('boom');
const Hapi = require('hapi');

const server = new Hapi.Server();
server.connection({ port: 4000 });

server.route({
    method: 'GET',
    path: '/v4/users',                                    Create a
    handler: function (request, reply) {          Boom.notImplemented error

        const err = Boom.notImplemented('Still working on this');
        reply(err);                              Set the Boom error
    }                                            as the response
});

server.start(() => {

    console.log('Server running at:', server.info.uri);
});
```

hapi will take our Boom error and create an HTTP response with the appropriate status code and a JSON response body containing the error information and our message:

```
HTTP/1.1 501 Not Implemented
content-type: application/json; charset=utf-8
cache-control: no-cache
content-length: 78
Date: Mon, 03 Aug 2015 09:26:33 GMT
Connection: keep-alive

{"statusCode":501,"error":"Not Implemented","message":"Still working on this"}
```

JSON error responses are great when our users are machines, such as in an API, but they're not so friendly for our human users, who like stylish-looking error pages.

5.3.4 *Friendly HTML error pages for websites*

When an error prevents you from performing an action on a website, you don't want to see a JSON message in your browser (especially if you don't know what JSON is!).

You want a nicely styled HTML error page with the details of what went wrong and what to do about it.

But we already know that hapi uses `Boom` internally to create "HTTP-friendly" error responses with a JSON payload. How can we intercept the response before it's sent to the client and alter it to be an HTML response?

We can use our knowledge of the request lifecycle and extension points to help us with this. Although it's possible for a response to be generated at several points in the lifecycle, we can always rely on the extension point `onPreResponse` being called, no matter what else happened, including hapi generating an error response for us. This looks like the right place to handle it. Figure 5.9 shows why this will work.

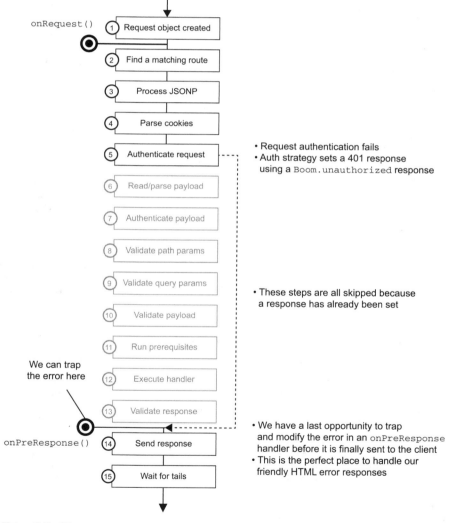

Figure 5.9 We can use an `onPreResponse` **extension function to trap an error response even if it was generated internally by hapi.**

We can use the special property isBoom that all Boom errors have to check if the outgoing response is indeed an error.

Listing 5.11   index.js: application that renders errors as HTML views

```
'use strict';

const Boom = require('boom');
const Hapi = require('hapi');
const Joi = require('joi');
const Path = require('path');

const server = new Hapi.Server();
server.connection({ port: 4000 });

server.route([{
    method: 'GET',
    path: '/error',
    handler: function (request, reply) {

        return reply(new Error('Something bad happened!'));

    }
}, {
    method: 'GET',
    path: '/newFeature',
    handler: function (request, reply) {

        return reply(Boom.notImplemented());

    }
}, {
    config: {
        validate: {
            params: {
                name: Joi.string().min(4)
            }
        }
    },
    method: 'GET',
    path: '/name/{name}',
    handler: function (request, reply) {

        return reply('OK');

    }
}]);

server.ext('onPreResponse', (request, reply) => {

    if (request.response.isBoom) {
        const err = request.response;
        const errName = err.output.payload.error;
        const statusCode = err.output.payload.statusCode;

        return reply.view('error', {
            statusCode: statusCode,
            errName: errName
```

Annotations:
- Pass Error object to reply interface, triggering 500 response in hapi's internals
- Pass Boom Error object to reply interface, which hapi uses as a response
- Set validation rule on name param: invalid value triggers 400 response in hapi's internals
- Register onPreResponse extension point function; always runs for all requests
- Check if response is Boom object
- Get name of Boom object
- Get statusCode of Boom object
- Render error template, passing error details as context

```
            })
            .code(statusCode);              ◁─┐  Set response's status code
        }                                       │  to match Boom object

    reply.continue();                        ◁─┐  If response wasn't Boom object,
});                                             │  hand control back to framework

server.register(require('vision'), (err) => {

    if (err) {
        throw err;
    }

    server.views({
        engines: {
            hbs: require('handlebars')
        },
        path: Path.join(__dirname, 'templates')
    });

    server.start((err) => {

        if (err) {
            throw err;
        }
        console.log('Server running at:', server.info.uri);
    });
});
```

NOTE Joi is a validation library you'll learn all about in the next chapter.

We're using Vision's view rendering function along with Handlebars to render an HTML view for our error pages, so we also need to make a simple template.

Listing 5.12 templates/error.hbs: error view

```html
<!DOCTYPE html>
<html lang="en">
<head>
    <meta charset="UTF-8">
    <title>{{title}}</title>

    <style>
        body {
            text-align: center;
            background: #B0B0B0;
            color: #222;
        }
        .error h1 {
            font-size: 80px;
            margin-bottom: 0;
        }
    </style>
</head>
```

```
<body>
    <div class="error">
        <h1>&#x26a0;<br/>{{statusCode}}</h1>
        <h2>{{errName}}</h2>
    </div>
</body>
</html>
```

We can start this application and navigate to different pages to see our spectacular HTML error pages in all their glory, as shown in figure 5.10.

Figure 5.10   The various pages shown for different error types

The important thing to note is that our error pages are shown for all error types, including ones we didn't create ourselves but rather hapi generated internally. This shows how understanding the request lifecycle and customizing it using extension points gives you a lot of power to bend hapi to your needs.

Toward the end of this chapter we looked into the importance of communicating errors in our application back to the client. What we didn't discuss is how to create meaningful and useful errors when clients give our applications bad input. For that, we need to jump into the world of validation.

5.4 Summary

- Every request to a hapi server is represented in a `request` object, decorated with all the information we have about a request.

- Every request travels along a path with distinct steps that we call the request lifecycle. We affect what happens during the request lifecycle by both the configuration and code that we write.

- There are extension points in the request lifecycle that we can hook into to customize the request lifecycle and add our own functionality.

- Depending on what happens during the request lifecycle, some extension points may be skipped or never called, but we can always be sure of `onRequest` and `onPreResponse` being called, which makes `onPreResponse` a good place to handle custom error reporting or inspect responses before they're sent.

- The `reply` interface is used for both generating responses to requests and handing control back to hapi inside handlers, extension points, and prerequisites.

- After generating a response by calling `reply()`, a `response` object is set as a property on the `request` object. You can inspect and modify this response before it's sent to the client at the end of the request lifecycle.

Validation with Joi

This chapter covers

- Working with Joi
- Adding validation to hapi.js apps
- Customizing validation errors
- Consuming and presenting validation errors

Humans often make mistakes, and as a result the systems we create need to be prepared for misuse. Validation is an essential part of almost every system we use in our daily lives. An example of such a system is a snack vending machine.

A vending machine has several inputs that it needs to validate. If any one input doesn't match its expectations, the machine will halt normal functioning and give feedback to the user on what went wrong. For instance, if you place a foreign coin in the slot, the machine will reject the coin, spitting it out into the coin return tray, as shown in figure 6.1.

We rely on the feedback we get from validation to make sure we can use systems the correct way. Without it, we'd be clueless about what we're doing wrong. We use the term *validation* to apply to software as well. This chapter shows you both the tools and methods hapi.js offers that allow you, in your applications, to define

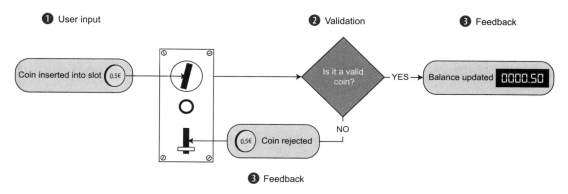

Figure 6.1   An example of validation that occurs in vending machines

your expectations and give useful feedback to users when things don't go according to plan.

6.1   Introducing Joi

Joi is an npm package for data validation. Joi can validate any kind of JavaScript values, from simple scalar data types such as strings, numbers, or Booleans, to complex values consisting of several levels of nested objects and arrays. To run the examples in this chapter, install Joi like any other npm package with `npm install joi@8`. If you use a different version of Joi, some of the examples in this chapter may not work.

> **NPM PACKAGE**   `joi` v8 (https://npmjs.com/package/joi)

If you're working with data in your application that comes from an unknown source, for example via a public API, Joi can help to ensure that data is in the required format. Checking these kinds of inputs and acting accordingly when they're incorrect will help to make your applications more stable and reliable.

Joi can be used as a standalone module in any Node application. Joi is used internally in a lot of the modules in the hapi ecosystem for this exact purpose. If you've used any of hapi's APIs incorrectly before and seen an error message, that message could likely have come from validation performed by Joi.

hapi has been designed with Joi in mind. The framework's built-in validation features, such as validation of HTTP headers and payloads, are designed to work seamlessly with Joi.

In this section I'll be showing you how Joi works and giving you a few examples to get you comfortable with using it.

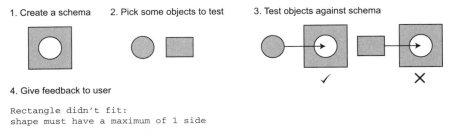

1. Create a schema   2. Pick some objects to test   3. Test objects against schema

4. Give feedback to user

```
Rectangle didn't fit:
shape must have a maximum of 1 side
```

Figure 6.2   The steps taken when validating with Joi

6.1.1   *How it works*

Working with Joi involves a process of four steps, shown in figure 6.2. The first step is to create a schema. A *schema* is an object that describes your expectations and is what you'll be checking your real data against. Think of a schema as a description of your ideal object.

There's a common sorting game given to toddlers, where they need to place different shaped blocks into different shaped holes. This game is a good analogy to using Joi. With Joi, the schema is like the hole, and the object you want to test is like the block. Any given object is either going to fit the schema or not.

Once you have a schema, you will use Joi to test the schema against some objects. If there was a validation error, Joi will tell you precisely what went wrong. You can then use that feedback to make a decision and respond to the user appropriately.

6.1.2   *A simple example: validating a scalar type*

Passwords are an example of data that we commonly need to validate in our applications. In the following simple example, I check the format of the `password` argument in an `updatePassword` function. If the format doesn't match the required format, an error is thrown. The password is required to be a string and must be between six and ten characters in length.

Here's the Joi schema for the password validation:

```
const Joi = require('joi');

const schema = Joi.string().min(6).max(10);
```
⟵ **String between 6–10 characters in length**

> ### Fluent interfaces
>
> *Fluent interfaces* are an approach to API design in software development. They're also commonly known as *chainable interfaces* because they consist of methods that are chained onto one another.
>
> Fluent interfaces can promote more readable code where a number of steps are involved and you're not interested in the intermediate returned values.

An example of a fluent interface to make toast could be:

```
const toast = new Toast()
    .cook('3 minutes')
    .spread('butter')
    .spread('raspberry jam')
    .serve();
```

The result of each method call is another `Toast` object, but we only care about that delicious final product, which is saved in the `toast` variable after all methods in the chain have executed.

Joi schemas are also built using a fluent interface. Here's an example of creating a schema for a JavaScript date that falls within the month of December 2015 and is formatted in ISO date format:

```
const schema = Joi.date()
    .min('12-1-2015')
    .max('12-31-2015')
    .iso();
```

To test a schema against a real value, you can use `Joi.assert(value, schema)`. When using this function, Joi will throw an error upon encountering the first validation failure. The error message logged will contain useful information about where the validation failed:

```
const Joi = require('joi');

const schema = Joi.string().min(6).max(10);

const updatePassword = function (password) {
    Joi.assert(password, schema);          // Error will be thrown here if validation fails
    console.log('Validation success!');    // If we got here, validation was successful.
};

updatePassword('password');   // Valid password (8 characters)
updatePassword('pass');       // Invalid password (4 characters)
```

If you run this small example in the console, you will see some output that resembles the following:

```
Validation success!          // Success message after validating value 'password'

index.js:121
            throw new Error(message + error.annotate());
            ^
ValidationError: "pass"      // Error thrown with value 'pass'

[1] value length must be at least 6 characters long   // Details about what went wrong
    ...
```

The previous example shows how to validate a simple scalar value, but Joi is capable of much more. Often the values you want to validate are more complex, compound values such as objects and arrays.

6.1.3   *A more complex example: validating a compound type*

Let's imagine that I'm creating an API that collects data from automated weather measuring stations around the world. This data is then persisted and can be retrieved by consumers of the API to get up-to-the-minute data for their region.

Each weather report sent by the stations has to follow a standard format. A weather report contains several bits of information and can be represented as a JavaScript object. A weather report from Taipei, at noon on a day in July, might look something like this listing.

Listing 6.1   Listing 6.1 Sample weather report

```
const report = {
    station: 'Taipei',
    datetime: 'Wed Jul 22 2015 12:00:00 GMT+0800'),
    temp: 93,
    humidity: 95,
    precipitation: false,
    windDirection: 'E'
};
```

The remote weather stations that are sending the data to the central API are out of my control. It would therefore be prudent to validate all the incoming data to ensure that it matches the standard format, as shown in figure 6.3. Accepting invalid data from a malfunctioning station could cause unknown problems for consumers of my API.

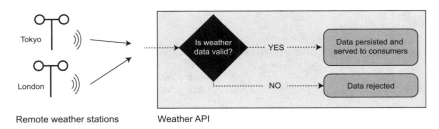

Figure 6.3   Validating incoming requests helps ensure the integrity of your data.

UNDERSTAND YOUR DATA

My first step is to think about the restrictions I want to put on each field in the report. I've outlined my requirements for the weather reports in table 6.1.

Table 6.1   Required format for weather reports

Field name	Data type	Required	Other restrictions
station	string	Yes	Max 100 characters
datetime	date	Yes	

Table 6.1   Required format for weather reports

Field name	Data type	Required	Other restrictions
temp(°F)	number	Yes	Between –140 and 140
humidity	number	Yes	Between 0 and 100
precipitation	boolean	No	
windDirection	string	No	One of N, NE, E, SE, S, SW, W, NW

CREATE A SCHEMA

In the previous subsection, you saw that we could specify a JavaScript string in a schema using Joi.string(). It won't come as a huge surprise to you that the equivalent for an object is Joi.object(). Like Joi.string(), Joi.object has methods you can *chain* onto it to further expand the schema. One of those methods is .keys(), which allows you to add sub-schemas for each of the object's properties. Here's an example of creating a schema for an object with keys:

```
const schema = Joi.object().keys({
    prop1: Joi.string(),          ←——  Property prop1        Top level schema
    ...                                 validates a string   validates an object
});
```

Creating schemas for objects with keys is so common that Joi also offers a convenient shorthand for the preceding. You can replace Joi.object().keys({...}) with only {...}:

```
const schema = {
    prop1: Joi.string(),          ←——  Property prop1        Top-level schema
    ...                                 validates a string   validates an object
};
```

This listing is the schema for validating the weather reports.

Listing 6.2   A schema for validating weather reports

```
const schema = {                                                        Required string of max
    station: Joi.string().max(100).required(),          ←——             100 character length
    datetime: Joi.date().required(),                ←—— Required date
    temp: Joi.number().min(-140).max(140).required(),        ←——
    humidity: Joi.number().min(0).max(100).required(),                  Required number
    precipitation: Joi.boolean(),                                       between –140 and 140
    windDirection: Joi.string()
        .valid(['N', 'NE', 'E', 'SE', 'S', 'SW', 'W', 'NW'])  ←——
};                                                                      Optional string with
                                                                        whitelist of values
```

Required number between 0 and 100 → humidity

Optional Boolean → precipitation

This schema can now be used to validate some real weather reports. You can run the script in the following listing to check the sample report from listing 6.1 against this schema.

Listing 6.3 Script to test the report against the schema

```
const Joi = require('joi');

const report = {
    ...
};

const schema = {
    ...
};

Joi.assert(report, schema);
```

There should be no output before the script finishes. That indicates that the value tested was valid. In the next listing let's try to modify the original report so it's no longer valid according to the schema.

Listing 6.4 Invalid sample weather report

```
const report = {
    station: 'Taipei',
    datetime: 'Wed Jul 22 2015 12:00:00 GMT+0000 (GMT)',
    temp: 34,
    humidity: 93,
    precipitation: false,              Oops, no such
    windDirection: 'WE'           ◁——┘ direction as WE
};
```

If you run the script again, with the modified report, you should see an error thrown. The error message will contain output to pinpoint exactly what caused the validation to fail:

```
...
ValidationError: {
  "station": "Taipei",
  "datetime": "2015-07-22T12:00:00.000Z",
  "temp": 93,
  "humidity": 95,
  "precipitation": false,
  "windDirection" [1]: "WE"
}

[1] windDirection must be one of [N, NE, E, SE, S, SW, W, NW]
```

You should now have a pretty good idea of the basics of working with Joi and you should recognize the usefulness of employing validation techniques in your apps.

6.2   *Mastering Joi*

This section dives deeper into the Joi API to show how you can build schemas to validate any kind of value in JavaScript.

6.2.1   *Getting to know the API*

The first step in mastering Joi is to know the API inside out. Let's first look at the main types of values you can validate.

TOP-LEVEL SCHEMA TYPES

All Joi schemas are created by first specifying a top-level object type. Some examples are `Joi.string()` and `Joi.array()`.

Table 6.2   Joi schema types

Schema type	Matches (JS value)	Example
`Joi.any()`	Any data type	`Joi.any().valid(6, 'six')`
`Joi.array()`	Arrays	`Joi.array().length(5)`
`Joi.boolean()`	Booleans	`Joi.boolean().required()`
`Joi.binary()`	Buffers (or Strings)	`Joi.binary().encoding('utf8')`
`Joi.date()`	Dates	`Joi.date().iso()`
`Joi.func()`	Functions	`Joi.func().required();`
`Joi.number()`	Numbers (or Strings)	`Joi.number().greater(100)`
`Joi.object()`	Objects	`Joi.object().keys({...})`
`Joi.string()`	Strings	`Joi.string().email()`

The table lists all the available types. Any Joi schema (or sub-schema) that you define will start with one of these types at its root.

METHODS ON SCHEMA TYPES

Each schema type in Joi has a set of methods that can be chained onto the type to qualify the schema further. Some of these methods are specific to one type, such as the `encoding()` method on `Joi.binary()`, or the `email()` method on `Joi.string()`.

There are other methods, such as `required()`, that can be called on any Joi type. All schema objects in Joi are optional by default. This means that the following code won't throw an error:

```
const schema = Joi.object().keys({
    name: Joi.string(),
    age: Joi.number()
});

Joi.assert({ name: 'Mark' }, schema);
```

To fix that, you can mark the age property as required:

```
const schema = Joi.object().keys({
    name: Joi.string(),
    age: Joi.number().required()
});

Joi.assert({ name: 'Mark' }, schema);
```

Will throw an error because age is missing

There are too many methods in the Joi API to reproduce fully in this book. Check out the Readme on GitHub (https://github.com/hapijs/joi/blob/master/API.md) for more.

By now you should have a good idea of how Joi works. You should be able to write schemas and validate your own objects. Joi is such a useful tool on its own that you'll probably find yourself using it in applications that don't use hapi. It's even more powerful when coupled with hapi, though. We'll be looking at that soon.

6.2.2 *Joi.assert() vs. Joi.validate()*

There are a couple of ways you can test an object against a schema using Joi. There's the Joi.assert() function that you've already seen. This will cause an exception in your program if the object you're testing doesn't validate against the schema. Joi.assert() is useful for cases where you want to stop executing the current call stack if the validation check fails:

```
const Joi = require('joi');

const fruits = ['mango', 'apple', 'potato'];
const schema = Joi.array().items(['mango', 'apple', 'grape']);

Joi.assert(fruits, schema);

console.log('This code will never execute');
```

Exception thrown here

There's also Joi.validate(), which won't cause an exception in your program if the tested object doesn't pass the validation. Instead it will provide you with the error object that contains the details of what happened during validation, and you can choose to act on this information however you want. Joi.validate() is much more flexible and can be used to create your own custom validation workflows:

```
const Joi = require('joi');

const fruits = ['mango', 'apple', 'potato'];
const schema = Joi.array().items(['mango', 'apple', 'grape']);

Joi.validate(fruits, schema, (err, value) => {

    if (!err) {
        console.log('The object was valid');
    }
    else {
```

err is null if the object was valid

```
        console.log('The object wasn\'t valid');
    }

    console.log('This code will still run');
});
```

The third argument to `Joi.validate()` is a callback, which is called synchronously and accepts two parameters, `err` and `value`. `err` is a JavaScript `Error` object that contains information about the validation failure. `value` is the resultant value of the tested object after validation. This might not be equal to the value that you originally tested because of the type conversion behavior in Joi, which we look at next.

6.2.3 Type conversion in Joi

Joi types don't have an exact one-to-one mapping to JavaScript types—they're a little more flexible than that. `Joi.number()` validates all JavaScript numbers, as we know. But it will also validate a JavaScript `string` that *looks* like a number, such as `'1625'`. Not only will Joi allow this value, it will also coerce the `string` into a `number` because it knows that you're expecting one.

```
const numberString = '16';
console.log(typeof numberString);              ⟵┐ Outputs string

Joi.validate(numberString, Joi.number(), (err, value) => {

    console.log(typeof value);                 ⟵┐ Outputs number
});
```

Joi will also convert strings into `Buffer` objects, Node's type for working with binary data, when validating against the `Joi.binary()` type. This is shown in figure 6.4.

This type conversion by Joi is usually a good thing. If you ever want to be more strict about the types you validate, though, you can disable it by setting the `convert` option to `false`, either by using the `.options()` method on a Joi schema or by

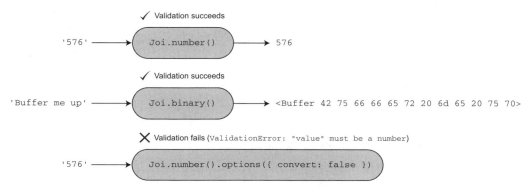

Figure 6.4 Joi will convert some values into other types.

supplying an options object to `Joi.validate()`. The latter approach is shown in the following code, and the former approach is shown in figure 6.4.

```
const numberString = '16';

Joi.validate(numberString, Joi.number(), { convert: false }, (err, value) =>
   {

    if (err) {
        throw err;                          ◁──┐  Throws Error: ValidationError:
    }                                            "value" must be a number
});
```

6.2.4   *The abortEarly option*

The `abortEarly` option, available when calling `Joi.validate()`, is set to `true` by default. This option tells Joi to stop validating any remaining data as soon as it hits upon the first validation error. This means if you try to validate an object with several invalid properties, it's going to report only the first problem it finds. That seems like a sensible default. If something's wrong, there's not much point in trying to validate any further, right?

In most cases, you do probably want `abortEarly` set to `true`. But sometimes you may want to validate the entire object and report all validation problems so they can be fixed in one go. You can do this, as shown in figure 6.5, by setting `abortEarly` to `false`.

An example of such a case would be when validating a web form. The user should know everything that was wrong with their form submission immediately. It would be tiresome to have to fix problems with the form, one field at a time. You'll see an example of this use case in section 6.4.

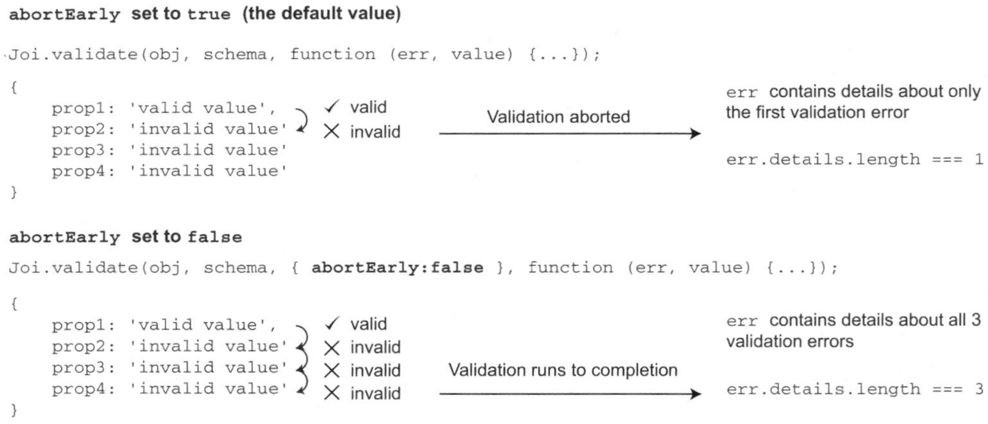

abortEarly set to `true` (the default value)

```
Joi.validate(obj, schema, function (err, value) {...});

{
    prop1: 'valid value',     ⎫  ✓ valid
    prop2: 'invalid value'    ⎭  ✗ invalid      Validation aborted
    prop3: 'invalid value'                    ─────────────────────────▶
    prop4: 'invalid value'
}
```

err contains details about only
the first validation error

err.details.length === 1

abortEarly set to false

```
Joi.validate(obj, schema, { abortEarly:false }, function (err, value) {...});

{
    prop1: 'valid value',     ⎫  ✓ valid
    prop2: 'invalid value'    ⎬  ✗ invalid
    prop3: 'invalid value'    ⎨  ✗ invalid    Validation runs to completion
    prop4: 'invalid value'    ⎭  ✗ invalid    ─────────────────────────▶
}
```

err contains details about all 3
validation errors

err.details.length === 3

Figure 6.5   Joi's behavior when setting abortEarly to true versus false

6.2.5 *Exploring Joi errors*

To use Joi's validation feedback in a useful way, it's important to understand exactly what information it provides when there's a validation failure. If a call to `Joi.validate()` results in an unsuccessful validation attempt, the `err` parameter in the callback will be an instance of a JavaScript `Error` object:

```
Joi.validate({ num: 'hello' }, Joi.number(), (err, data) => {

    console.log(err instanceof Error);                    ⟵──  Outputs true
});
```

The `Error` object created by Joi has several properties that you can inspect to understand more about exactly what went wrong. One of those properties is `message`, which is a `string` containing a summary of the validation error.

The `details` property will contain an array of objects. Each object represents a single validation error. If `abortEarly` is set to `true`, this array will contain only a single item. This listing shows an example of validating an object that has multiple validation errors.

Listing 6.5 Object with multiple validation errors

```
const Joi = require('joi');

const product = {
    id: 5489,
    name: 'Trouser press',
    price: {
        value: 34.88,
        currency: 'GBP'
    }
};

const schema = {
    id: Joi.number().max(4000),
    name: Joi.string(),
    price: {
        value: Joi.number(),
        currency: Joi.string().valid(['USD', 'EUR'])
    }
};
```

Pretty-print the full details array └─▷
```
Joi.validate(product, schema, { abortEarly: false }, (err, data) => {

    console.log(JSON.stringify(err.details, null, 2));
});
```

Running the code in the previous listing yields the following output:

Path to validated value from root value └─▷
```
[
    {
        "message": "\"id\" must be less than or equal to 4000",    ⟵──┘  Description of validation error
        "path": "id",
```

Type of validation rule that caused error

```
"type": "number.max",
"context": {
    "limit": 4000,
    "value": 5489,
    "key": "id"
}
},
{
    "message": "\"currency\" must be one of [USD, EUR]",
    "path": "price.currency",
    "type": "any.allowOnly",
    "context": {
        "valids": [
            "USD",
            "EUR"
        ],
        "key": "currency"
    }
}
]
```

Contains other data, specific to validation rule type used, properties different between different error types

By knowing your way around the error object that Joi provides, including the err.details array, you can build your own custom validation responses, which is what exactly what I'll be showing you in section 6.3.4.

6.3   *Validation in hapi*

Joi and hapi go together like peas and carrots. The framework offers built-in input validation that works seamlessly with Joi by allowing you to specify Joi schemas in the configuration of your routes. Validation is usually a tricky matter and involves writing a lot of conditional statements. How many times have you seen ugly code like the following?

```
const handler = function (req, res) {

    const url = require('url').parse(req.url, true);

    if(!url.query.firstName || typeof url.query.firstName !== 'string'){
        res.writeHead(400);
        res.end('Bad request');
    }

    ...
}
```

By taking care of validation at the framework level, once again hapi can help eradicate messy boilerplate code from your applications. hapi will also automatically take care of responding to requests with bad inputs, without even touching your code.

But what exactly do we need to validate? In the vending machine example, I mentioned that we needed to validate the *inputs* into our systems. In the case of a hapi application, the inputs are the bits of data that we may get sent in HTTP requests—path parameters, query parameters, headers, and payloads.

6.3.1   *Validating inputs with Joi*

Every route in hapi has an optional `config` object, used to specify additional options. One of the properties available in `config` is `validate`.

CONFIGURATION OPTIONS

Figure 6.6 shows an example HTTP request with the input types you can validate with hapi identified. The `validate` option is used to specify validation criteria for the route's inputs.

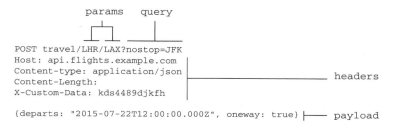

Figure 6.6   The input types you can validate in hapi

The value defined for `validate` should be an object, consisting of several optional keys. You can specify validation rules for the inputs shown in table 6.3.

Table 6.3   Available input validation options

Property	Explanation
headers	Validates the HTTP headers stored in `request.headers`
query	Validates the query parameters stored in `request.query`
params	Validates the URL path parameters stored in `request.params`
payload	Validates the HTTP payload stored in `request.payload`

Each of the properties in table 6.3 can be assigned one of several allowable values:

- `true`, meaning no validation will be performed. All inputs are set to this by default.
- `false`, a no-no. Inputs of this type are explicitly forbidden.
- A function, a custom validation function (not covered in this book).
- A Joi validation schema.

VALIDATING PATH PARAMETERS

Imagine we're building an API that accepts a product ID as a path parameter and then makes a query to a database. We should check that the ID is a positive, non-zero integer before making the database query. It would be inefficient to make a database query that we know is going to fail beforehand. By adding validation, we can ensure our API allows URLs like http://localhost:4000/products/389 and not http://local-host:4000/products/horses or http://localhost:4000/products/-16.5. To achieve this, we can set a `params` validation rule in the route config.

Listing 6.6   Validating path parameters

```
const Hapi = require('hapi');
const Joi = require('joi');

const server = new Hapi.Server();
server.connection({ port: 4000 });

server.route({
    method: 'GET',
    path: '/products/{id}',
    handler: function (request, reply) {

        reply('Success');
    },
    config: {
        validate: {
            params: {
                id: Joi.number().integer().min(1)
            }
        }
    }
});

server.start(() => {

    console.log('Started server');
});
```

If you spin up the server from the previous listing and visit http://localhost:4000/products/389 in a browser, you should see a success message. If you change the ID parameter to a string value, like `'eggs'`, you'll get a different message. We can get a better idea of what is happening by using cURL:

```
$ curl -i http://localhost:4000/products/eggs

HTTP/1.1 400 Bad Request
content-type: application/json; charset=utf-8
cache-control: no-cache
content-length: 123
Date: Wed, 04 Mar 2015 23:38:40 GMT
Connection: keep-alive
```

HTTP response head

```
{"statusCode":400,"error":"Bad Request","message":"\"id\" must be a
    number","validation":{"source":"params","keys":["id"]}}
```

HTTP response body

You should recognize the payload of this response as JSON—it's another `Boom` error response.

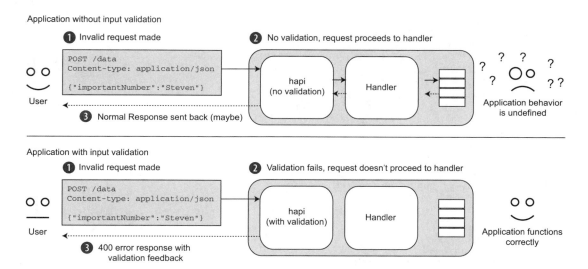

Figure 6.7 Input validation protects your app from undefined behavior.

6.3.2 Validating payloads

If your application accepts payload data and then acts on that data, you should validate it to ensure your application behaves correctly (see figure 6.7). If you don't validate it and someone sends you bad data, several things could happen. At best your handler will throw an error, and the client will get a 500 response code and internal server error message. At worst you could store invalid data, which is passed on to consumers, undermining your whole app.

Earlier, I defined a format for an imaginary API that receives weather reports. Here's another example of a report in that format, from a chilly day in Toronto:

```
const report = {
    station: 'Toronto',
    datetime: 'Fri Jan 24 2014 12:00:00 GMT+0000 (GMT)',
    temp: -14
};
```

The weather API is going to accept that data as a payload. I can add the schema that I defined earlier to the payload validation option in a route.

Listing 6.7   Validating path parameters

```
const Hapi = require('hapi');
const Joi = require('joi');

const server = new Hapi.Server();
server.connection({ port: 4000 });
```

```
const schema = {
    station: Joi.string().max(100).required(),
    datetime: Joi.date().required(),
    temp: Joi.number().min(-140).max(140).required(),
    humidity: Joi.number().min(0).max(100),
    precipitation: Joi.boolean(),
    windDirection: Joi.string()
        .valid(['N', 'NE', 'E', 'SE', 'S', 'SW', 'W', 'NW'])
};
```
The payload schema definition

```
server.route({
    method: 'POST',
    path: '/reports',
    handler: function (request, reply) {

        reply('Thanks for the report!');
    },
    config: {
        payload: {
            output: 'data'
        },
        validate: {
            payload: schema
        }
    }
});
```
Handler will only run if validation passes

hapi should try to parse incoming payload

Set payload validation rule

```
server.start((err) => {

    if (err) {
        throw err;
    }

    console.log('Started server');
});
```

You can start this server and make test requests using a tool of your choice. Here's a test using cURL, sending the Toronto example as a payload:

```
curl -X POST \
-i \
-H "Content-Type: application/json" \
-d '{"station":"Toronto","datetime":"2014-01-24T12:00:00.000Z",
    "temp":-14}' \
    http://localhost:4000/reports
```

Running the preceding command yields the following output:

```
HTTP/1.1 200 OK
content-type: text/html; charset=utf-8
cache-control: no-cache
content-length: 22
Date: Fri, 06 Mar 2015 10:40:16 GMT
Connection: keep-alive

Thanks for the report!
```

Seeing the "Thanks for the report!" output means that the payload passed our validation, and the handler was executed as usual. Let's see what happens if I make another request but forget to include the `station` property:

```
curl -X POST \
-i \
-H "Content-Type: application/json" \
-d '{"datetime":"2014-01-24T12:00:00.000Z","temp":-14}' \         ⟵ Oops,
http://localhost:4000/reports                                        no station!
```

The response this time is different:

```
HTTP/1.1 400 Bad Request          ⟵ 400 status code
content-type: application/json; charset=utf-8    Indicates "client error"
cache-control: no-cache                          ⟵ Response body is
content-length: 129                                 JSON error object
Date: Fri, 06 Mar 2015 10:45:36 GMT
Connection: keep-alive
```

Error response object ⟶ `{"statusCode":400,"error":"Bad Request","message":"\"station\" is required","validation":{"source":"payload","keys":["station"]}}`

hapi has default behavior when it encounters an input validation error. It won't go ahead and execute your handler. Instead it will respond early to the request with a 400 status code. It will also create an error object to respond with. Here's the error from earlier, formatted so it's easier to read:

```
{
    "statusCode":400,                              ⟵ HTTP status code
    "error":"Bad Request",
    "message":"\"station\" is required",           ⟵ Error message
    "validation":{
        "source":"payload",
        "keys":[                                    Additional info about
            "station"                               which input and which
        ]                                           keys validation failed on
    }
}
```
Name of error ⟶ (points to `"error":"Bad Request"`)

6.3.3 Validating responses

In the previous few sections, you've learned why validating your inputs is important. You've also seen how this can be done in hapi applications by adding Joi schemas to your route configuration. In this section we're going to look at another area in your applications where validation could be important: the outputs.

It's all very well if I've built an API that is demanding valid data from its clients. But if that API is then potentially giving out invalid data, I'm kind of a hypocrite, aren't I? You might ask, "If you're validating all your inputs correctly, why would you ever be giving out any bad data?" The truth is that most applications these days aren't isolated systems—they often pull in data from several external sources during the lifetime of a request. You might fetch some tweets to display on a promotional web page or contact an external supplier for updated prices on an e-commerce website.

You add validation options to response payloads much as you did for input validation, except rather than specifying them under `config -> validate` property you do so under the `config -> response` property.

Listing 6.8 is a simple API that responds to GET requests for a person resource on the path /people/{id}. The data for the people objects is stored in a simple JavaScript array. Adding a Joi schema to the response validation `config` property, we ensure that responses are validated before being sent out, which prevents serving bad data to any clients.

Listing 6.8   Specifying outgoing response payload validation

```
const Hapi = require('hapi');
const Joi = require('joi');

const server = new Hapi.Server();
server.connection({ port: 4000 });

const schema = {
    firstName: Joi.string().required(),        ┐
    lastName: Joi.string().required(),          │ Schema for
    age: Joi.number().required(),               ├ person object
    location: Joi.string().required(),          │
    dob: Joi.date().required()                  ┘
};

server.route({
    method: 'GET',
    path: '/people/{id}',
    handler: function (request, reply) {

        const people = [{
          .firstName: 'Xiang',               ┐
            lastName: 'Zheng',                │
            age: 48,                          ├ Valid person
            location: 'Singapore',            │
            dob: '1967-03-02'                 ┘
        }, {
            firstName: 'Emma',                ┐
            lastName: 'Ashdown',              │ Invalid person,
            age: 'millennial',                ├ age is not a number
            location: 'UK',                   │
            dob: '1990-01-01'                 ┘
        }];

        reply(people[request.params.id - 1]);
    },
    config: {
        response: {
            schema: schema          ┐ Provide Joi schema object to
        }                           ┘ response schema option
    }
});
```

```
server.start((err) => {

    if (err) {
        throw err;
    }

    console.log('Started server');
});
```

The default action when encountering an invalid payload is to respond to the request with a 500 status code and internal server error response. You can see this by running the example from listing 6.8 and visiting http://localhost:4000/people/1 and http://localhost:4000/people/2 in your browser, as shown in figure 6.8.

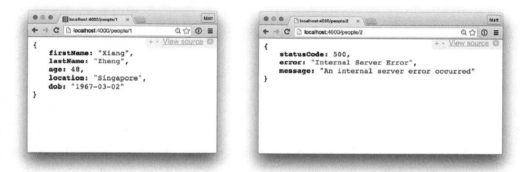

Figure 6.8   Response from hapi when sending a valid (left) and an invalid (right) response payload

6.3.4   *Customizing the validation response with failAction*

As you've seen, hapi's default behavior is to send back a 400 error response to the client as soon as it knows that a request is invalid. For some applications, you may want to have a bit more control over how exactly to respond to invalid requests. By using the `failAction` option, you can define a custom function that will get executed when a request fails validation.

It's important to understand the signature that the `failAction` function should have:

```
function failAction (request, reply, source, error) { }
```

The first two parameters are the same `request` object and `reply` interface that you already know well from writing handlers. The `source` parameter is set to a string value indicating which input source was invalid. `source` will be one of the following values:

- `'headers'`
- `'params'`
- `'query'`
- `'payload'`

The `error` parameter is an instance of the JavaScript `Error` type. This is a `Boom` error prepared for an HTTP error response, rather than the error generated by Joi's validation step. `Boom` is a package created by the hapi core team, for generating HTTP friendly errors. A `Boom` object is an instance of the native JavaScript `Error` type, with extra properties. You can access the original error that came from Joi at `error.data`. The following listing shows an example of using `failAction` to respond to invalid requests with a message indicating which input was the culprit for the failure.

Listing 6.9   Custom validation response using `failAction`

```
server.route({
    ...
    config: {
        validate: {
            ...
            failAction: function (request, reply, source, error) {

                reply(source + ' contained an invalid field.').code(400);
            }
        }
    }
});
```

6.4   *Bringing it all together: web form validation with hapi and Joi*

The content in this chapter, so far, has been general and can be applied to any scenario where validation is required. One thing I've not touched on yet is what happens after validation has failed. How can the error from Joi then be consumed and used, in a useful way, by the client? This section shows you an example of the full process of:

- Building a client (web form)
- Identifying server inputs
- Defining validation rules
- Validating input data
- Customizing the validation output
- Receiving feedback on the client
- Acting on feedback

Pretty much everyone who's ever used the web is familiar with form validation, whether or not they've known it as that. And we all know how frustrating it can be when it doesn't work properly. Thankfully, with a little tweaking, hapi and Joi can take the pain out of this normally tedious task. In this section, I'll be creating a simple registration form application to illustrate this.

6.4.1   *How it works*

The mini-application I'm going to create is a registration process for a conference consisting of a form page and a success page. I will be using the techniques shown in chapter 3 to render HTML documents using the Handlebars templating language. I will also be employing Handlebars layouts and helpers. If you need a refresher have a look at chapter 3 again. The two pages are shown in figure 6.9.

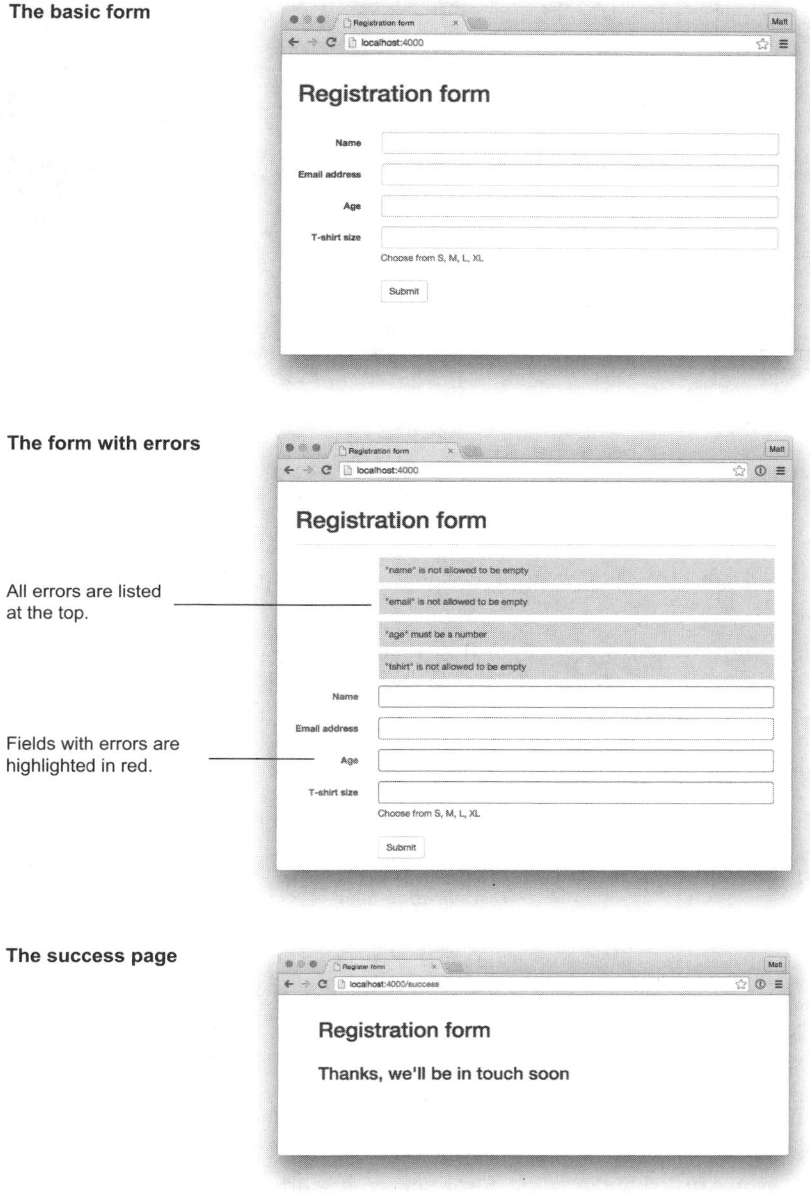

The basic form

The form with errors

All errors are listed at the top.

Fields with errors are highlighted in red.

The success page

Figure 6.9   The pages that make up the registration application

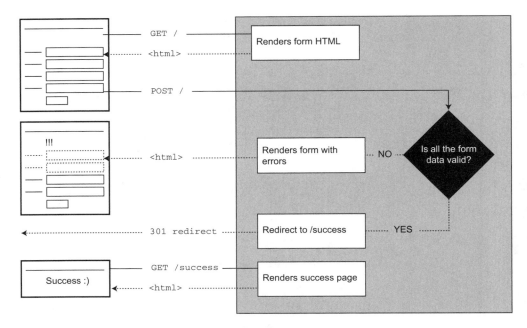

Figure 6.10   **How a user flows through the registration process**

If the form is submitted with validation errors, the server will render the form again but with errors shown. Once the form is submitted without errors, the user will be redirected to the success page. This flow is shown in figure 6.10.

You should have a good sense of how the app is intended to work now. Let's move on to writing some code.

6.4.2 *Creating the skeleton*

Create a directory to hold the app anywhere you want and flesh out the following structure:

Make sure to install all the required dependencies: hapi@13, joi@8, vision@4, and handlebars@4.

Next, you can create a basic hapi server in index.js and configure Handlebars using server.views(). So far, this should all be pretty familiar to you. This listing shows the initial skeleton app.

Listing 6.10   index.js: the application main file

```
'use strict';

const Hapi = require('hapi');
const Path = require('path');

const server = new Hapi.Server();
server.connection({ port: 4000 });

server.register(require('vision'), (err) => {          ⟵─┐ Load vision
                                                           │ plugin
    if (err) {
        throw err;
    }

    server.views({
        engines: {                                      ⟵─┐ Use Handlebars to render
            hbs: require('handlebars')                     │ views with .hbs extensions
        },
        path: Path.join(__dirname, 'views'),               ─────┐ Look here
        layoutPath: Path.join(__dirname, 'views/layouts'),  ⟵───┘ for layouts
        isCached: false,                                ⟵─┐
        layout: true                                       │ Re-render templates
    });                                                    │ on each request (useful
                                                           │ for development)
    server.route(require('./routes'));              ⟵─┐ Load
                                                       │ routes
    server.start((err) => {

        if (err) {
            throw err;
        }

        console.log('Started server at', server.info.uri);
    });
});
```

Look here for views points to `path: Path.join(__dirname, 'views'),`

Use layout points to `layout: true`

Next up, we'll create all the necessary views and set up the routing with hapi, shown in listing 6.12.

6.4.3   Creating the routes and views

You need to create three routes: one to handle the GET requests for the form, one for POST requests from the form submission, and one for the GET request of the success page (listing 6.11). The GET and POST requests from the form page can share the handler. You'll learn how to distinguish between them later.

> **NOTE** Remember all the code for this book is also available on GitHub (https://github.com/mtharrison/Hapi.js-in-action).

Listing 6.11   routes.js: the routes module

```
'use strict';

const Handlers = require('./handlers');

module.exports = [{
    method: 'GET',
    path: '/',
    handler: Handlers.form
}, {
    method: 'POST',
    path: '/',
    handler: Handlers.form
}, {
    method: 'GET',
    path: '/success',
    handler: Handlers.success
}];
```

At this stage, the handlers need only render the appropriate views using `reply.view()`. You'll be adding the additional logic later.

Listing 6.12   handlers.js: the handlers module

```
exports.form = function (request, reply) {

    reply.view('form');
};

exports.success = function (request, reply) {

    reply.view('success');
};
```

Both the views used in this application share a common layout so you can place that wrapper HTML inside `layout.hbs`. Remember the `{{{content}}}` tag is where your rendered view will go.

The head section of the layout contains a script tag to load the Bootstrap CSS file. Bootstrap is a front end framework that allows you to style HTML with ease. One of the components Bootstrap has support for is HTML forms. We'll use it here because it will save us from adding any CSS ourselves. Learn more about Bootstrap at http://getbootstrap.com. The following listing contains the layout template.

Listing 6.13   views/layouts/layout.hbs: the layout

```
<!DOCTYPE html>

<html lang="en">
<head>
    <meta charset="UTF-8">
```

```
    <title>Registration form</title>
    <link href="//maxcdn.bootstrapcdn.com/bootstrap/3.3.2/css/boot-
    strap.min.css" rel="stylesheet">
</head>
```
◁── **Load CSS from Bootstrap**

```
<body>
    <div class="container">
        <div class="page-header">
            <h1>Registration form</h1>
        </div>
```
│ **The page title**

```
        {{{content}}}
```
◁── **The view content will be outputted here**

```
    </div>
</body>
</html>
```

The HTML for the registration form should be placed inside `views/form.hbs`. If you're wondering what all the classes such as `form-horizontal` and `form-group` are, they're classes that are automatically styled by the CSS from Bootstrap. This is the form view template.

Listing 6.14 views/form.hbs: the form view

```
<div class="row" id="formErrors">
    <div class="col-sm-10 col-sm-offset-2">
        {{!-- Error summary goes here --}}
    </div>
</div>
```
◁── **Handlebars comment**

```
<form action="/" class="form-horizontal" method="post">
    <div class="form-group">
        <label class="col-sm-2 control-label">Name</label>
        <div class="col-sm-10">
            <input class="form-control" name="name" type="text">
        </div>
    </div>
```
Name input ──▷

```
    <div class="form-group">
        <label class="col-sm-2 control-label">Email address</label>
        <div class="col-sm-10">
            <input class="form-control" name="email" type="text">
        </div>
    </div>
```
Email input ──▷

```
    <div class="form-group">
        <label class="col-sm-2 control-label">Age</label>
        <div class="col-sm-10">
            <input class="form-control" name="age" type="text">
        </div>
    </div>
```
Age input ──▷

```
    <div class="form-group">
        <label class="col-sm-2 control-label">T-shirt size</label>
```

T-shirt
size input

```
        <div class="col-sm-10">
            <input class="form-control" name="tshirt" type="text">
            <p class="help-block">Choose from S, M, L, XL</p>
        </div>
    </div>

    <div class="form-group">
        <div class="col-sm-offset-2 col-sm-10">
            <button class="btn btn-default" type="submit">Submit</button>
        </div>
    </div>
</form>
```

Finally you can create the view for the success page, as shown in the following listing. This is a simple view, containing only a quick message.

Listing 6.15   views/success.hbs: the success page view

```
<h2>Thanks, we'll be in touch soon</h2>
```

Phew, that was quite a bit of work, but you can now start the hapi server (node index) and behold the result. If you open http://localhost:4000/ and http://localhost:4000/ success in a browser, you should see the styled form and success pages. If you submit the form, nothing interesting will happen yet. Let's work on that now.

6.4.4   *Adding validation*

The data from the submitted registration form will be sent as a payload. You can add validation rules for the payload to the POST route, which processes the form.

Listing 6.16   routes.js: adding validation rules

```
...
const Joi = require('joi');

    ...
}, {
    method: 'POST',
    path: '/',
    handler: Handlers.form,
    config: {
        validate: {
            payload: {
                name: Joi.string().required(),
                email: Joi.string().email().required(),
                age: Joi.string().required().regex(/^[1-9][0-9]+/),
                tshirt: Joi.string().required().valid(['S','M','L','XL'])
            }
        }
    }
}, {
    ...
```

ABORT EARLY

Because I want to collect and display all the validation errors at once, I will set
`abortEarly` to false in the Joi options:

```
...
validate: {
    payload: {
        ...
    },
    options: {
        abortEarly: false
    },
}
...
```

FAIL ACTION

Upon a validation error, I want the form to be rendered again rather than the default,
so I need to write a custom `failAction` function. Here's an example of the contents
of `error.details` for a submission of my form, which fails validation:

```
[ { message: '"name" is not allowed to be empty',
    path: 'name',
    type: 'any.empty',
    context: { key: 'name' } },
  { message: '"email" is not allowed to be empty',
    path: 'email',
    type: 'any.empty',
    context: { key: 'email' } },
  { message: '"email" must be a valid email',
    path: 'email',
    type: 'string.email',
    context: { value: '', key: 'email' } }]
```

I don't need all that information available to my view context. Ideally what I want is an
object with keys for the field names and the value equal to the first error message for
that key. I can achieve this easily by building up my own `errors` object:

```
...
validate: {
    payload: {
        ...
    },
    options: {
        ...
    },
    failAction: function (request, reply, source, error) {
        const errors = {};                          // Object to hold errors
        const details = error.data.details;         // Details of Joi error

        for(let i = 0; i < details.length; ++i) {
            if (!errors.hasOwnProperty(details[i].path)) {
                errors[details[i].path] = details[i].message;
            }
        }
    }
```

Loop through each error in details and grab first error for each key

```
        reply.view('form', {
            errors: errors,
            values: request.payload
        }).code(400);
    }
}
...
```

Render form view, passing in
original submitted values and errors

Send 400
response code

FRIENDLY ERROR MESSAGES

Machines and developers are the intended audience for the error messages that Joi produces. For that reason, the messages are precise and unambiguous. The flipside of this is that they're not suitable for consumption by end users. For instance, the regex validator we're using in this example for the age field will produce this error message:

```
"age" with value "Twenty!" fails to match the required pattern: /^[1-9][0-9]+/
```

That message is going to be totally meaningless to any user who isn't also a software developer or familiar with regular expressions. There's also the issue of internationalization. The error messages coming from Joi are always English. There's been some debate in the hapi community about this. Some consider Joi to only be a solution for use on the back end of systems and never exposed to the client in any way. Others, myself included, think that Joi is a powerful tool and we should extend its use to the front end too, rather than finding yet another validation tool. I hope to see further development on Joi in the future to make this dual-use easier. For now, we have an interim solution in the form of the language option.

Earlier in the chapter, we saw that for any Joi validator we can supply additional options by chaining on the options method. One of those available options is the language option, which lets us specify a custom error message to use. In the case of the age validator, we want to provide a custom message for the string.regex.base validator type. Here's how that will look in our validator:

```
age: Joi.string().required().regex(/^[1-9][0-9]+/).options({
    language: {
        string: {
            regex: {
                base: 'should be a numeric string with no leading zeros'
            }
        }
    }
}),
```

Using this approach, we can then substitute any of the possible default error messages for one of our own.

Okay, we're almost there. We've got our form submissions validated and we have the errors available in the view now. The last thing to do is use those errors to render the invalid form correctly.

6.4.5 Rendering errors on the form

It's common practice when returning a user to an invalid form to leave their submitted values in the fields. This saves them from typing the correct ones all over again. The original values are available in `values` in the template context so we can update our form view to output those values for each field, as shown in the following listing.

Listing 6.17   views/form.hbs: setting the form field values

```
...

<input class="form-control" name="name" type="text" value="{{values.name}}">

...

<input class="form-control" name="email" type="text"
  value="{{values.email}}">

...

<input class="form-control" name="age" type="text" value="{{values.age}}">

...

<input class="form-control" name="tshirt" type="text"
     value="{{values.tshirt}}">
```

We can use the class `bg-danger` from Bootstrap to render a list of all the errors above the form (see figure 6.11):

```
<div class="row" id="formErrors">
    <div class="col-sm-10 col-sm-offset-2">
        {{#each errors}}
            <p class="bg-danger">{{this}}</p>
        {{/each}}
    </div>
</div>
```

Loop through each error → `{{#each errors}}` ... `{{/each}}`

Print value of error in bg-danger paragraph tag ←

Figure 6.11   List of errors above the form

A finishing touch is to add the `has-error` class on each field that has an error associated with it (see figure 6.12). We can check whether the field has an error using the `{{#if}}` conditional helper in Handlebars:

```
<div class="form-group {{#if errors.email}}has-error{{/if}}">
    <label class="col-sm-2 control-label">Email address</label>
    <div class="col-sm-10">
        <input class="form-control" name="email" type="text"
        value="{{values.email}}">
    </div>
</div>
```

Name	
Email address	somebody@email.com
Age	
T-shirt size	L
	Choose from S, M, L, XL

Figure 6.12   The highlighted form fields using the `has-error` class

You should start the hapi server and play around with the form, testing different combinations of valid and invalid values to see what happens. Even though this example has used Bootstrap as a front end framework, the same principles can be applied to any HTML form.

6.4.6   *Redirecting users after successful form submission*

When a user has successfully submitted a form without validation errors, the user should see a success page. We can implement this by checking whether the request was a POST request in the form handler in handlers.js and then redirecting to `/success` if it is. In a real web application, this might be where you then store the form submission in a database or trigger email alerts to the relevant people. Here is this redirect on POST.

Listing 6.18   handler.js: redirecting successful submissions

```
exports.form = function (request, reply) {

    if (request.method === 'post') {             Redirect to success page—in a
        return reply.redirect('/success');       real web app this is where you'd
    }                                            process form submission

    reply.view('form');
};

...
```

In the next chapter we'll look at a particularly exciting and important feature of hapi: plugins. I won't lie to you, I think plugins are awesome. I hope you'll agree.

6.5 *Summary*

- Joi is a validation library you can use to validate JavaScript values against their expected format.
- Joi can be used outside of hapi.js projects, but it's also well integrated with the framework.
- You can use Joi schemas when creating hapi routes to specify input validation for headers, query params, path params, and payloads.
- You can validate your hapi responses using Joi.
- You can customize the errors that Joi produces by specifying a `failAction` function for hapi routes.

7

Building modular applications with plugins

This chapter covers

- Defining plugins and why you should use them
- Creating and loading plugins
- Building applications in a modular way using plugins
- Communicating and sharing data between plugins

When building software we strive for modularity at many different layers. We package reusable statements into functions and functions into modules and classes. More recently we've started using tools like Browserify and React to split our front end into modules and components too.

Modularizing helps us to draw a line around something and says *this does X*, without anyone else (or our future selves) having to worry about how it does X. When working on a modular application, the cognitive load is reduced. We can lock away in the back of our minds all the messy details of the rest of the system and focus on the piece that we're working on.

Despite developers having been aware of these benefits for a long time, the way we often see servers being built with Node.js is in a monolithic fashion. I've seen many Node applications with a single app.js or server.js file that contains the entire logic for the server. What happened to the modularity?

The hapi plugin system exists to give you a way to achieve modularity in how you build servers. You can think of hapi plugins as mini hapi servers that all come together to create a single, unified server. This approach gives great scalability and maintainability, especially when dealing with extensive codebases or a large number of developers.

Plugins are my favorite feature in hapi. The ability to build up my apps from many small and focused chunks of server logic, neatly packaged into modules, brings me a great sense of inner peace and satisfaction. I hope by the end of this chapter you'll be as sold on this approach as I am.

7.1 Plugged-in thinking

I'm going to say this up front to avoid any confusion later: it's time to forget most of what you know about plugins from other frameworks. In most other frameworks, plugins are usually *only* about extending the framework's capabilities beyond what's offered out of the box. Plugins are usually an advanced topic that you probably only bother learning once you've mastered the framework and want to add more new features that you feel are missing.

Plugins are quite different in hapi, they're much *simpler* but also much more *powerful* than other frameworks. And you should start creating your own plugins straight away. Why?

- They're *simple* because they're super easy to *create, use,* and *share* with others.
- They're *powerful* because there's practically no limit to what you can put inside a plugin. If you can do it inside any other hapi application, you can do it inside a plugin.

If you develop a piece of functionality in a plugin that's useful to others, you can share that via a plugin in a public npm package. You could also split a large internal application into several small plugins that are hosted on npm via private packages. If you don't want to manage the overhead of separate packages, you can keep all of your plugins in a single codebase until it makes sense (if it ever does) to split these apart.

Another benefit of building an application from many small plugins is that there's a relatively small cost (in time or money) of replacing or removing an entire part of the system. This means you don't need to be too precious about your code. If something's not working out how you expected, you can remove the plugin and write a new one.

Plugins are also ideal when developing with a microservices architecture. *Microservices* are what you get when a large monolithic application is split into separate processes, perhaps running on separate machines or datacenters, as illustrated in

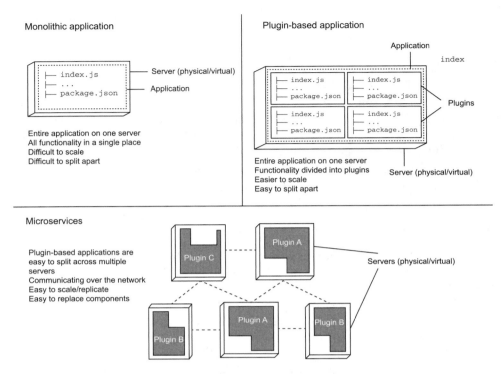

Figure 7.1   Plugins lend themselves well to a microservices architecture.

figure 7.1. The self-contained nature of hapi plugins means it's incredibly simple to move a chunk of functionality from one application to another with a simple configuration change.

Let's take a step back and look at what a plugin is.

7.1.1   *What is a plugin?*

A hapi plugin is created simply by writing a function and defining an attributes object:

```
const plugin = function (server, options, next) {

    ...
};

plugin.attributes = { name: 'my-simple-plugin', version: '0.0.1' };
```

Inside the body of the function is where you work your magic and put any code that you want to write to build the plugin. The server argument is the same you get from calling new Hapi.Server(), so all the usual methods like server.route() and friends are available. Let's see how to create a route in a plugin:

```
const plugin = function (server, options, next) {
```

```
server.route({
    method: 'GET',
    path: '/',
    handler: function (request, reply) {

        reply('Welcome home!');
    }
});

...
};
```

Nothing too different, right? When your plugin has finished doing what it needs to do to set itself up, you call next() to let the parent application know that the plugin has finished being loaded:

```
const plugin = function (server, options, next) {

    server.route({
        method: 'GET',
        path: '/',
        handler: function (request, reply) {

            reply('Welcome home!');
        }
    });

    next();
};
```

Note that you *never* create or start servers inside plugins—you leave that up to the parent application, which is the thing that loads and uses the plugin. Speaking of which, listing 7.1 shows that loading the plugin works by calling server.register(), as you've seen before when loading plugins that you've downloaded with npm, like Inert and Vision.

HAPI API server.register(plugins, [options], [callback]) (http://hapijs.com/api#serverregisterplugins-options-callback)

Listing 7.1 Creating and loading a simple plugin

```
const Hapi = require('hapi');

const server = new Hapi.Server();
server.connection({ port: 4000 });

const plugin = function (server, options, next) {          Define plugin by creating
                                                            plugin registration function

    server.route({
        method: 'GET',
        path: '/',                                          Add new route
        handler: function (request, reply) {                inside plugin
```

```
        reply('Welcome home!');
    }
});

next();                              Call next callback to signify
};                                   plugin registration is complete

plugin.attributes = { name: 'my-simple-plugin', version: '0.0.1' };

server.register(plugin, (err) => {

    if (err) {
        throw err;
    }

    server.start((err) => {

        if (err) {
            throw err;
        }

        console.log('Started server');
    });
});
```

Add new route
inside plugin

Define some
required plugin
attributes

Load plugin with
server.register()

Handle any errors that
occurred when loading plugin

7.1.2   What can go in a plugin?

A plugin can contain practically anything that you'd put inside a normal hapi application (and by *normal*, I mean one that doesn't use any plugins). Plugins can contain routes, server methods, extension points, custom handlers, and decorators.

Normally, most plugins are either containers of *business logic* or *utilities*. Let's talk about those two types now.

BUSINESS LOGIC PLUGINS

Imagine we're building a bookstore application. Customers will use it to browse and purchase books. Staff members will use it to manage inventory and shipping.

Even though we're building a single application here, it serves multiple roles. If our book company is of a decent size, separate groups of developers might be working on different parts of our application. We might have an inventory team that works in relative isolation from the shipping team, sharing only a database.

Ideally, one team shouldn't have to be worried about stepping on the toes of another when working on their part of the application. This kind of large-scale enterprise setting is an environment that hapi and hapi plugins were specifically designed for.

This bookstore application could be built up from separate hapi plugins, each controlling one facet of the application. This architecture is shown in figure 7.2.

Inside the Browsing plugin would be all the routes, handlers, and server methods that implement the browsing side of the application. The same would be the case with the other plugins.

This is an example of using hapi plugins to divide business logic. Business logic plugins are usually isolated from each other. A change in one plugin shouldn't—usually—affect another plugin.

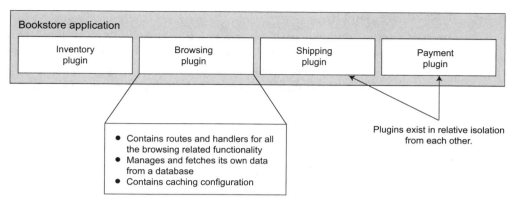

Figure 7.2 Bookstore application split into business logic plugins that individually manage different areas of the same application

It would be naïve to suggest that plugins are always in total isolation, though. After all, they're part of the same application. In a real-world application there's always some crossover between plugins, which is why we'll be looking into inter-plugin communication in section 7.4.

Business logic plugins are normally kept private to your organization or team (or you), because they make sense only within your app. They could all be kept inside a single repository or packaged as npm modules.

EXTENSION/UTILITY PLUGINS

An *extension* or *utility* plugin is the other main type of plugin. This kind implements something on a scale global to an application. All the plugins we've used so far such as Good, Inert, Vision, Yar, and `hapi-auth-cookie` are examples of extension/utility plugins. They extend the framework in a global sense, offering new functionality to your application.

In the bookstore application, if we add Inert as a registered plugin, we could take advantage of static file serving in each of our other plugins, as shown in figure 7.3.

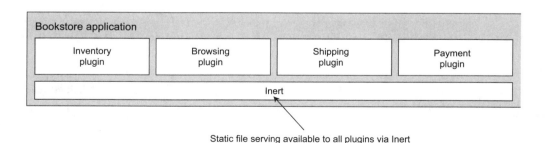

Figure 7.3 Extension/utility plugins add functionality to all other plugins.

7.1.3 *Plugin all the things!*

You may wonder on what occasion you should put something inside a plugin, and when you should have it as part of a root application. Here's a simple answer to that dilemma: *put everything inside a plugin.*

Everything? Yes, everything. Unless you're building an extremely basic application with a few routes you should always adopt a plugin approach. Why not? You've seen how easy plugins are to create and you now know the benefits they offer, so use them—all the time.

Recapping, plugins:

- Are self-contained chunks of application functionality that come together to make an application
- Help create modular, maintainable applications
- Can contain pretty much anything you'd put in a normal hapi app:
  - Routes
  - Server methods
  - Extension points
  - Decorations
- Are created by defining a plugin registration function and a set of attributes
- Are loaded with `server.register()`
- Usually implement either business logic or add utilities/extend the framework

We've covered some of the theory behind plugins. Now it's time to see how to use plugins in the real world.

7.1.4 *The Pingoo application*

Technical discussions and abstract explanations are all well and good, but it always helps to ground these in a real example. This section describes a hapi application called Pingoo, shown in figure 7.4.

Pingoo is a fictional product consisting of a web application that receives "pings" from a device on airborne commercial aircraft. Each ping is received as an HTTP request containing a JSON payload, which represents the plane's current position. This listing shows an example payload.

Listing 7.2   Example JSON "ping" received by Pingoo

```
{
    "code": "SA2490",
    "lat": 53.470721,
    "lng": -2.240567,
    "timestamp": "2015-08-22T11:00:00+00:00"
}
```

Flight code

Flight's current latitude (decimal)

Flight's current longitude (decimal)

ISO 8601 datetime ping was generated

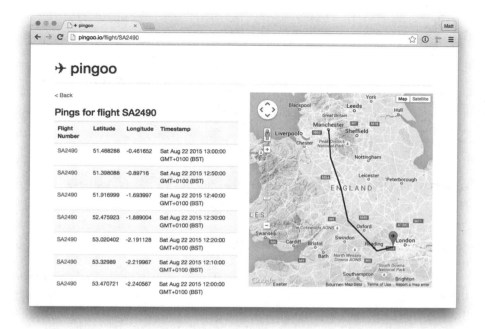

Figure 7.4   Map view of the Pingoo application

The Pingoo app validates these payloads and inserts them into a RethinkDB database table.

> **RethinkDB**
>
> RethinkDB is a NoSQL JSON database with a fully featured official Node.js library. To get started with it, follow the installation instructions for your platform at http://rethinkdb.com/docs/install/.
>
> The supplied code for this chapter has a script (CH07 - Creating Modular Applications with Plugins/db-setup.js) that you can run to create a database with the sample data for this chapter.

NPM PACKAGE   `rethinkdb` v2 (https://www.npmjs.com/package/rethinkdb)

Another part of the Pingoo application is a web portal, which lets you view the most recent pings from aircraft and see the flight path of a single flight on a Google Map (shown in figure 7.4). Currently this application is structured in a flat fashion with all the routes and login in a single file, but we're going to convert it to use a plugin

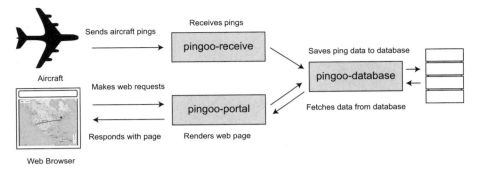

Figure 7.5 Plugin structure and the different actors that use the Pingoo application

architecture. Figure 7.5 shows a few of the plugins that we're going to create in order to split up this application.

We're not going to get deep into the details of how Pingoo works or how to build the features. It's pretty simple, and you can check the code for that. Rather, we're going to walk through taking the app from a flat structure with all the logic in a single file to a plugin-based approach, along the way meeting the important features in hapi's plugin system. The code for both the starting point of Pingoo (in the folder `initial_application`) and the finished plugin-based app is available on GitHub, along with the rest of the book's code.

7.2   *Creating and loading plugins*

This section looks at ways to create plugins and load them into a server. We'll check out passing options into plugins to allow them to be configured from the outside. We'll also see how to manage situations where one plugin depends on another.

We're going to be working on splitting up the Pingoo application from a single big hapi app contained in a single file into several small, focused plugins. Let's get started.

7.2.1   *Creating a plugin*

Creating a plugin with hapi is as simple as writing a JavaScript function. We call this function the *registration function*, and it has the following format:

```
const plugin = function (server, options, next) {

    ...
    next();
};

plugin.attributes = { name: 'my-plugin', version: '0.0.1' };
```

Table 7.1 shows what those three parameters given to the registration function are.

Table 7.1   Parameters given to a plugin registration function

Parameter	Explanation
server	A hapi server (or single connection) object, as would be returned from new `Hapi.Server()`. Supports all the usual server methods such as `server.route()`, `server.method()`, and so on.
options	Optional settings that are handed directly to the plugin. Allows for outside configuration of the plugin. See section 7.2.3.
next	A callback that you need to call to let hapi know when the plugin has finished setting itself up and is ready to be used.

You add all the features that you want your plugin to implement before calling the `next()` callback. The registration function also has an `attributes` property, which tells hapi a little bit about your plugin.

> **NOTE** If attaching a property to a function looks unusual to you, don't worry—it's perfectly valid JavaScript. Functions in JavaScript are a special kind of object. Try typing `new Function() instanceof Object` into your browser's dev console, and you'll see `true`.

Normally, when developing hapi plugins, we like to keep a plugin in a module of its own. In this case, we need to export the registration function from the plugin as `exports.register`:

```
exports.register = function (server, options, next) {

    ...
    next();
};

exports.register.attributes = { ... };
```

If we're releasing this plugin as an npm package with its own package.json file, we can use the data in there as the plugin's attributes:

```
exports.register.attributes = { pkg: require('./package') };
```

OUR PLUGIN'S JOB

Our starting point is the project in the directory `initial_application` in the supplied source code from GitHub. You'll see that all the code for Pingoo is all contained in a single index.js file. We're going to change that by slicing things into plugins.

There's a route in index.js that's responsible for receiving the pings from aircraft:

```
server.route({
    config: {
        validate: {
            payload: {
                code: Joi.string().required(),
                lat: Joi.number().required(),
```

```
                        lng: Joi.number().required(),
                        alt: Joi.number().required(),
                        timestamp: Joi.date().required()
                    }
                }
            },
            method: 'POST',
            path: '/api',
            handler: function (request, reply) {

                server.methods.database.addPing(request.payload, reply);

            }
        });
```

We're going to put this route in its own dedicated plugin called pingoo-receive. First we'll add a plugins directory and a package.json for the new plugin. Our directory structure now looks like this:

```
├── index.js
├── package.json
├── plugins
│   └── receive
│       ├── index.js
│       └── package.json
└── templates
    ...
```

This listing creates a minimal package.json for the pingoo-receive plugin.

Listing 7.3 Pingoo: plugins/receive/package.json

```
{
  "name": "pingoo-receive",
  "version": "1.0.0"
}
```

CREATING THE PINGOO-RECEIVE PLUGIN

Now we can get to adding the content of the plugin. We can remove the receiver route from the index.js file and place it in our new plugin's index.js file, as shown in the following listing. We also need to make sure we load Joi, as it's required by the plugin.

Listing 7.4 Pingoo: plugins/receive/index.js

```
const Joi = require('joi');

exports.register = function (server, options, next) {        ◁── Define and export
                                                                 plugin's registration
    server.route({                                               function
        config: {
            validate: {
                payload: {
                    code: Joi.string().required(),
                    lat: Joi.number().required(),
```

Add receiver route

```
                            lng: Joi.number().required(),
                            alt: Joi.number().required(),
                            timestamp: Joi.date().required()
                        }
                    }
                },
                method: 'POST',
                path: '/api',
                handler: function (request, reply) {

                    server.methods.database.addPing(request.payload, reply);
                }
            });

    next();                          Call next() callback to
};                                   signal plugin is fully loaded        Use plugin's
                                                                   package.json info as
                                                                     plugin's attributes
exports.register.attributes = { pkg: require('./package'); }
```

Now that we've created our first plugin, it's time to see how we can load it into our application.

> **EXERCISE** See if you can separate the rest of the logic from index.js in the provided sample code for section 7.2.1 into plugins. We should have three plugins: database, portal, and receive. The portal plugin should contain view configuration and the routes for GET / and GET /flight/{code}. The database plugin should contain the RethinkDB connection and the database server methods. Look at the sample code for section 7.2.2 to see how close your attempt is.

7.2.2 Loading plugins with server.register()

We load our own custom plugins, as we do with core hapi plugins, by using `server.register()`. There are a few syntaxes that we can use with `server.register()`, and you're likely to encounter them all at some point. If we're loading a single plugin we can do this:

```
const Plugin = require('plugin');

server.register(Plugin, (err) => {

    ...
});
```

The `err` parameter will be an `Error` object if an error occurred while registering the plugin. Sometimes you may see somebody skip the initial assignment and load the plugin inline. There's no difference in behavior here. It saves a little typing:

```
server.register(require('plugin'), (err) => {

    ...
});
```

WITH PLUGIN OBJECTS

You can also specify the plugin argument as an object with a register property instead:

```
server.register({ register: require('plugin') }, (err) => {

    ...
});
```

MULTIPLE PLUGINS

We can use server.register() to register multiple plugins simultaneously by providing an array of plugins. We can use any of the single plugin syntaxes from earlier for each element in the array:

```
const plugins = [
    Plugin1,
    require('plugin2'),
    { register: require('plugin3') }
];

server.register(plugins, (err) => {

    ...
});
```

Although slightly more verbose, I prefer the object syntax because it's more flexible and allows you to pass options to the plugin too, which you'll see in the next section.

Now that all the Pingoo application logic is divided into plugins, we can load those external plugins in index.js using the multiple plugin array syntax for server .register().

Listing 7.5 Pingoo: index.js, loading the plugins

```
server.register([
    { register: require('vision') },
    { register: require('./plugins/database') },    Register the
    { register: require('./plugins/portal') },      required plugins
    { register: require('./plugins/receive') }
], (err) => {

    if (err) {
        throw err;
    }
    server.start((err) => {

        if (err) {
            throw err;
        }
        console.log('Server started at: ' + server.info.uri);
    });
});
```

7.2.3   *Plugin dependencies*

It's common to have a situation where one plugin depends on another. For instance, in our Pingoo application, the pingoo-portal plugin uses the `server.views()` method in its registration function. This method isn't built in to hapi—it's added by the Vision plugin—so we say that *pingoo-portal has a dependency on Vision*.

If Vision isn't loaded by the time pingoo-portal is loaded, it will fail to register with an exception. Try it. Swap the order of these two plugins in the `register` call, as shown here.

Listing 7.6   Pingoo: index.js

```
server.register([
    { register: require('vision') },
    { register: require('./plugins/database') },
    { register: require('./plugins/portal') },
    { register: require('./plugins/receive') }
], (err) => {

    ...

});
```

Swap these lines and see what happens

If you run listing 7.6 with the plugin ordering swapped, you'll get a message like this:

```
TypeError: Object [object Object] has no method 'views'
```

Now, you may think a simple solution to this problem would be to make sure you always load plugins in the correct order. And it would be, but this is a fragile approach. It may be easy to keep track of things when you're working with only a few plugins, but it's going to be a nightmare when you have a lot of plugins, and if lots of people are collaborating on the project, to keep track of ordering and dependencies. hapi has a better way.

You can declare a dependency on one or more other plugins inside a plugin using the `server.dependency()` method.

> **HAPI API**   `server.dependency(dependencies, after)` (http://hapijs.com/api#serverdependencydependencies-after)

`server.dependency()` lets you list the dependencies that your plugin depends on and a callback that will execute only once after those plugins have finished loading. The following listing uses this inside pingoo-portal to express its dependency on Vision.

Listing 7.7   Pingoo: plugins/portal/index.js, using `server.dependency()`

```
const after = function (server, next) {

    server.views({
        engines: {
            hbs: require('handlebars')
        },
```

Executes only after all dependencies have loaded

```
            relativeTo: __dirname,
            helpersPath: 'templates/helpers',
            partialsPath: 'templates/partials',
            path: 'templates',
            layout: true,
            isCached: false
        });

        ...

    next();
};

exports.register = function (server, options, next) {

    server.dependency('vision', after);        ◁─┐ Declare dependency on
    next();                                         │ vision, provide a callback
};
```

The application will start correctly now, even with the plugins out of order. Let's look at another, more subtle issue.

The pingoo-portal plugin also has a dependency on pingoo-database because it uses the server methods added by the plugin inside some of its route handlers. But if we remove pingoo-database altogether from our array of loaded plugins in index.js, the application will start normally without any errors. Everything will work until we attempt to access one of those routes. Then we see the problem:

```
TypeError: Uncaught error: Cannot call method 'getRecent' of undefined
```

We want to avoid this problem by ensuring our application *doesn't start* when we have missing dependencies. We can achieve this by adding pingoo-database as an additional dependency inside pingo-portal, as shown next.

Listing 7.8 Pingoo: plugins/portal/index.js

```
exports.register = function (server, options, next) {

    server.dependency(['pingoo-database', 'vision'], after);   ◁─┐ Add pingoo-
    next();                                                        │ database as a
};                                                                 │ dependency
```

This time if we try to start the application with the missing pingoo-database plugin, we'll meet an error immediately:

```
Plugin pingoo-portal missing dependency pingoo-database in connection: http:/
    /localhost:4000
```

7.2.4 Configuring plugins with options

There are a couple of distinct ways to configure a plugin. First, and probably what you'll use the most, is what we'll refer to as *plugin options*.

PLUGIN OPTIONS

When loading a plugin with the object syntax, you can specify options to be passed to the plugin:

```
server.register([
    {
        register: require('plugin1'),
        options: {
            option1: 'something'
        }
    }
], (err) => {

    ...
});
```

These options get passed along unchanged to the plugin as the second parameter in the register function:

```
exports.register = function (server, options, next) {

    const option1 = options.option1;   // 'something'
    ...
};
```

It's useful to be able to do this. If you're building a plugin that you intend to share, one that will be used in many applications or by many different people, it's probable that you'll need at least some user-configurable behavior.

If your plugin isn't for public consumption, it may still be useful to pass options into it. You might want all of your configuration kept in a single place and then passed into your plugins as options. This can make it easier to test plugins in isolation too.

As an example, let's look again to the Pingoo application. Inside the pingoo-database plugin there are references to both the database name and table that we're using.

Listing 7.9   Pingoo: plugins/database/index.js

```
...

server.method({
    name: 'database.addPing',
    method: function (payload, callback) {

        R
        .table('pings')
        .insert(payload)
        .run(server.app.db, (err) => {

            if (err) {
                throw err;
            }
```

This db name and table hardcoded into plugin would make good plugin options

```
                callback();
            });
        }
    });

    R.connect({ db: 'pingoo' }, (err, conn) => {

        if (err) {
            return next(err);
        }

        server.app.db = conn;
        next();
    });

    ...
```

⟵ This db name and table
hardcoded into plugin would
make good plugin options

These are currently strings that are hardcoded into our plugin. It's better to keep configuration like this outside the plugins themselves. To make these values into plugin options, we need to supply them when registering the plugin.

Listing 7.10   Pingoo: index.js, specifiying options when loading a plugin

```
server.register([
    {
        register: require('./plugins/database'),
        options: {
            dbName: 'pingoo',
            dbTable: 'pings'
        }
    },
    { register: require('./plugins/portal') },
    { register: require('./plugins/receive') },
    { register: require('vision') }
], (err) => {

    ...
});
```

This listing shows we can update the references with the plugin itself so it uses this option.

Listing 7.11   Pingoo: plugins/database/index.js, using the plugin options

```
...

server.method({
    name: 'database.addPing',
    method: function (payload, callback) {

        R
        .table(options.dbTable)
```

```
        .insert(payload)
        .run(server.app.db, (err) => {

            if (err) {
                throw err;
            }

            callback();
        });
    }
});

R.connect({ db: options.dbName }, (err, conn) => {

    if (err) {
        return next(err);
    }

    server.app.db = conn;
    next();
});

...
```

PLUGIN REGISTRATION OPTIONS

There's a second set of options available when registering plugins. These options can be confusing for developers new to hapi because getting them mixed up is easy. But they're different. The second set of options can be passed as an optional argument before the callback in `server.register()`. We'll refer to this set of options as *registration options*:

```
server.register({ register: require('./myplugin') }, { ... }, (err) => {

    ...
});
```

These options aren't passed directly to the plugin, but rather are used by hapi internally when registering your plugin. The available options you can supply are listed in table 7.2.

Table 7.2 `server.register()` optional register options

Option	Explanation
`select`	A string or array of strings. Each string should correspond to a connection label. All routes within the plugin will only be attached to the matching server connections.
`routes.prefix`	A string prefix. All routes inside the plugin will have this prefix prepended to their path. For example, a route with a path `/api` inside a plugin with a prefix `/v1` will respond to requests to `/v1/api`.
`routes.vhost`	A string virtual host. All routes inside the plugin will only match a given request if the host header matches this value. Useful for limiting all routes with a plugins to certain domains/subdomains.

Here's an example that uses all three register options from table 7.2:

```
server.connection({ port: 4000, labels: ['api'] });
server.connection({ port: 4001, labels: ['web'] });
server.register(require('myplugin'), {
    select: ['api'],
    routes: {
        prefix: '/v1',
        vhost: 'api.example.com'
    }
}, (err) => {

});
```

Make server connection with api label

Make server connection with web label

Routes only matched when request host header equals api.example.com

Only connections with api label passed as server option to plugin

All routes created inside plugin have their paths prefixed with /v1.

It's important to recognize that even when loading multiple plugins at once using an array, there's only one `register` options object. Any specified options will be applied to all plugins.

If you want to specify different `register` options per plugin, you could nest calls to `server.register()`:

```
server.register(require('plugin1'), { ... }, (err) => {

    ...
    server.register(require('plugin2'), { ... }, (err) => {

        ...
    });
});
```

This approach is neither scalable nor pretty. Once you start looking at plugin loading situations like this, with many options or complex configuration needs, it's time to take a look at Glue.

7.3   Composing plugins with Glue

We've seen how to load plugins with `server.register()`, a method which is a fairly low-level utility function. It works great when you're loading a plugin or two, but becomes unwieldy and awkward when loading lots of plugins. You can end up writing a lot of boilerplate code to load all of your plugins. You should recognize by now that this is definitely not the hapi way. This is where Glue comes to the rescue.

> **NPM PACKAGE**   glue v3 (https://www.npmjs.com/package/glue)

7.3.1   What is Glue?

It's a core philosophy of hapi to reduce repetitive boilerplate code and in place present configuration-driven APIs. When we start building applications in a modular way from plugins, we put all the important logic inside our plugins, so we tend to keep writing code that does the following, as the entrypoint to our applications:

- Creates hapi server with options
- Adds server connections
- Loads all our plugins
- Starts the server

In code, this normally looks something like the following.

Listing 7.12   Common boilerplate code when working with plugins

```
const Hapi = require('hapi');

const server = new Hapi.Server({
    debug: {
        request: ['error'],
        log: ['error']
    }
});                                           Create hapi server

server.connection({ port: 4000, labels: ['api'] });
server.connection({ port: 4001, labels: ['web'] });   Add connections

server.register([...], (err) => {              Load
                                               plugins
    ...
    server.start((err) => {                    Start
                                               server
        ...
    });
});
```

Glue is a utility designed for use with hapi (it's not a hapi plugin, but a normal package from npm) that does this legwork for us. It lets you define an entire application in a configuration object called a manifest. A *manifest* is nothing special—it's a plain-old JavaScript object with a specific set of properties. Glue takes a manifest and builds a server with all the connections and plugins loaded how you specified. It's pretty awesome to see it in action. Let's see an example.

To get started with Glue, add it to your project as a dependency:

```
npm install --save glue@3
```

Then load it:

```
const Glue = require('glue');
```

Once you have Glue loaded, the next step is to create a manifest.

7.3.2   Creating a manifest

We'll now use Glue to replace the boilerplate code currently sitting in the index.js file of our Pingoo application. Let's first take another look in the following listing at that index.js file so we can see a side-by-side comparison of the end result.

Listing 7.13   Pingoo: index.js

```
const Hapi = require('hapi');

const server = new Hapi.Server({
    debug: {
        request: ['error'],
        log: ['error']
    }
});

server.connection({ port: 4000 });

server.register([
    {
        register: require('./plugins/database'),
        options: {
            dbName: 'pingoo',
            dbTable: 'pings'
        }
    },
    { register: require('./plugins/portal') },
    { register: require('./plugins/receive') },
    { register: require('vision') }
], (err) => {
    if (err) {
        throw err;
    }
    server.start((err) => {

        if (err) {
            throw err;
        }
        console.log('Server started at: ' + server.info.uri);
    });
});
```

What Glue does is write the code in our index.js for us, based on our manifest. This is explained in figure 7.6.

First we need to write the Glue manifest, a JavaScript object that contains configuration that the Glue utility will use to build your server. A manifest has three top-level properties, shown in table 7.3.

Table 7.3   Top-level Glue manifest properties

Property	Purpose
server	Defines the options that would usually be passed when calling: `new Hapi.Server(options)`.
connections	An array of options. Glue will use each item to create a new connection by calling `server.connection(options)`.
registra-tions	An array of objects describing which plugins to load. Each object must have a `plugin` property, which may be a string (passed to `require()`) or an object with a `register` and `options` properties nested within. There's also an optional `options` property at the same level as the `plugin` property, which defines any registration options.

The configuration manifest that you write

```
{
    "server": {
        "debug": {
            "request": ["error"],
            "log": ["error"]
        }
    },
    "connections": [
        { "port": 4000 }
    ],
    "registrations": [
        {
            "plugin": {
                "register": "./plugins/database",
                "options": {
                    "dbName": "pingoo",
                    "dbTable": "pings"
                }
            }
        },
        { "plugin": "./plugins/portal" },
        { "plugin": "./plugins/receive" },
        { "plugin": "vision" }
    ]
}
```

The code that Glue executes for you

```
const Hapi = require('hapi');

const server = new Hapi.Server({
    debug: {
        request: ['error'],
        log: ['error']
    }
});

server.connection({ port: 4000 });

server.register({
    register: require('./plugins/database'),
    options: {
        dbName: 'pingoo',
        dbTable: 'pings'
    },
    (err) => {

        server.register({
            register: require('./plugins/portal')
        }, (err) => {

            server.register({
                register: require('./plugins/receive')
            }, (err) => {

                server.register({
                    register: require('vision')
                }, (err) => {

                    ...
                });
            });
        });
    });
});
```

Figure 7.6   Glue translates your configuration manifest into boilerplate code.

Because the manifest is purely configuration, it can be written as a JSON document. We'll store that in a file called config.json at the root of our project, as shown here.

Listing 7.14   Pingoo: config.json, our Glue manifest

```
{
    "server": {
        "debug": {
            "request": ["error"],
            "log": ["error"]
        }
    },
    "connections": [
        { "port": 4000 }
    ],
    "registrations": [
        {
            "plugin": {
                "register": "./plugins/database",
                "options": {
                    "dbName": "pingoo",
                    "dbTable": "pings"
                }
            }
```

```
        },
        { "plugin": "./plugins/portal" },
        { "plugin": "./plugins/receive" },
        { "plugin": "vision" }
    ]
}
```

Next we'll need to write the code that loads this manifest and gives it over to Glue to construct a server. We can get rid of all of the code currently in the index.js file and replace it with the following listing.

Listing 7.15 Pingoo: index.js

Load Glue →
```
const Glue = require('glue');
const Manifest = require('./config');        ← Load manifest object

const options = { relativeTo: __dirname };   ← Specify options for Glue

Glue.compose(Manifest, options, (err, server) => {    ←

    if (err) {                               Call Glue.compose()
        throw err;                           method to build server
    }

    server.start((err) => {                  ← Start server
                                               like normal
        if (err) {
            throw err;
        }

        console.log('Server started at: ' + server.info.uri);
    });
});
```

And that's it. We have the same application, but now it's powered by a JSON configuration and Glue. We could now add more functionality by building new plugins, and we'd only need to update our manifest in config.json to add them to our application.

7.3.3 *Smart configuration with the Confidence utility*

Configuration is pretty dumb. It's not dynamic in the same way code can be. If we define configuration in JSON, it's not influenced by external factors, such as whether our app is running in development or production. But we often need to vary our configuration slightly based on such factors. We need our configurations to be a little smarter. Therefore we'll often see code that looks like this next listing.

Listing 7.16 Varying configuration based on environment

```
const configuration = {
    ...
    'connections': [
        { 'port': 4000 }
    ],
```

```
    ...
};

if (process.env.NODE_ENV === 'production') {
    configuration.connections = [
        { 'port': 80 }
    ];
}
```

This kind of conditional configuration can lead to messy, ugly code.

NPM PACKAGE   confidence v1 (https://www.npmjs.com/package/confidence)

Confidence is a hapi utility for capturing more complex configuration requirements entirely in a single JavaScript object (or a JSON document), as shown in figure 7.7.

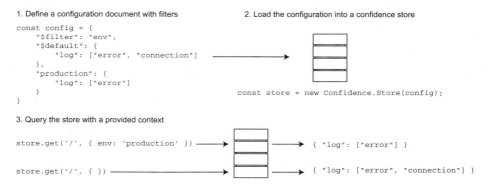

Figure 7.7   How Confidence works

Confidence starts with a configuration *document* that follows a specific format defined by Confidence. This format is a simple extension of JSON. All existing JSON-based configuration objects are valid Confidence documents.

Listing 7.17   Valid Confidence document

```
const config = {
    activity: 'walking'
};
```

A Confidence *store* is created and a document loaded into the store. We can retrieve the configuration from the store at a later time.

Listing 7.18   Retrieving a value from a Confidence store

```
const Confidence = require('confidence');

const config = {
```

```
        activity: 'walking'
};

const store = new Confidence.Store(config);
console.log(store.get('/'));
```

Logs { activity: 'walking' }

> **NOTE**   To retrieve configuration from a store, we pass a location string to
> `store.get()`. The `'/'` means retrieve the root object. `'/a/b/c'` means
> retrieve the value at `a.b.c`, if it exists.

Confidence's power lies in the concept of *filters*, which can be defined at any level of a
document to conditionally alter the configuration. When configuration is retrieved
from the store, we can specify an optional context, which the filters in our document
will use to determine how the configuration should be built.

Listing 7.19   Using a Confidence filter property

```
const Confidence = require('confidence');

const config = {
    activity: {
        '$filter': 'weather',
        '$default': 'walking',
        'rain': 'watch movie',
        'sun': 'play tennis'
    }
};

const store = new Confidence.Store(config);

console.log(store.get('/'));
console.log(store.get('/', { weather: 'rain' }));
console.log(store.get('/', { weather: 'sun' }));
```

Default value should be walking

Filter property on value of weather in context

If weather is rain, value should be watch movie

If weather is sun, value should be play tennis

Logs { activity: 'watch movie' }

Logs { activity: 'walking' }

Logs { activity: 'play tennis' }

Now we're going to use Confidence to implement a smart configuration for Pingoo.
We're going to vary the server connections and the logging events depending on the
environment the app is running in. First, we need to update our Glue manifest in con-
fig.json with the appropriate filters.

Listing 7.20   Pingoo: pingoo:config.json, add Confidence filters to manifest

```
{
    "server": {
        "debug": {
            "$filter": "env",
            "$base": {
                "request": ["error"]
            },
            "$default": {
                "log": ["info", "error", "connection", "client"]
            },
```

Always include property no matter the context

Filter property based on value of env in context

If no value for env, use this default

```
                    "production": {
                        "log": ["error"]          ◁──┐  If env === production,
                    }                                 │  include this property
                }
            },
            "connections": {
                "$filter": "env",
                "production": [
                    { "port": 5000 }
                ],
                "$default": [
                    { "port": 4000 }
                ]
            },
            "registrations": [
                {
                    "plugin": {
                        "register": "./plugins/database",
                        "options": {
                            "dbName": "pingoo",
                            "dbTable": "pings"
                        }
                    }
                },
                { "plugin": "./plugins/portal" },
                { "plugin": "./plugins/receive" },
                { "plugin": "vision" }
            ]
}
```

Now, we need to update the index.js that loads our manifest to process this configuration, passing the context, which includes the env variable. For the value of env, we'll use the standard NODE_ENV environment variable, as shown next.

Listing 7.21 Pingoo: index.js, working with Confidence

```
const Confidence = require('confidence');       ◁──┐  Load
const Glue = require('glue');                        │  Confidence
                                                          ┌─ Create Confidence
                                                          │  store using config file
const store = new Confidence.Store(require('./config'));   ◁──┘
const manifest = store.get('/', { env: process.env.NODE_ENV });   ◁────────

const options = { relativeTo: __dirname };
                                                    Retrieve manifest from
                                                    store, passing in context
Glue.compose(manifest, options, (err, server) => {

    if (err) {
        throw err;
    }

    server.start((err) => {

        if (err) {
            throw err;
        }
```

```
            console.log('Server started at: ' + server.info.uri);
    });
});
```

You can try spinning up the Pingoo app both with `node index` and with `NODE_ENV =production node index` to test the conditional configuration.

By combining Glue and Confidence, you can build powerful workflows for plugin-based hapi applications driven by flexible configuration. Next up, we're going to look at how we can communicate between plugins.

7.4   *Plugin communication*

Plugins aren't part of their own universe—they need to interact with the application outside, and sometimes with each other. This section looks at ways we can share data and communicate between plugins.

7.4.1   *Global server configuration*

Whenever we create a hapi server object, we can specify custom configuration properties using the `app` option in the server constructor function. These values can then be accessed globally across our application, wherever the server object is available. This is a useful place to store static configuration—for example, email addresses—as shown in the next listing.

Listing 7.22   Setting custom application configuration when creating a hapi server

```
const server = new Hapi.Server({
    app: {                                ◁──┐  Set custom configuration
        mail: {                                │  values here
            adminEmail: 'admin@pingoo.io'
        }
    }
});

...

server.route({
    method: 'GET',                            Values can be accessed from
    path: '/',                                server.settings.app wherever
    handler: function (request, reply) {      server object is available

        const mailSettings = request.server.settings.app.mail;   ◁──
        const adminEmail = mailSettings.adminEmail;
        reply(adminEmail);
    }
});

...
```

When we're working with a plugin-based application that uses Glue, we can add this configuration data to our manifest instead.

Listing 7.23   Adding custom application configuration to a Glue manifest

```
{
    "server": {
        "app": {
            "appName": "pingoo"
        },
        . . .
}
```

These settings will then be inherited inside all of our plugins, and can be used inside handlers.

Listing 7.24   Custom application configuration is inherited by plugins too

```
const after = function (server, next) {

    const appName = server.settings.app.appName;

    server.route({
        method: 'GET',
        path: '/',
        handler: function (request, reply) {

            server.methods.database.getRecent((err, pings) => {

                if (err) {
                    throw err;
                }

                reply.view('home', {
                    pings: pings,
                    appName: appName
                });
            });
        }
    });
};

. . .
```

Server-wide configuration gives you a simple way to communicate static values downstream into plugins, but what about communicating in the other direction?

7.4.2   *Exposing properties from within a plugin with server.expose()*

You can expose some data or functionality that is internal to a plugin to code outside of the plugin using server.expose(). If you think of a hapi plugin in terms of a class from an object-oriented programming (OOP) language, all properties and methods inside a plugin are private by default. Using server.expose() is equivalent to making one of those properties or methods public and accessible from outside the plugin.

HAPI API server.expose(key, value) (http://hapijs.com/api#serverexposekey-value)

The exposed value can be any kind of value such as an object or function. It will be available outside the plugin at `server.plugins[pluginName][key]`.

> **NOTE** Be aware when using `server.expose()` that primitive values such as strings and numbers will be copied rather than passed as reference. If you want access to a primitive value that will change over time, you should expose an object or a function to return a primitive value.

As an example, let's add a simple page view counter to our pingoo-portal plugin. The counter is incremented each time the home page is visited. We'll expose a function that returns this counter variable using `server.expose()` so the counter can be retrieved outside of the pingoo-portal plugin, as shown next.

Listing 7.25   Pingoo: plugins/portal/index.js, using `server.expose()`

```
...
let counter = 0;                          ←┐ Initialize counter
server.expose('viewCount', () => {          │ variable to zero
                                                    ←┐ Expose function that
    return counter;                                  │ returns value of counter
});                                                  │ using server.expose()
server.route({
    method: 'GET',
    path: '/',
    handler: function (request, reply) {    ←┐ Increment counter
                                               │ with each page view
        counter++;

        server.methods.database.getRecent((err, pings) => {

            if (err) {
                throw err;
            }

            reply.view('home', {
                pings: pings,
                appName: appName
            });
        });
    }
});
```

To test this exposed function from outside the plugin, set a loop in our index.js file to log the number of views every second, as shown here.

Listing 7.26   Pingoo: index.js, use exposed `viewCount()` function from pingoo-portal

```
...
Glue.compose(manifest, options, (err, server) => {

    setInterval(() => {
```

```
        const views = server.plugins['pingoo-portal'].viewCount();
        console.log('homepage has been viewed %d times', views);
    }, 1000);

    if (err) {
        throw err;
    }
    server.start((err) => {

        if (err) {
            throw err;
        }
        console.log('Server started at: ' + server.info.uri);
    });
});
```

Try this by starting the application and refreshing the home page a few times to see the counter increment in your terminal.

7.4.3 *Using an event system*

In this section we're going to build a simple logging plugin for Pingoo. We want to log important events such as when a new ping is received. Rather than writing to the log in the place where the event happens, we want to have all our logging managed in a single place. For now we want to log to the console, but in the future we may want to write logs to a file or ship them to a remote logging service. Keeping our logging functionality centralized makes this easier to change in the future.

But how can we keep all logging centralized in one place when the events that are happening could be occurring in any part of our application, including inside of plugins?

THE OBSERVER PATTERN AND EVENT EMITTERS

The observer pattern is a great approach in software development for uncoupling separate parts of code. In the Node world, we use the built-in `events` module, specifically the `EventEmitter` class, to use the observer pattern.

The concept is simple. We have an object that emits or publishes events and we have one or more subscribers. In JavaScript our subscribers are callback functions, as shown here.

Listing 7.27 Using the observer pattern with Node's `EventEmitter` object

```
const EventEmitter = require('events').EventEmitter;
                                                          Create an
const emitter = new EventEmitter();                       EventEmitter object

emitter.on('myEvent', () => {                            Subscribe to
                                                          myEvent event
    console.log('Notified about a `myEvent` event');
});

setTimeout(() => {
                                                     Emit myEvent event
    emitter.emit('myEvent');                         (has 1 listener)
```

```
    emitter.emit('somethingElse');
}, 2000);
```

◁─┐ **Emit somethingElse**
    event (0 listeners)

If we run listing 7.27, we'll see the message Notified about a `myEvent` event after 2 seconds. Events are different from functions because there's only one-way communication.

Subscribers don't return anything to the emitter; the emitter doesn't care who's listening. It's fire-and-forget. In listing 7.27 there are no listeners for the somethingElse event, but there's no error when it's emitted, as there would be if we called a function that's not defined.

Think of the thing emitting the event as a radio transmitter and the listeners as radios. The transmitter doesn't need to know anything about who's listening.

These properties make events a great decoupling strategy. We can emit events when important things happen in our plugins and allow other parts of our application to react (or not) to those events without the event emitter (or producer) caring.

BUILDING PINGOO-EVENTS AND PINGOO-LOGGER

We're ready to build our centralized logging plugin for Pingoo. Figure 7.8 shows how our solution is going to work.

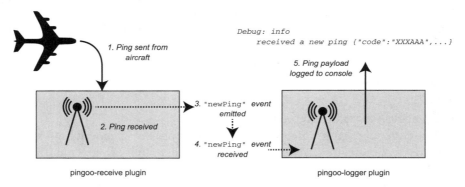

Figure 7.8   pingoo-logger will listen for events from other plugins and log them to the console.

First we need a way to expose an EventEmitter interface across our whole application. Server settings aren't appropriate for this because they're designed for static values. We can do it with a plugin and server decorations. Let's make a utility plugin for this called pingoo-events. As the next listing shows, its implementation is going to be simple.

Listing 7.28   Pingoo: plugins/events/index.js

```
const EventEmitter = require('events').EventEmitter;

exports.register = function (server, options, next) {
```

```
        const emitter = new EventEmitter();
        server.decorate('server', 'events', emitter);      ◄──┐  Decorate server object with
        next();                                                │  events property, which is
};                                                             │  an EventEmitter object

exports.register.attributes = { pkg: require('./package') };
```

This plugin decorates our server object with a new property events, which is an instance of an EventEmitter object. We can now emit events in our other plugins. For example, let's emit an event inside the pingo-receive plugin every time a new ping is received.

Listing 7.29   Pingoo: plugins/receive/index.js

```
...
server.route({
    config: {
        validate: {
            payload: {
                code: Joi.string().required(),
                lat: Joi.number().required(),
                lng: Joi.number().required(),
                alt: Joi.number().required(),
                timestamp: Joi.date().required()
            }
        }
    },
    method: 'POST',
    path: '/api',
    handler: function (request, reply) {

        server.methods.database.addPing(request.payload, reply);
        server.events.emit('newPing', request.payload);            ◄──┐
    }                                                                  │
});                                                                    │
...                              Emit newPing event, also passing      │
                                 request payload to any listeners ─────┘
```

We also need a consumer for these events. Let's create an additional plugin called pingoo-logger. This plugin will listen for newPing events and log the received payload.

Listing 7.30   Pingoo: plugins/logger/index.js

```
exports.register = function (server, options, next) {

    server.events.on('newPing', (data) => {

        server.log('info', 'received a new ping ' + JSON.stringify(data));
    });

    next();
};
```

```
exports.register.attributes = { pkg: require('./package') };
```

We need to ensure that we add a new package.json for each of these plugins and also that we load them into our app by adding them to our Glue manifest.

Listing 7.31 Pingoo: config.json, adding the new plugins to the manifest

```
...
"registrations": [
    {
        "plugin": {
            "register": "./plugins/database",
            "options": {
                "dbName": "pingoo",
                "dbTable": "pings"
            }
        }
    },
    { "plugin": "./plugins/events" },
    { "plugin": "./plugins/logger" },
    { "plugin": "./plugins/portal" },
    { "plugin": "./plugins/receive" },
    { "plugin": "vision" }
]
...
```

We can test this decoupled logging solution by starting the application and posting a new example ping payload to the application:

```
curl -X POST -H "Content-Type: application/json" -d '{
    "code": "TEST",
    "lat": 51.50722,
    "lng": -0.12750,
    "alt": 12000,
    "timestamp": "2015-08-22T11:20:00+00:00"
}' 'http://localhost:4000/api'
```

The event will be propagated into the logging plugin, and we'll see a message in our console:

```
Debug: info
    received a new ping {"code":"XXXAAA","lat":51.50722,"lng":-
    0.1275,"alt":12000,"timestamp":"2015-08-22T11:20:00.000Z"}
```

Using an event system like this has many real-world applications, such as an email notification system that sends out emails when certain events happen within your application.

Okay, so you now can build a super-duper, modular, plugin-based hapi application, and it's all ready to go into production. Whoa there, steady on! We haven't even mentioned caching. *Caching* is a way to make your applications faster and your users happier, and give your servers a much-needed breather.

7.5 Summary

- Plugins are like miniature hapi.js apps. You can combine them into an application.

- You can do all sorts of things in a plugin, including add routes, server methods, and extension points and much more.

- You should try to split your application entirely into plugins, with the root level of your application purely defining configuration and loading those plugins into a server.

- You can configure plugins by setting options when you load them with `server.register()`.

- Plugins should be indifferent to the order they're loaded. For this reason you should declare any dependencies within plugins using `server.dependency()`.

- You can use Glue to simplify composing application from plugins using a manifest.

- You can make smart manifests with Confidence.

- There are several methods for communicating into, out of, and horizontally across plugins, including server configuration, `server.expose()`, and using `EventEmitters`.

Cache me if you can

There are two things that we always want to do in web applications:

- Give users the most up-to-date, relevant data that we can get our hands on
- Make the experience as quick as possible

We can't always have both at the same time, so we find a compromise. *Caching* is the name of that compromise. Caching lets us serve data that is *fresh enough,* with the benefit that we can serve it a lot faster. It's common sense, and sometimes this isn't much of a compromise to make as figure 8.1 illustrates—in particular, when your data changes infrequently.

It's faster to serve from a cache for a few reasons. The obvious one is that it's usually physically a lot faster to pull data from a cache than it is to get it from its source. This is either because the cache is located closer to you—for example, your browser cache is on the same machine as your browser—or it's stored in a physical

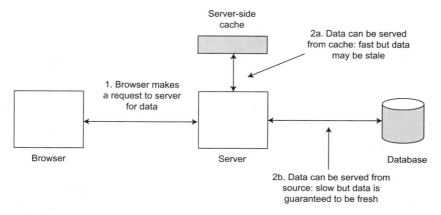

Figure 8.1   The server-side caching trade-off

form which is faster to read from. For instance, RAM is ~80x faster to read from than an optical disk and probably several thousand times faster than requesting the same amount of data via a network request.

Before we dive into server-side caching we should recognize that caching begins at home. HTTP clients, such as browsers and mobile applications, have access to their own caches. And we can control how those clients choose to cache our data, such as images, web pages, and other media, saving our servers from ever receiving a request. Let's start by looking at client-side caching.

8.1   Client-side caching

Although server-side caching can improve the experiences of your users and help keep your servers healthy, sometimes we can even do one better by using client-side caching. After all, the fastest transactions are the ones that never need to even touch the network.

When a web browser requests an image from a server, there are mechanisms in HTTP for the server to tell the browser whether it should subsequently cache the image and for how long. If the image is requested again by the browser before the cache has expired, the cached image can be used, instead of making a whole new request over the network to fetch it again. The same applies to any kind of HTTP client with a cache—for example, those often embedded in mobile or desktop applications. See figure 8.2.

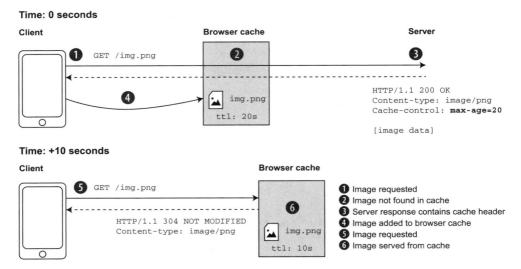

Figure 8.2   Servers control client caches by setting response headers

The way we specify the client-caching policy in an HTTP response is by setting response headers. The headers that we developers use have changed slightly over the years. The main ones you should be interested in now are listed in table 8.1.

Table 8.1   HTTP response cache headers

Header	Purpose
Cache-control	The Swiss army knife of caching headers. Used to communicate when and how to cache the resource
ETag	A unique identifier used to revalidate a cached resource
Vary	Tells the user-agent which request headers when varied will invalidate a previously cached response for the same resource. A convenient way to think about the vary header, is as if the values of the listed headers form part of the cache key. Changing one of those headers will mean a different cache key altogether and thus a different cached value.

Table 8.1 doesn't attempt to give a complete understanding of all the headers. Probably the best resource I know of for a detailed but clear explanation is *Leverage Browser Caching* (https://developers.google.com/speed/docs/insights/LeverageBrowserCaching) on Google Developers. If you're feeling brave, you can also read the HTTP specification, which, although rather dense, has the most precise description of the headers and their roles.

In this section we're going to look at working with client-side caching with hapi. First, I'll show you how to manually set headers with hapi. Then I'll show you a convenient feature in hapi that lets you control cache headers by setting policies in configuration. Finally, we'll take a look at ways of dealing with revalidation and ETags.

8.1.1 Setting headers manually

Implementing client-side caching is all about setting the appropriate headers on responses. We can set response headers explicitly in hapi by using the `response` `.header()` method inside a handler.

> **HAPI API** `response.header(name, value, options)` (http://hapijs.com/api #response-object)

Let's say we have a hapi route to serve a single image (using Inert) and we've determined that 24 hours is a suitable maximum age for this particular image. Inside the handler, we can specify that the image should be cached for 24 hours. This desired policy can be expressed by the response header: `Cache-Control: max-age=86400` (86,400 seconds being equal to 24 hours).

Listing 8.1 Manually setting a Cache-Control header in a handler

```
server.route({
    method: 'GET',
    path: '/image.png',
    handler: function (request, reply) {

        const response = reply.file(Path.join(__dirname , 'image.png'));
        response.header('Cache-Control', 'max-age=86400');
    }
});
```

Set Cache-Control header on the response with response.header()

Create response object using the reply interface

When the image is now served, it will be accompanied by this Cache-Control header and the client will store the image in its cache.

8.1.2 Setting a cache policy in configuration

Rather than manually adding headers inside of handlers for each route, hapi offers a way to set the client-caching policy in the configuration for the route. Listing 8.2 shows the example from the previous section, but this time using the `config.cache` property in the route configuration. As mentioned before when talking about the philosophy of hapi, this configuration-over-code approach helps to separate the concerns of your business logic (inside your handlers) from orthogonal concerns like caching.

Listing 8.2 Setting a client-caching policy in the route configuration

```
server.route({
    method: 'GET',
    path: '/image.png',
    handler: function (request, reply) {

        reply.file(Path.join(__dirname , 'image.png'));
```

```
    },
    config: {
        cache: {
            privacy: 'private',
            expiresIn: 86400 * 1000
        }
    }
});
```

Sets client-caching policy for route through configuration

If we were to set up a server with the route in listing 8.2 and send a request to the server using cURL, we'd see the following response:

```
$ curl -I localhost:4000/image.png

HTTP/1.1 200 OK
content-type: image/png
last-modified: Sat, 16 May 2015 06:55:53 GMT
etag: "da39a3ee5e6b4b0d3255bfef95601890afd80709"
cache-control: max-age=86400, must-revalidate, private
Date: Sat, 16 May 2015 10:24:33 GMT
Connection: keep-alive
```

You can see that hapi has added the Cache-Control header for you now from inspecting the policy for the route.

You may notice that hapi has also added a couple of extra things to the headers. There's now also an ETag header and a `must-revalidate` directive in the Cache-Control header. What's that all about then?

8.1.3   *Revalidation and ETags*

If your browser caches a 100 MB video for 24 hours, when that 24 hours is up, the video in the cache is no longer valid. If you want to watch that video again in five minutes, your browser needs to speak to the server again.

But what if the expired video in your cache is still identical to the one on the server? It's wasteful to download the full 100 MB over the network again, to get exactly what you already have in your cache. HTTP has a solution to this dilemma in the form of revalidation.

Revalidation is a mechanism for the browser to ask the server something along the lines of "Hey, I've already got some data here for this resource, is it still valid? If it's not, give me the new version." This kind of request is often referred to as a *conditional GET request*—because we're requesting the resource on the condition that it hasn't changed.

During a conditional GET request, the server needs a way to compare your cached version with its own current version. The way it does this is using an *ETag*, a string that identifies the state of the resource in time, kind of like a version number.

The ETag string may take any form you want, but a common approach is for the ETag to be the result of calculating an asymmetric hash function (such as SHA-1) over the contents of the resource itself and encoding as a base64 string. This ensures a unique ETag for every possible state of the resource. Figure 8.3 illustrates this.

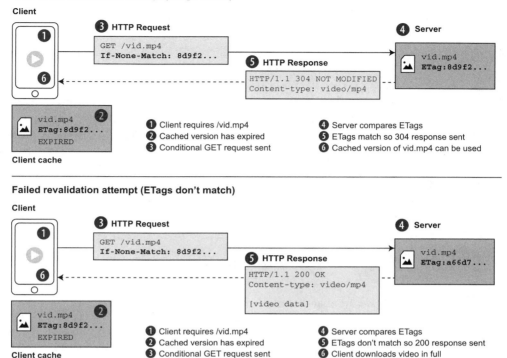

Figure 8.3   Example of the revalidation process

Let's look again at the example from the previous section. We made a request for an image and hapi automatically added an ETag to the response:

```
$ curl -I localhost:4000/image.png

HTTP/1.1 200 OK
content-type: image/png
last-modified: Sat, 16 May 2015 06:55:53 GMT
etag: "da39a3ee5e6b4b0d3255bfef95601890afd80709"
cache-control: max-age=86400, must-revalidate, private
Date: Sat, 16 May 2015 10:24:33 GMT
Connection: keep-alive
```

We can then use that ETag to make a conditional GET request to see how that works. To make a conditional GET request, we need to add a request header called If-None-Match:

```
$ curl -I -H 'If-None-Match: "da39a3ee5e6b4b0d3255bfef95601890afd80709"'
    localhost:4000/image.png

HTTP/1.1 304 Not Modified
```

```
content-type: image/png
last-modified: Sat, 16 May 2015 06:55:53 GMT
etag: "da39a3ee5e6b4b0d3255bfef95601890afd80709"
cache-control: no-cache
Date: Sat, 16 May 2015 10:35:38 GMT
Connection: keep-alive
```

In this case, the server is telling us that our resource, identified by the ETag we supplied, is still valid. We can save our client from downloading the image again.

hapi will calculate and set ETags for you automatically only when using the file and directory handlers from Inert. You might want to use ETags in other cases too. We see ETags used in some JSON APIs such as Facebook's Graph API and Github's API. The benefits here are the same. An API client can avoid downloading a whole new resource if it has an efficient way to revalidate a previously cached response.

If you want to set ETags for non-file responses, you'll have to manage setting them yourself. Rather than manually setting the ETag header and managing the If-None-Match comparison yourself, hapi has the convenience method response.etag().

> **API METHOD** response.etag(tag, options) (http://hapijs.com/api#response -object)

Listing 8.3 shows an example of setting the ETag on a JSON response. We use the built-in Crypto module in Node.js to calculate a SHA-1 hash to use as an ETag.

Listing 8.3   Setting the ETag manually using `response.etag()`

```
...
const Crypto = require('crypto');
...

server.route({
    method: 'GET',
    path: '/users',
    handler: function (request, reply) {

        const users = [
            {
                gender: 'female',
                name: {
                    title: 'ms',
                    first: 'manuela',
                    last: 'velasco'
                },
                location: {
                    street: '1969 calle de alberto aguilera',
                    city: 'la coruña',
                    state: 'asturias',
                    zip: '56298'
                }
            }
        ];
```

```
        const hash = Crypto.createHash('sha1');
        hash.update(JSON.stringify(users));
        const etag = hash.digest('base64');
        const response = reply(users);
        response.etag(etag);
    },
    config: {
        cache: {
            privacy: 'private',
            expiresIn: 86400 * 1000
        }
    }
});
```

Get SHA-1 hash of stringified response payload to use as ETag

Set ETag on response to value of hash

In listing 8.3, the ETag is calculated by performing a SHA-1 hash on the stringified JSON. The hash is converted into a base64 encoded string so it can be used in the ETag header. hapi will ensure this value is sent in the response ETag header for the route. hapi will also determine whether to send a 304 Not Modified response code when the value of an `If-Not-Modified` request header matches the ETag.

You should be aware that revalidating this route still requires the handler to run for the ETag to be calculated, meaning there is a performance cost to pay. The benefit when using ETags comes in the bandwidth saving of not needing to download the full response body.

In summary, you should identify reasonable caching policies for your application's resources and then set appropriate response headers for these, either manually with `response.header()` or by setting policies in the configuration of your routes.

Client-side caching is one side of the story. Next up let's move on to exploring caching on the server-side.

8.2 *Introducing Catbox: a multi-strategy object-caching library*

We employ caching on the server-side as well as the client side. You may be building a finance app that displays news stories relevant to your user's stock portfolio on the home screen. If you're using the New York Times API from your app's back-end servers to search for news stories, you could cache the most read stories in a server cache to ensure your users get a faster experience in your app.

In more general terms, we want to cache something on the server-side if one or more of the following are true:

- The data is relatively slow to retrieve or produce (for instance, requires I/O, such as reading from disk or making one or more network requests, or it has high CPU demand).
- The data has a reasonable lifetime of being useful.
- The data is in high demand from our users.

Server-side caching involves identifying the data you want to cache, storing that data somewhere (the *cache*), and then later retrieving it again. In a JavaScript application, a cache could be as simple as a JavaScript object that's kept in scope between multiple requests.

Typically, though, we will use a separate, dedicated data store for our cache. There are numerous data stores suitable for use as a cache, such as Redis and Memcached. These pieces of software are referred to as *key-value stores*.

The basic interface we use to work with key-value stores is simple: We store a value at a location determined by a key. We can then use the same key to retrieve the value later, as shown in figure 8.4.

set operations store data	key-value store		get operations retrieve data
	KEY	**VALUE**	
set('key1', 'hello'); ──────▶	'key1'	'hello'	get('key1', === 'hello'); ──────▶
set('key2', 'world'); ──────▶	'key2'	'world'	get('key2', === 'world'); ──────▶

Figure 8.4   Basic API of a key-value store

Although at this abstract level, all key-value stores look the same, each has a different set of characteristics, including their performance, persistence, and scaling model. Every key-value store also has a different API or client library to work with it. You'd think that means you need to pick one and stick with it, right? Well, no. It's time to meet Catbox.

8.2.1   *What is Catbox?*

Working with a cache data store usually involves finding a decent client library, including it as a dependency, and then writing all your code against that one library. Switching to another store usually means refactoring all your code that uses the library.

> **NPM PACKAGE**   catbox v7 (www.npmjs.com/package/catbox)

The hapi contributors have eased the pain here by producing a package called Catbox. Catbox can be thought of as a caching adapter that gives you a common caching API that you can use in your application. You can then connect Catbox to one of several supported back-end data stores. Whether you use Riak or MongoDB, your code that uses Catbox is exactly the same. This means it's easier to use multiple caching strategies in an application or change your mind later without a painful refactoring required, as shown in figure 8.5.

You may be wondering where hapi fits into all this? The server-side caching functionality offered by hapi is enabled by Catbox behind the scenes. Before we move on to seeing some examples of interacting with caching in a hapi application, we're going to take a brief foray into the world of Catbox. By understanding a little of what's

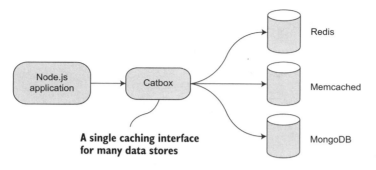

Figure 8.5   Catbox sits between your application and a choice of data stores or "engines."

A single caching interface for many data stores

happening under the hood, you'll have a deeper understanding of how to use and configure caching in hapi.

GETTING STARTED

In order to see how Catbox works, we first need an example. Remember the example I gave at the beginning of this chapter of searching the New York Times API for articles? We're going to implement that example in code and add some caching capabilities using Catbox.

> **NOTE**   To run the following examples yourself, head to http://developer
> .nytimes.com and register for API keys for the Article Search and Movie
> Reviews APIs. You'll need to add these in place of API_KEY in the following
> examples to get things to work properly.

Listing 8.4 shows an example that queries the NYT API every two seconds for articles about Node.js. The reason for doing this on a timer is to make it easier to illustrate the lifetime of objects in the cache later in this section.

Listing 8.4   index.js: Search the NYT API for "Node.js" articles every two seconds

```
const Wreck = require('wreck');

const search = function (id, next) {
    const baseUrl = 'http://api.nytimes.com/svc/search/v2/articlesearch';
    const apiKey = 'API_KEY';
    const query = 'Node.js';

    const url = baseUrl + '.json?q=' + query + '&api-key=' + apiKey;

    Wreck.get(url, { json: true }, (err, res, payload) => {

        if (err) {
            return next(err, null);
        }

        const numArticles = payload.response.meta.hits;
        next(err, numArticles);
```

Build API query URL

Make GET request using Wreck

Get number of articles found

```
        });
    };

    const loop = function () {

        const startTime = Date.now();

        search('node.js', (err, value) => {                    ◁─┐ Call search
                                                                 │ function
            if (err) {
                throw err;
            }

            const endTime = Date.now() - startTime;
            console.log('Found %d articles in %dms', value, endTime);
        });
    };

                                                               ┌─ Run loop function
    setInterval(loop, 2000);                              ◁────┘  every two seconds
```

Log time for search to complete and number of articles found (points to the `console.log` line)

Running this code with `node index`, you should see output (probably with slightly different timing depending on your internet connection) similar to the following:

```
$ node index.js
Found 12 articles in 880ms
Found 12 articles in 712ms
Found 12 articles in 802ms
...
```

Each time the search function is called, we kick off a fresh new HTTP request to the NYT API. A timeline to illustrate what is happening is shown in figure 8.6.

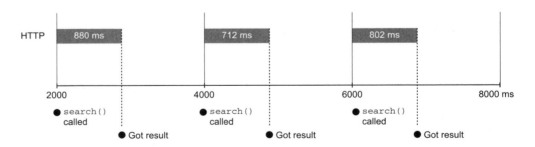

Figure 8.6   Timeline for example in listing 8.4

If this were a real application, we'd probably want to cache those responses if we needed them so often, to reduce the number of HTTP requests. We will do this using Catbox. First let's look at how to install and configure Catbox.

INSTALLING CATBOX AND STRATEGY PACKAGE

The first step to using Catbox is to install the package as a dependency. If you're following along, start a project the usual way by creating a new directory and making a `package.json` (either manually or by using `npm init`). Install and save the Catbox version 7 dependency with `npm install --save catbox@7`.

Next, we also need to load a caching *strategy*. A strategy is how Catbox stores data under the hood, be it with MongoDB or Redis or any other supported data store. Strategies are implemented in separate packages to Catbox, so they need to be added as dependencies too. See figure 8.7.

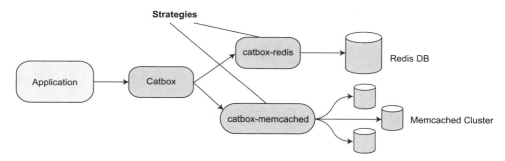

Figure 8.7   Every supported data store is implemented by a strategy package.

The simplest strategy to get started with is the `catbox-memory` strategy. This is a strategy that stores cached data in the memory of the current Node process. It's handy for developing with, but because of this you should be aware it's not suitable for serious production use. But later we'll see that swapping it out for another strategy is straightforward.

> **NPM PACKAGE** `catbox-memory` v2 (https://www.npmjs.com/package/catbox-memory)

Catbox strategies are distributed as npm packages. A full list can be found in the Catbox readme on Github (https://github.com/hapijs/catbox). To install `catbox-memory` and add it to your dependencies, run `npm install --save catbox-memory@2`.

8.2.2   *Catbox clients and policies*

There are two ways to interact directly with Catbox. There is a lower-level interface called *Client* and a higher-level interface called *Policy*. We're not going to cover working with `Client` in this book. Instead we're going to look at the `Policy` interface, which offers a more convenient abstraction for caching.

`Policy` builds upon the `Client` interface, so we first need to make a client object. Let's create a client using the `catbox-memory` strategy. The signature for the `Client` constructor is `new Client(engine, options)`, where `engine` is a loaded Catbox strategy. We can ignore the `options` object and thus accept the defaults, as in the next listing.

Listing 8.5   Creating a Catbox client

Load catbox module

```
const Catbox = require('catbox');
const CatboxMemory = require('catbox-memory');

const client = new Catbox.Client(CatboxMemory);

client.start((err) => {

    if (err) {
        throw err;
    }
    ...
});
```

Load catbox-memory strategy module

Create new Catbox Client

Client must be started by calling start() before cache can be used

The `Policy` constructor signature is new `Policy(options, [cache, segment])`, where `cache` is an instance of a Catbox client. We'll look at what segments are later in the chapter. For now we can use the value `'default'`.

The `options` object is where we define how the policy behaves. A full list of the available policy options can be found at https://github.com/hapijs/catbox#policy. For this first example, we're going to look at two options:

- `expiresIn`—How long a new value should be stored in the cache until it expires, in milliseconds
- `generateFunc`—A function to generate a new value if one can't be found in the cache

The object that we get back when calling the `Policy` constructor has only one method that we care about: `get(id, callback)`. As its name suggests, `get()` tries to get an item out of the cache with a matching `id`. If one can't be found in the cache, it will use your `generateFunc` function to generate one, store it in the cache, and hand it back to you.

Listing 8.6 rewrites the New York Times API example from earlier in this section to make use of a Catbox policy. You can place this inside a new file policy.js.

Listing 8.6   policy.js: caching responses from the NYT Articles API

```
const Catbox = require('catbox');
const CatboxMemory = require('catbox-memory');
const Wreck = require('wreck');

const search = function (id, next) {

    const baseUrl = 'http://api.nytimes.com/svc/search/v2/articlesearch';
    const apiKey = 'API_KEY';
    const query = 'Node.js';
```

Search function unmodified from original example

```
        const url = baseUrl + '.json?q=' + query + '&api-key=' + apiKey;

        Wreck.get(url, { json: true }, (err, res, payload) => {

            if (err) {
                return next(err, null);
            }

            const numArticles = payload.response.meta.hits;
            next(null, numArticles);
        });
};

const loop = function () {                                      Call policy.get() to
                                                                retrieve search result
    const startTime = Date.now();

    policy.get('node.js', (err, value, cached, report) => {     ◁

        if (err) {
            throw err;
        }

        const endTime = Date.now() - startTime;
        console.log('Found %d articles in %dms %s', value, endTime, cached ?
    '(CACHED)' : '');
        });

};
                                                                Create new
const client = new Catbox.Client(CatboxMemory);     ◁          Catbox Client

const options = {
    expiresIn: 3000,                                           Define policy
    generateFunc: search,                                      options
    generateTimeout: 10000
};

const policy = new Catbox.Policy(options, client, 'default');   ◁    Create new
                                                                     Catbox Policy
client.start((err) => {                          ◁   Start client

    if (err) {
        throw err;
    }

    setInterval(loop, 2000);                        ◁   Once client is
});                                                     started, start loop
```

A key thing to note here is that the `Policy` interface gives us a clean separation between the concerns of caching (encapsulated by the `Policy` object) and the business logic of our application, which is, in our case, the `search()` function. We didn't have to modify the `search()` function to make use of caching.

Start this program by running `node policy.js` in your terminal. The output should be quite different than last time:

```
$ node policy.js
Found 12 articles in 825ms
Found 12 articles in 0ms (CACHED)
Found 12 articles in 795ms
Found 12 articles in 0ms (CACHED)
...
```

We can see that every second call to `policy.get()` is returning an item from the cache immediately rather than triggering a new HTTP request. Figure 8.8 illustrates exactly what is happening in this example.

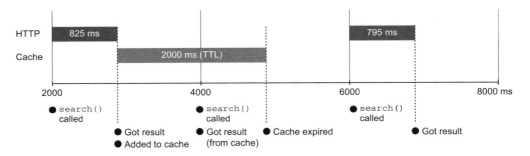

Figure 8.8   Timeline for example in listing 8.6

Although this example clearly shows the advantage of our cache policy, there is a bit of a problem. If this example exists in the context of a web application, it means some users are going to get their responses quickly and others will sometimes have to wait quite a while for the cache to be primed again.

To fix the issue and ensure a good experience for all requests, we can take advantage of the staleness options of Catbox policies.

8.2.3   *Staleness*

Going back to the fictional finance app example, your manager might set a performance target that all API requests should be fulfilled within 100 ms. Clearly our policy from the previous section isn't going to cut it. As we identified, some users will have to wait the full ~800 ms for the cache to be filled again. How can we solve this tricky problem?

When we need to make a new HTTP request to the NYT API, what if we could set a timer for 90 ms? If the response comes back within that 90 ms, we serve it to the user—if it takes longer, we serve whatever we have in the cache.

You can configure a Catbox policy to behave this way using the staleness options. After the time specified in `staleIn`, a value in the cache will be marked stale.

staleTimeout indicates how long you're willing to wait for a fresh value to be acquired before serving the stale value instead.

The neat thing about this is that the new fresh value continues to be fetched in the background even after the original request has been responded to with the stale value. This means that the cache is warmed with a fresh value shortly after, which can be used to serve subsequent requests.

The best way to understand what is happening is with another example. To add this powerful functionality, we only need to make a few small changes to the caching policy from listing 8.6, as shown in listing 8.7.

Listing 8.7   policy.js: adding a staleness policy

Items in cache marked stale after 2 s

Items in cache finally expire after 20 s

Stale item can be returned if generating fresh item takes more than 90 ms

Wait this long before returning error from generateFunc

```
...
const options = {
    expiresIn: 20000,
    staleIn: 2000,
    staleTimeout: 90,
    generateFunc: search,
    generateTimeout: 10000
};
...
```

We can also update the logged output to indicate whether the value retrieved from the cache was stale, as seen in the following listing.

Listing 8.8   policy.js: determining whether a cache policy value was stale

```
...
policy.get('node.js', (err, value, cached, report) => {

    if (err) {
        throw err;
    }

    const endTime = Date.now() - startTime;
    console.log('Found %d articles in %dms %s %s', value, endTime, cached ?
    '(CACHED)' : '', cached && cached.isStale ? '(STALE)' : '');
});
...
```

Running the example again should give output that looks like this:

```
Found 12 articles in 681ms
Found 12 articles in 0ms  (CACHED)
Found 12 articles in 95ms (CACHED) (STALE)
Found 12 articles in 0ms  (CACHED)
Found 12 articles in 95ms (CACHED) (STALE)
...
```

Aside from the initial search where the cache was empty, every search returned a value within the target of 100 ms. Figure 8.9 shows what's happening here visually.

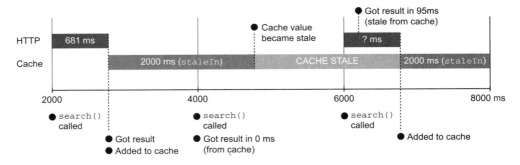

Figure 8.9   Timeline for example in listing 8.8

An important thing to keep in mind when using staleIn and staleTimeout is that the total amount of time an object is kept in the cache is still dictated by the value of expiresIn. Once the cache value for a specific key has truly expired, any subsequent requests for that value will have to wait the full time for a new value to be generated. For this reason, you should set your expiresIn as high as your use case allows.

8.2.4   *Which cache strategy should I use?*

Catbox provides a consistent API between several caching engines. This is a convenience, but it can also belie their inner differences. Which caching strategy you choose to use with hapi may be influenced by a few factors:

- Which technology is most appropriate
- What you are currently using in your stack
- What you already have experience with
- What you/your team's personal preference is

You should always thoroughly research the strategy you choose to ensure it meets your needs. Table 8.2 contains a brief overview of some of the main caching strategies supported by hapi and Catbox. It might help to steer your decision.

Table 8.2   Comparison of popular Catbox strategies

Memory—(provided by catbox-memory)
■ **Key feature:** Convenience
■ Stores cache data in the memory (JavaScript heap) of the running Node process
■ Data is not persisted, will be lost on process crash/termination
■ No setup required, perfect for development
■ Not suitable for production use

Table 8.2 Comparison of popular Catbox strategies

Redis—(provided by `catbox-redis`)

- **Key feature:** Extremely fast
- In-memory key-value store
- Data stored in memory with persistence on disk
- Can run on separate hosts
- Provides replication and automatic failover
- Cache should fit in memory of Redis box

Riak—(provided by `catbox-riak`)

- **Key feature:** Fault tolerance and high-availability
- Provides masterless replication
- Focus on scalability and big data support

Memcached—(provided by `catbox-memcached`)

- **Key feature:** Support for large amounts of transient data
- In-memory key-value store
- Typical installation involves shared-nothing farm of multiple servers
- Data is not persisted, will be lost on process crash/termination
- Least-used data is purged when cache is full
- Keys are limited to 250 bytes, values are limited to 1 MB each

In this section you've seen what Catbox is and how to integrate it within an application in a standalone manner. You've learned how to define cache policies that take advantage of automatically cache expiry and staleness.

In the next section we're going to shift the focus back onto hapi and see how you can add caching to your API and website projects using the knowledge you've already learned about Catbox.

8.3   Server-side caching in hapi applications

The techniques shown in the previous section are applicable to any Node.js application, and we could use exactly the same techniques to add caching to a hapi app. But hapi offers extra sugar on top of Catbox to make caching easier and more convenient to work with.

8.3.1   Configuring clients

When you create a hapi server, a default cache client is provisioned using the `catbox-memory` strategy. Next you'll see how you can create additional cache clients when instantiating a hapi server by providing the configuration with the `cache` option.

Listing 8.9   Provisioning additional cache clients

```
const server = new Hapi.Server({
    cache: [
        {
```

Common options required for all cache strategies

```
        engine: require('catbox-redis'),
        name: 'redis-cache',
        host: '127.0.0.1',
        port: 6379
    },
    {
        engine: require('catbox-memcached'),
        name: 'memcached-cache',
        location: [
            '127.0.0.1:9000',
            '127.0.0.1:9001'
        ]
    }
    ]
});
```

Specific options for the strategy

In listing 8.9, engine and name are required options for all cache clients you want to create. The additional options are specific to the cache strategy being used. You should check the documentation for any other strategy to find out which options are needed.

Once you've provisioned a cache client with hapi, there are a couple of ways to interact with it. The first is by using server.cache().

8.3.2 *Creating and using a Catbox Policy with server.cache()*

You can create a Catbox cache Policy object by using the server.cache() method in hapi. This will return exactly the same kind of object that we worked with in section 8.2.2. One difference is that there's no direct interaction with the Catbox module—it all happens through hapi.

> **HAPI API** server.cache(options) (http://hapijs.com/api#servercacheoptions)

The only other difference is that you can supply a cache option, which is one of the names of a cache client that you provisioned when the server was created. In the previous section's listing, we created a cache client with the name 'redis-cache'.

> **NOTE** If you want to run this example, you'll need a local installation of Redis. To get that you can follow the instructions on the Redis download page: http://redis.io/download. If you're on a Mac, you can also use Homebrew to install Redis: brew install redis.

This next example is an API that acts as a thin wrapper around the NYT Movie Reviews API. Users can make a request to the API—for example, GET /movies/the%20matrix will make a request to the Movie Reviews API to search for all reviews of *The Matrix*, adding the result to the Redis cache instance. Be sure to install all dependencies to run this (npm install --save catbox-redis@1 hapi@13 qs@6 wreck@7).

Listing 8.10   Using a cache `Policy` provisioned by hapi with `server.cache()`

```
'use strict';

const Hapi = require('hapi');
const Qs = require('qs');
const Wreck = require('wreck');

const server = new Hapi.Server({
    cache: [
        {
            engine: require('catbox-redis'),          Provision cache
            name: 'redis-cache',                       called redis-cache
            host: '127.0.0.1',
            port: 6379
        }
    ]
});

server.connection({ port: 4000 });

const searchReviews = function (query, callback) {

    const baseUrl = 'http://api.nytimes.com/svc/movies/v2/reviews/
    search.json';
    const queryObj = {
        'api-key': 'YOUR_API_KEY',
        query: query
    };
    const queryUrl = baseUrl + '?' + Qs.stringify(queryObj);

    const options = { json: true };

    Wreck.get(queryUrl, options, (err, res, payload) => {     Make request to NYT
                                                              Movie Reviews API
        callback(err, payload);
    });
};
                                              Provision cache
const movieCache = server.cache({             policy object
    generateFunc: searchReviews,                           Use searchReviews function
    expiresIn: 60000,                                      to generate values for cache
    staleIn: 10000,
    staleTimeout: 100,
    cache: 'redis-cache',
    segment: 'movies',                         Store cache values in
    generateTimeout: 10000                     movies segment
});

server.route({
    method: 'GET',
    path: '/movies/{movie}',
    handler: function (request, reply) {
```

Build API query URL using qs package →

Use redis-cache to store/find cache values →

```
                const start = Date.now();
                const query = request.params.movie;
```

Query cache ⟶   `movieCache.get(query, (err, value, cached, report) => {`

```
                    console.log('Got reviews for %s in %dms %s %s',
                        query,
                        Date.now() - start,
                        cached ? '(CACHED)' : '',
                        cached && cached.isStale ? '(STALE)' : '');

                    if (err) {
                        throw err;
                    }

                    reply(value);                    ⟵┐  Respond with either
                });                                    │  cached or fresh result
            }
        });

        server.start((err) => {

            if (err) {
                throw err;
            }
            console.log('Server running at:', server.info.uri);
        });
```

This is a perfectly good way to add caching to a hapi application. Let's look at another, slightly different way that you might prefer.

8.3.3   *Caching server methods*

If your application is using server methods, there's a slightly more convenient way to use caching. You can skip creating a cache policy with `server.cache()` altogether and supply the same cache policy configuration as an additional option when creating the server method.

Here is the movie reviews example from the previous section rewritten to use a server method.

Listing 8.11   Caching movies reviews using a server method

```
...

server.method('reviews', searchReviews, {
    cache: {
        expiresIn: 60000,
        staleIn: 10000,
        staleTimeout: 100,            ┐  Supply cache option with
        cache: 'redis-cache',          │  desired cache policy when
        segment: 'movies',             │  creating server method
        generateTimeout: 10000
```

```
        }
    });

    server.route({
        method: 'GET',
        path: '/movies/{movie}',
        handler: function (request, reply) {

            const query = request.params.movie;

            server.methods.reviews(query, (err, reviews) => {

                if (err) {
                    throw err;
                }

                reply(reviews);
            });
        }
    });

    ...
```

Use server method normally (except it returns cached value if in cache)

The great thing about using this method is that caching becomes mostly transparent and all happens behind the scenes for you, managed internally by hapi. You use the server method exactly the same as normal, and hapi will decide whether to give you a cached value or generate a new value for you based on your policy.

If you want to switch to a whole different caching engine, it's as easy as changing the `cache` option in the configuration. Because of this convenience, using server methods is my favorite way of working with server side caching in hapi.

8.3.4   *Organizing cache data using keys, partitions, and segments*

There are two pieces of information that together give the location of an item in a Catbox managed cache: the key and the partition. The key itself comprises both an ID and a segment name.

- Key
    - Segment
    - ID
- Partition

PARTITIONS

A *partition* is an isolated area in a cache where cache data is stored. Two partitions with separate names have no overlap. This is implemented differently by different strategies. Using MongoDB, two different partitions would correlate to two different databases. With Riak they would be separate buckets. See figure 8.10.

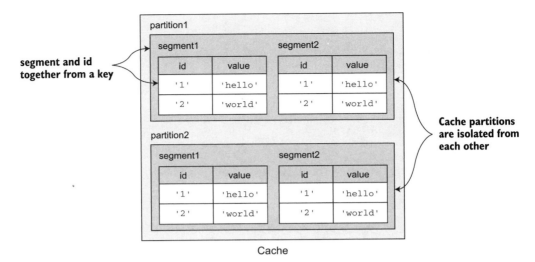

Figure 8.10   Sets of key-value pairs in a Catbox cache are stored within a partition and a segment.

You can define the partition you want to use when you create cache clients. It probably makes good sense to use partitions if you're sharing a database between multiple applications. That way you can be sure to isolate your data.

Listing 8.12   Using a partition in a Redis cache

```
const server = new Hapi.Server({
    cache: [
        {
            engine: require('catbox-redis'),
            name: 'redis-cache',
            host: '127.0.0.1',
            port: 6379,
            partition: 'real-estate-app'
        }
    ]
});
```

If you omit the partition option when creating a cache client, hapi will choose a default of 'hapi-cache' for you. If you want to create multiple clients and have them share the same cache data, you should ensure they use the same cache partition.

SEGMENTS

Often you'll want to store different values in the cache that have the same IDs. For instance, you may have built an e-commerce app driven by a MySQL database. Most likely you'll have a products and a customers table, with incremental primary keys.

It's convenient if you can use the database ID as the cache ID. But using the ID alone will lead to conflicts between the customers and products value that you cache, so you'll need an extra degree of separation.

A *segment* is a grouping of IDs within a single partition of a cache. By using different segments, you can store cache items with the same ID without a conflict. The segment and the ID together form the cache key.

Listing 8.13   Using cache segments to isolate values

```
const products = server.cache({
    expiresIn: 10 * 60 * 1000,
    cache: 'redis',
    generateFunc: getProduct,
    segment: 'products',
    generateTimeout: 10000
});

const customers = server.cache({
    expiresIn: 10 * 60 * 1000,
    cache: 'redis',
    generateFunc: getCustomers,
    segment: 'customers',
    generateTimeout: 10000
});

server.route([{
    method: 'GET',
    path: '/products/{id}',
    handler: function (request, reply) {

        products.get(request.params.id, (err, value) => {

            if (err) {
                throw err;
            }

            reply(value);
        });
    }
}, {
    method: 'GET',
    path: '/customers/{id}',
    handler: function (request, reply) {

        customers.get(request.params.id, (err, value) => {

            if (err) {
                throw err;
            }

            reply(value);
        });
    }
}]);
```

Both caches using same cache client

Two caches using separate cache partitions to keep data isolated

Possibly conflicting IDs can be used safely.

You should use partitions to separate unrelated cache data or when you're sharing a database across multiple applications. And you should separate cache data into segments within an application to allow you to use similar IDs, such as database primary keys, for multiple data sets.

Whether or not you know it, there are some mischievous folks out there who are up to no good. I've got your back, though, so worry not! Keep turning those pages and you'll learn all about security and authentication next.

8.4   *Summary*

- Implementing client-side caching policies is all about manually setting headers or adding cache policy configuration to routes.
- To manually add ETags to non-file responses you can use convenience methods.
- Catbox can be thought of as a caching adapter.
- How to create and use Catbox policies.
- Strategies are implemented in separate packages to Catbox.

Part 3

Creating rock-solid apps

At this point in the book, you should be pretty confident putting together functional web applications using hapi. You also know some more about advanced features like validation and caching, and how to organize your apps using plugins. This final part is about making sure your apps are reliable and secure and as bug-free as possible.

Previous chapters have touched on authentication, but in chapter 9 you're going to explore the subject in a lot more depth. You'll also be looking at other security considerations, like protecting your apps from cross-site request forgery attacks and some security best practices.

Chapter 10 is all about testing. You'll meet tools like lab, code, sinon, and proxyquire, which we're going to employ to make sure your code is as bug-free as possible before you release anything to production.

Last but not least, chapter 11 covers getting your app into production and keeping it there. You'll address several topics including logging, documentation, monitoring, and debugging.

Authentication and security

Web application security can be a daunting topic. Most literature on it is drowning in acronyms like XSS, CSRF, and TLS. It seems like every few months a new game-changing security exploit appears too, with names intended to scare the bejeebies out of you: Heartbleed, BEAST, CRIME, POODLE, and FREAK. Okay, so maybe not POODLE.

Where do we even begin to deal with all this? Well, first breathe . . . and relax. A lot of security starts with plain common sense. You should use strong random passwords/encryption keys. You shouldn't check secrets like security credentials into your source control system. You should run your app with the fewest privileges it needs. If you know this stuff, you're already a long way there.

A big chunk of the security iceberg is out of your hands as an application developer. When you decide to use Node.js, you're inheriting *a lot* of work already done for you by the Node core developers. You don't need to worry about patching OpenSSL or checking for buffer overruns. You need to make sure you update Node when security patches come out.

The piece of the security puzzle this chapter concentrates on is application security. That's the part that's your responsibility as an application developer. Things like authentication, security headers, protecting against CSRF (Cross-Site Request Forgery), and making use of CORS (Cross-Origin Resource Sharing). You'll be pleased to hear that you're not on your own with these matters. hapi has already done a huge amount to make these things as painless as possible.

9.1   Authentication in depth

You've already taken a short foray into authentication back in chapter 2. We used a simple *Bearer token* authentication strategy to secure the DinDin API application we built in that chapter. This section begins by briefly revisiting the basic authentication concepts and then following up with more advanced material.

9.1.1   hapi authentication recap

Authentication is all about confirming *identity*. When a user makes a request to a route that requires authentication, the server wants to know *who* they are. The user's browser (or app or other HTTP client) makes that known to the server by including some form of credential in their request (see figure 9.1). Maybe the credentials are in a cookie, an HTTP header, or some combination—or are something totally different.

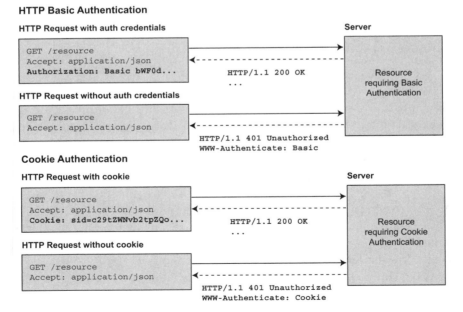

Figure 9.1   Authentication schemes often require a credential be provided in an HTTP header.

The way that you've decided users should authenticate with a route, is called the *authentication scheme*. You can also think of a scheme as a protocol. Examples of schemes are basic authentication, bearer token authentication, and cookie authentication. To make use of an authentication scheme in hapi, you first create an authentication strategy from that scheme (see figure 9.2).

A *strategy* is a named instance of a scheme that you can use in hapi to authenticate requests to a route. For instance, you might use the basic authentication scheme to create a strategy called `website`. You then apply the `website` auth strategy to a route. Now whenever a user makes a request to that route, they'll need to authenticate using basic authentication.

The core hapi package doesn't have any authentication schemes built in. Instead they must be loaded via plugins. You don't have to go out and invent any yourself, though, because many are already available on npm to use.

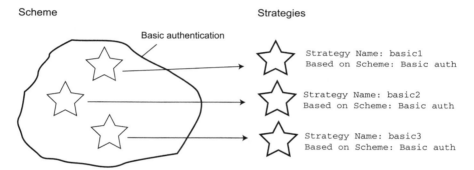

Figure 9.2 Authentication schemes are a template for creating strategies.

To refresh your memory, let's see a quick example of how you would use the hapi-auth-basic authentication plugin.

NPM PACKAGE hapi-auth-basic v4 (www.npmjs.com/package/hapi-auth-basic)

This plugin provides a scheme called `basic`. We can use the `basic` scheme to create a new auth strategy by calling `server.auth.strategy()`.

HAPI AP `server.auth.strategy(scheme, name, options)` (http://hapijs .com/api#serverauthstrategyname-scheme-mode-options)

The name you give the strategy is totally up to you. For this simple example, I'll pick `simple`. When creating a strategy from the `basic` scheme, only one option is required: a `validateFunc` function. This `validateFunc` function is where you write code to decide whether the username and password given in the request resolve to a valid user. A full example with annotations is shown here.

Listing 9.1   Authenticating requests using hapi-auth-basic

```
const validUsers = {
    john: 'secret'          <─── Usernames and passwords
};                                of valid users

const validate = function (request, username, password, callback) {

    const err = null;                           Compare username and
    let isValid = false;                        password in request
    let credentials = {};                       with known values

    if (validUsers[username] && validUsers[username] === password) {   <───
        isValid = true;
        credentials = { username: username };   <─── Prepare user credentials
    }                                                to expose to hapi route

    callback(err, isValid, credentials);
};

server.register(require('hapi-auth-basic'), (err) => {    <─── Register
                                                               hapi-auth-basic plugin
    if (err) {
        throw err;
    }

    server.auth.strategy('simple', 'basic', { validateFunc: validate });   <───
    server.route({
        method: 'GET',
        path: '/',                              Create strategy called
        config: {                               simple from basic scheme
            auth: 'simple',                     provided by hapi-auth-basic
            handler: function (request, reply) {

                reply('Hi ' + request.auth.credentials.username + '!' );   <───
            }
        }                                       If authenticated, route has access
    });                                         to provided user credentials in
});                                             request.auth.credentials
```

Set up route to use simple auth ──→

NOTE The plaintext password is only shown for the simplicity of the example—never store plaintext passwords in real apps, only hashed passwords! Additionally, a constant time comparison function should be used in place of = = = when comparing hashes and passwords. For more info on this look up timing attacks.

Listing 9.1 uses the hapi-auth-basic plugin, which defines a basic scheme. We use this basic scheme to create a strategy called simple. The simple strategy is applied to the GET / route. This means to access this route, we need to authenticate using basic authentication.

9.1.2   *Which authentication scheme should I choose?*

There numerous available authentication schemes for hapi. Three are within the hapijs organization on Github itself and maintained by the core project maintainers:

- *hapi-auth-basic*—Supports HTTP basic authentication. Usable for both websites and APIs. Recommended for use only over SSL/TLS as username/password are sent as cleartext over the network.
- *hapi-auth-cookie*—Implements cookie authentication and basic session support. Highly useful for websites. Often coupled with form-based login.
- *hapi-auth-hawk*—New authentication scheme for APIs created by Eran Hammer (author of hapi). Intended to be an improvement over HTTP Digest authentication. Relies on a shared secret key between client and server.

There are also many more available auth plugins from other contributors and the wider community. You should always be wary when running someone else's code in production—even more so when the code is intended to secure your app. If you can, always study the code yourself before using an auth plugin or use a popular, well-documented, and well-tested plugin such as the ones published under the hapijs Github organization.

9.1.3 *Authentication scopes*

Authentication is often conflated and confused with another similar concept: authorization. The difference between the two is an important one to grasp:

- *Authentication*—Identity or figuring out who you are
- *Authorization*—Permissions or figuring out what you're allowed to do or see

When you check in at an airport, you need to show two things. You show your passport to prove *who* you are—that's authentication. You show your ticket or boarding pass to prove that *you're allowed* on that particular flight. That's authorization.

The computer scientist Melvin Conway made the observation (known now as Conway's law) that when organizations build software, they tend to mimic the same structure as the organization themselves. In organizations there are typically different roles, and along with these roles come different permissions. An example is security clearance level.

As users of web applications, we often have roles too. On a blog, for instance, an admin user will have different permissions and be able to use a larger or different subset of features than an editor.

hapi offers a rudimentary role-like authorization feature called *scopes*. You can define a set of scopes for every resource (route) that requires authentication. To do so you provide an array of scope names as part of the configuration, as shown here.

> **Listing 9.2 Specifying a list of authentication scopes on a route**

```
server.route({
    ...
    config: {
        auth: {
            strategy: 'simple',
            scope: ['user', 'admin']
        }
    }
    ...
});
```

Whenever a user is authenticated, a `scope` property can be set in their credentials to indicate which scope(s) should be assigned to the user.

Listing 9.3   Setting a user's assigned scopes

```
const validate = function (request, username, password, callback) {

    ...
    callback(err, isValid, { scope: ['user', 'admin'] });
};
```

The two lists are compared when a user accesses a scoped route in order to know whether they should be allowed access, as shown in figure 9.3.

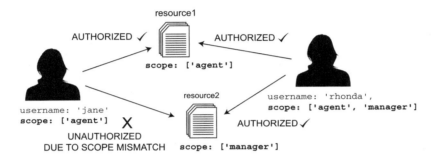

Figure 9.3   A user's scope(s) must intersect with a resource's scope(s) to be allowed access.

9.1.4   *Authentication modes*

So far, all the examples of authentication have been mandatory authentication. That is to say, when we specify an auth strategy for a route, such as `basic`, we expect users to successfully identify themselves to access the route. If they don't, they're not allowed access to that route.

Sometimes we may *desire* a user to authenticate with a route, but if they don't or can't, we may still allow them access to the route. As an example, imagine an online shop web page that displays details for a product. If a user is logged in, we may also show them recommended products based on what they bought in the past. If the user isn't logged in, they can still see the page but without the recommendations.

hapi permits this optional authentication by setting the authentication `mode` to `try` or `optional` instead of the default value of `required`, as shown in the following listing and figure 9.4.

Listing 9.4   Using an authentication strategy in `try` mode

```
server.route({
    method: 'GET',
    path: '/',
```

```
config: {
    auth: {
        strategy: 'simple',
        mode: 'try'
    },
    handler: function (request, reply) {

        if (request.auth.isAuthenticated) {
            return reply('Hi ' + request.auth.credentials.username);
        }

        reply('Hi guest!');
    }
}
});
```

All requests try to authenticate with simple strategy, but handler still executed for requests with invalid or missing credentials

request.auth.isAuthenticated set to true or false depending on whether auth successful

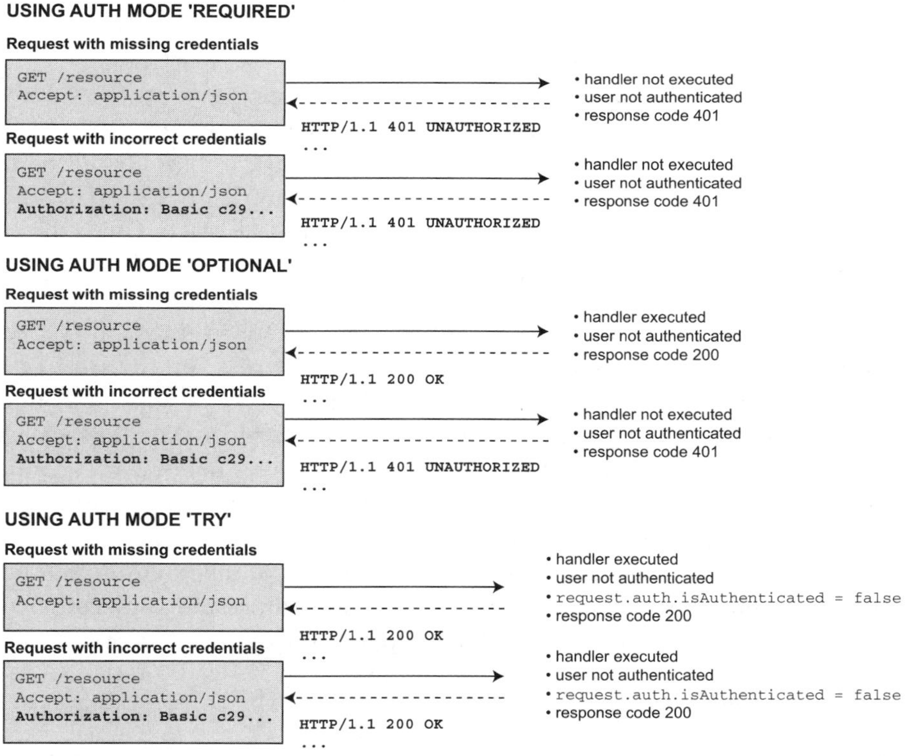

USING AUTH MODE 'REQUIRED'

Request with missing credentials
```
GET /resource
Accept: application/json
```
HTTP/1.1 401 UNAUTHORIZED
...
- handler not executed
- user not authenticated
- response code 401

Request with incorrect credentials
```
GET /resource
Accept: application/json
Authorization: Basic c29...
```
HTTP/1.1 401 UNAUTHORIZED
...
- handler not executed
- user not authenticated
- response code 401

USING AUTH MODE 'OPTIONAL'

Request with missing credentials
```
GET /resource
Accept: application/json
```
HTTP/1.1 200 OK
...
- handler executed
- user not authenticated
- response code 200

Request with incorrect credentials
```
GET /resource
Accept: application/json
Authorization: Basic c29...
```
HTTP/1.1 401 UNAUTHORIZED
...
- handler not executed
- user not authenticated
- response code 401

USING AUTH MODE 'TRY'

Request with missing credentials
```
GET /resource
Accept: application/json
```
HTTP/1.1 200 OK
...
- handler executed
- user not authenticated
- request.auth.isAuthenticated = false
- response code 200

Request with incorrect credentials
```
GET /resource
Accept: application/json
Authorization: Basic c29...
```
HTTP/1.1 200 OK
...
- handler executed
- user not authenticated
- request.auth.isAuthenticated = false
- response code 200

Figure 9.4   Behavior between auth modes differs for requests with missing or incorrect credentials

The difference between try and optional modes is optional mode requires that if credentials are present, they must be valid. Using try mode will still allow a request to proceed to the handler, even if the credentials are present but invalid. The differences are shown in figure 9.4.

9.2   *Implementing third-party authentication with Bell*

Unless you've stumbled upon this book while living under a proverbial rock (no offense meant to any cave-dwelling readers), you will have used or at least seen examples of third-party authentication on the web or in mobile applications. I'm talking about "Login with Facebook" or "Sign up using Google" buttons.

In this section we're going to learn how to implement this functionality in our own web applications using a hapi plugin called Bell. I cover what third-party auth is all about and how Bell works. I finish up with a working example that can act as a template for your own applications.

9.2.1   *What is third-party authentication?*

Third-party authentication is all about delegating responsibility for identifying a user to another party—trusting someone else to vouch for a user. If you trust that third party, and they trust the user, then you implicitly trust the user too. What's the point of all this? Let's look at a real-world example.

Credit cards are a convenient way to pay for products, but a store doesn't want to keep a vast database of all credit cards and how much money their owners have. Because the store trusts the bank, they let the bank identify you, and the bank tells them, "Yes, they can afford it," or, "No, they can't afford it." The shop trusts the bank, the bank now trusts you too, and the transaction can take place. This is the essence of third-party authentication.

In the same way, a web application might not want to keep a database of all of its user passwords. It may only want to know who you are so it can show you relevant information. If the user is already a user of Facebook, the app can trust Facebook to identify you and then Facebook can communicate back to the app a little information about the user, such as Facebook user ID and email address. You'll typically then use this data to create an account for them in your app. Every time the user comes back to your app, they can then log in again using Facebook. This is more convenient for the user too. It's one less password to remember.

The magic that makes all this happen is a protocol called OAuth. OAuth can be complicated to understand in detail. It's even more difficult to implement it well yourself. The good news is that you don't have to do either.

NPM PACKAGE   `bell` v4 (www.npmjs.com/package/bell)

Bell implements the whole OAuth flow for you and comes with built-in support for a number of OAuth providers, including Facebook, Twitter, Google, and GitHub.

9.2.2   *Introducing Bell*

First, let's clear up some terminology that we'll be using when discussing Bell:

- *User*—A person who wants to use your app
- *Application*—The thing you are building

- *Provider*—The third party that will authenticate your users (for example, Facebook or Twitter)

Before we write any code, let's briefly take a look at the process that happens when a user authenticates with your app using Bell. This general process is the same when working with any Bell provider and is outlined in figure 9.5.

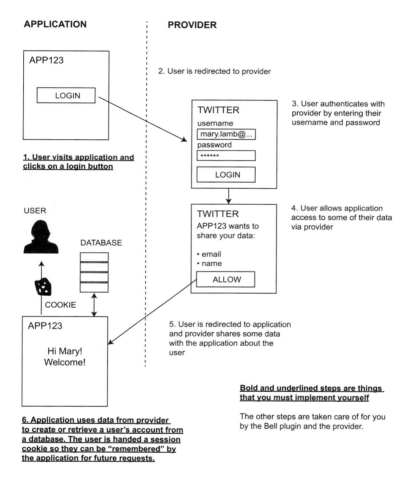

Figure 9.5 The flow of authentication with Bell

Of the six steps in figure 9.5, you only have to take care of two: providing a button and an endpoint/handler for the login link on your application and then handling the data that comes back from the provider. Bell and the third party take care of everything in between. Pretty neat huh? This should appeal to the laziness in all of us.

Enough theory and diagrams. Let's use this in an app.

9.2.3   *Integrating Bell into a hapi app*

We're going to build a simple app to showcase Bell. It's going to consist of a single page. When the user is logged out, they have the option to log in with Facebook. After successful login, they'll be greeted with a message and a logout link. The flow of this app is shown in figure 9.6.

Figure 9.6   The functionality of our simple Bell application

CREATING A FACEBOOK APP

Before we can get started with our app, we need to create a Facebook application. This way we can get the necessary credentials that Bell needs to implement the OAuth flow with Facebook. This is pretty simple to set up, and the process will be similar across different providers (look up the developer's documentation for your provider, if you're not using Facebook). You will need a Facebook account first. The steps to set up a new Facebook application are outlined in figure 9.7. Please be aware that Facebook updates its app creation process quite frequently, so the exact pages and order of steps may be slightly different than those outlined here.

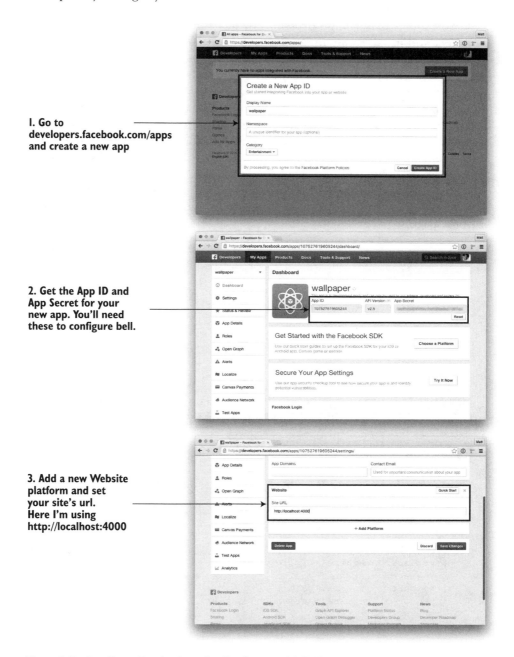

1. Go to
developers.facebook.com/apps
and create a new app

2. Get the App ID and
App Secret for your
new app. You'll need
these to configure bell.

3. Add a new Website
platform and set
your site's url.
Here I'm using
http://localhost:4000

Figure 9.7   Creating a Facebook application for use with Bell

BUILDING OUR APP

Okay, so you understand how Bell works, and you should have set a Facebook application and gotten the relevant credentials. Now it's time to get started writing some code for our application.

You should know these first steps by heart now. We create a package.json for our project and install some initial dependencies. To get started, we're going to run npm install bell@7 handlebars@4 hapi@11 hapi-auth-cookie@6 vision@4.

You might wonder why we need hapi-auth-cookie if we're using Facebook for authentication? Remember that HTTP is a stateless protocol—it has no memory of what came before. Having to authenticate with Facebook every time someone requests a page on your website would be inefficient and annoying. Instead, we only contact Facebook for the initial login stage. Once we know who the user is, we can create a session for them and hand them a cookie so we can identify them for subsequent requests.

As we're all big fans of plugins now after the previous chapter, we're going to split this app up into a couple of separate plugins: one plugin to handle the auth side of things (logging in and logging out) and one plugin to handle everything else (the home page):

```
.
.
├── index.js
├── package.json
└── plugins
    ├── auth
    │   └── index.js
    └── web
        ├── index.js
        └── views
            └── index.hbs
```

All we need in our index.js file is to load the plugins and start the server. The interesting stuff is all going to be within the plugins themselves.

Listing 9.5   index.js: the application's main file

```
const Hapi = require('hapi');

const server = new Hapi.Server();
server.connection({ port: 4000 });

server.register([
    { register: require('./plugins/web') },       Business logic plugins that we'll
    { register: require('./plugins/auth') },      develop in this example app
    { register: require('vision') },
    { register: require('bell') },
    { register: require('hapi-auth-cookie') }
], (err) => {

    if (err) {
        throw err;
    }
```

```
        server.start((err) => {

            if (err) {
                throw err;
            }

            console.log('Started server');
        });
    });
```

Let's start with the auth plugin. Let's first add the route that's going to take care of the Facebook login (see the following listing).

Listing 9.6   plugins/auth/index.js: the plugin that deals with authentication

```
exports.register = function (server, options, next) {

    server.dependency(['bell'], (server, next) => {          ◁── Declare plugin's
                                                                 dependency on Bell
        server.auth.strategy('facebook', 'bell', {
            provider: 'facebook',                            Create auth strategy
            isSecure: false,                                 called facebook using
            password: 'password-that-is-at-least-32-chars'   bell scheme, passing
            clientId: 'your Facebook App ID goes here',      along required options
            clientSecret: 'your Facebook App Secret goes here'
        });

        server.route({
            method: ['POST', 'GET'],      ◁──  Bell login route must be accessible
            path: '/login',                    for both GET and POST requests
            config: {
                auth: 'facebook'                       ◁──  Configure route for
            },                                              Facebook authentication
            handler: function (request, reply) {

                if (request.auth.isAuthenticated) {
                    const credentials = request.auth.credentials;
                }

                // Custom login code goes here

                return reply.redirect('/');
            }
        });

        next();
    });

    next();
};

exports.register.attributes = {
    name: 'auth'
};
```

True if login successful ──▷ (points to `if (request.auth.isAuthenticated) {`)

Will contain requested user's Facebook data ──▷ (points to `const credentials = request.auth.credentials;`)

When the user is authenticated successfully with Facebook, they will be sent back to the same /login route via a POST request from Facebook. Their shared Facebook data (name, email address, and so on) will be available inside request.auth.credentials. At this point we want to add some of this data to the user's session so we can recognize them for future requests. We need to integrate hapi-auth-cookie to get simple session support. We also need to make a basic logout route, which is going to clear our session.

At this point, we'll also refactor some hardcoded settings from inside the auth plugin as plugin options, as shown in the following listing.

Listing 9.7 plugins/auth/index.js: adding support for user sessions

```
exports.register = function (server, options, next) {

    server.dependency(['bell', 'hapi-auth-cookie'], (server, next) => {

        server.auth.strategy('facebook', 'bell', options.bell);
        server.auth.strategy('session', 'cookie', options.cookies);

        server.route({
            method: ['POST', 'GET'],
            path: '/login',
            config: {
                auth: 'facebook'
            },
            handler: function (request, reply) {

                if (request.auth.isAuthenticated) {
                    const credentials = request.auth.credentials;
                    request.cookieAuth.set({ account: credentials });
                }

                return reply.redirect('/');
            }
        });

        server.route({
            method: 'GET',
            path: '/logout',
            config: {
                auth: 'session'
            },
            handler: function (request, reply) {

                request.cookieAuth.clear();
                reply.redirect('/');
            }
        });
```

Use plugin options to configure Bell

Create session auth strategy using hapi-auth-cookie

Create session for user containing their Facebook data

Create logout route that clears user's session

```
        next();
    });

    next();
};
```

We must also remember to pass along the refactored plugin options when loading our plugins.

Listing 9.8   index.js: passing the required options to our plugins

```
...

server.register([
    { register: require('./plugins/web') },
    { register: require('./plugins/auth'), options: {        ⊲─┐ Pass configuration
        bell: {                                                │ options into plugins
            provider: 'facebook',                              │ when registering
            isSecure: false,
            password: 'password-that-is-at-least-32-chars',
            clientId: 'your Facebook App ID goes here',
            clientSecret: 'your Facebook App Secret goes here'
        },
        cookies: {
            password: 'password-that-is-at-least-32-chars',
            cookie: 'wallpaper-session',
            isSecure: false
        }
    } },
    { register: require('vision') },
    { register: require('bell') },
    { register: require('hapi-auth-cookie') }
], (err) => {

    ...
});
```

That's auth all done and dusted. Now we can focus on the web plugin. The web plugin is going to manage our home page route. It's going to render a simple Handlebars view. Our view context will show whether or not we're logged in and our name from Facebook to show in a greeting.

Listing 9.9   plugins/web/index.js: plugin that renders the homepage view

```
'use strict';

const Path = require('path');

exports.register = function (server, options, next) {
```

```
server.dependency(['vision', 'auth'], (server, next) => {

    server.views({
        engines: {
            hbs: require('handlebars')
        },
        path: Path.join(__dirname, 'views')
    });

    server.route({
        method: 'GET',
        path: '/',
        config: {
            auth: {
                strategy: 'session',
                mode: 'try'
            }
        },
        handler: function (request, reply) {

            let context = { loggedIn: false };

            if (request.auth.isAuthenticated) {
                const account = request.auth.credentials.account;
                context = {
                    loggedIn: true,
                    name: account.profile.displayName
                };
            }

            reply.view('index', context);
        }
    });

    next();
});

next();
};

exports.register.attributes = {
    name: 'web'
};
```

Add session authentication strategy to home page, use try mode to allow access even if not authenticated

If user has authenticated, pass some of their credentials to view context

Finally we need to make a Handlebars view for our home page. We're not going to bother with layouts and partials in this example because the app only has one page. Everything is going to go inside a single index.hbs view.

Listing 9.10   plugins/web/views/index.hbs: homepage view template

```
<!DOCTYPE html>
<html lang="en">
<head>
    <meta charset="UTF-8">
    <title>Facebook Login Application</title>
```

```
</head>
<body>
    {{#if loggedIn}}
        <h1>Hi {{name}}!</h1>
        <a href="/logout">Logout</a>
    {{else}}
        <a href="/login">Log in with Facebook</a>
    {{/if}}
</body>
</html>
```

⊲ **If user is logged in, print name and show logout button**

⊲ **Otherwise, show login button**

WHERE NEXT?

The example that we've built is about as simple as an app can get with Bell. Any real application would most likely have a database of some sort integrated. After a user has logged in, an account would be created (or retrieved) for the user from the database using their Facebook ID. Rather than storing their entire Facebook credentials in the user's session as we did, you'd probably store what data you needed in your database and only store the user's session ID in their cookie.

Aside from the fact that the user is doing the authentication stage on another site, Bell apps are no different than any other apps built with hapi. You should use Bell and third-party authentication whenever you don't want to handle authenticating users yourself or when you want to provide the convenience to users of using their preexisting accounts elsewhere.

It also makes sense to use a third-party auth provider if the available user information being shared from the provider is relevant to your app. For instance, if your app has social features, it might be useful to know some of your user's Facebook data, such as their friends list, when signing up.

9.3 *Managing cross-origin requests with CORS*

Sometimes you want to include data from other applications or services on websites. However, browsers conform to a restriction called the *same-origin policy*. This policy says that scripts can only access resources that are contained within the same origin as the script. This extends to making HTTP requests using XMLHttpRequest (AJAX requests). A script loaded from mysite.com can't make an HTTP request to load a resource from yoursite.com under the same-origin policy.

This restriction exists for security reasons. As it turns out, though, the ability to make cross-origin requests can be extremely useful. From the perspective of the service provider, if we're building an API, we may want to open it and allow it to be used client-side from other applications.

One of the early ways to circumvent the same-origin policy for these cases was JSONP. JSONP relies on a sort of loophole in the same-origin policy: the fact that it doesn't apply to <script> tags. JSONP is an ugly hack, though, in my opinion, and thankfully it's pretty much had its day.

A better solution finally appeared in the form of CORS. CORS allows a resource owner to explicitly define a policy that allows resources on their origin to be loaded

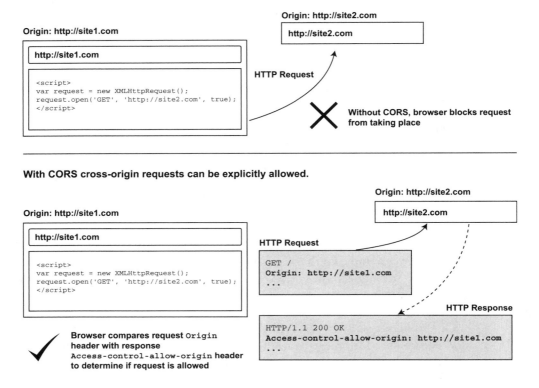

Figure 9.8 CORS allows cross-origin requests to take place that were previously disallowed by the same-origin policy.

from another origin with a fine degree of control over who can load what. See figure 9.8.

All modern browsers handle this for you on the client side. But on the server, we need to manage which resources are allowed to be loaded with CORS. You do that by setting certain response headers, all named with the prefix `Access-Control-*`. The browser will inspect these headers and determine whether the script is allowed access to the resource.

FURTHER READING   We're not going to be discussing in depth the various CORS headers and the differences between simple and preflighted requests. hapi provides a set of convenient options to take care of all of this for you. But an in-depth knowledge of CORS can be useful when debugging. For further reading, MDN (Mozilla Developer Network) is a great resource. https://developer.mozilla.org/en-US/docs/Web/HTTP/Access_control_CORS.

9.3.1 Allowing cross-origin requests from anywhere

Every route in a hapi application can have CORS options set for it. First we're going to look at the most simple and most heavy-handed way to allow cross-origin requests to a route.

Let's create a small example of a case where we need to enable CORS. This will be a simple web page that attempts to make a cross-origin request. It's going to consist of a couple of different files. There's a server portion that has two routes—one to serve an HTML file and the other intended as a resource that we'll attempt to load across origins, as shown in the next listing.

Listing 9.11 index.js: CORS example server script

```
const Hapi = require('hapi');
const Path = require('path');

const server = new Hapi.Server();
server.connection({ port: 4000 });

server.register(require('inert'), (err) => {

    if (err) {
        throw err;
    }

    server.route([
        {
            method: 'GET',
            path: '/',
            handler: function (request, reply) {

                reply.file(Path.join(__dirname, 'index.html'));
            }
        }, {
            method: 'GET',
            path: '/resource',
            handler: function (request, reply) {

                reply('A resource');
            }
        }
    ]);

    server.start((err) => {

        if (err) {
            throw err;
        }

        console.log('Started server');
    });
});
```

Respond with HTML file →

Our "resource" we're trying to load cross-origin, responds with simple string

We're using Inert because we need to serve an HTML file. The index.html page attempts to make an XMLHTTPRequest request to http://127.0.0.1:4000/resource. If we've loaded the home page in the browser by navigating to http://localhost:4000/, this will be a cross-origin request, as shown in the following listing.

Listing 9.12   index.html: CORS example HTML page

```html
<!DOCTYPE html>
<html lang="en">
<head>
    <meta charset="UTF-8">
    <title>CORS</title>
</head>
<body>
    <h1>CORS</h1>
    <script>
        var request = new XMLHttpRequest();
        request.open('GET', 'http://127.0.0.1:4000/resource', true);

        request.onload = function () {

            console.log('Loaded successfully');
            console.log(request.responseText);
        };

        request.onerror = function () {

            console.log('An error occurred');
        };

        request.send();
    </script>
</body>
</html>
```

Make AJAX request for /resource (will be cross-origin if we load this page on localhost)

We can start the server and load the home page in a browser with the address http://localhost:4000. If you have the console open, you should see an error message that the resource couldn't be loaded because of the absence of an "Access-Control-Allow-Origin" header (see figure 9.9).

Figure 9.9   The browser error shown when a cross-origin request fails

NOTE Even though http://127.0.0.1:4000 and http://localhost:4000 ultimately resolve to the same IP address and port, making a request from one to the other is still considered to be a cross-origin request by a browser, and thus CORS is required. The same goes for different subdomains and ports: a request from a.example.com to example.com is also considered cross-domain, as would a request from example.com:4000 to example.com:4001.

To allow the browser to request the resource across origins, we need to ensure that the `Access-Control-Allow-Origin` header is set on our response. We're not going to set that header manually though—we're going to set an option in our route configuration, as shown in the next listing.

Listing 9.13 index.js: setting the `cors` route option to allow all origins

```
server.route([
    {
        ...
    }, {
        config: {                         Allow cross-origin
            cors: true              ◁──── requests from any origin
        },
        method: 'GET',
        path: '/resource',
        handler: function (request, reply) {

            reply('A resource');
        }
    }
]);
```

Restart the app, try to load the page again, and the cross-origin request will succeed. By setting the `cors` option to `true`, we've told hapi that we want any origin to be able to load this resource freely. This sets a response header `Access-Control-Allow-Origin` with the value of `*`, the wildcard origin that matches any origin.

If you're building a publicly available API that will be used directly from browsers and can be embedded into clients on other domains, this wide-open access could be exactly what you need. Otherwise you're probably going to want to restrict exactly which origins are permitted.

9.3.2 *Restricting access to resources to specific origins only*

If you've built an API hosted on api.mysite.com and are serving a front-end client to this API, such as a single-page app on mysite.com, you're going to need to use CORS to allow cross-origin requests. There's no need to allow all origins to make CORS requests to the API, though. You should go with the most limited permissions model that allows your app to work.

To get finer-grained control over CORS in hapi, you can provide an `options` object to the `cors` route-configuration option. One of the options is `origin`, which accepts an array of permitted origins. The following listing takes the example from the previous section and modifies it so it only allows requests from http://localhost:4000.

```
server.route([
    {
        ...
    }, {
        config: {
            cors: {
                origin: ['http://localhost:4000']       ⊲─┐  Allow cross-origin requests from
            }                                              http://localhost:4000 origin
        },
        method: 'GET',
        path: '/resource',
        handler: function (request, reply) {

            reply('A resource');
        }
    }
]);
```

Note that the `origin` option should include both scheme (http:// versus https://), the hostname, and the port. This should match the value of the `Origin` request header sent by the browser. When debugging CORS issues, it can be helpful to check this in the Network tab of the developer tools of your browser.

9.3.3   *Dealing with custom headers*

CORS also enforces restrictions on which headers can be sent in a request and exposed from a response.

REQUEST HEADERS

If we attempt to set a custom request header when making the AJAX request in our prior example, the request is going to fail, as in the following listing.

```
var request = new XMLHttpRequest();
request.open('GET', 'http://127.0.0.1:4000/resource', true);
request.setRequestHeader('x-custom-header', 'custom value');   ⊲─┐  Set custom request
...                                                               header on AJAX request
```

A set of request headers is permitted with any cross-origin request by default:

- `Accept`
- `Authorization`
- `Content-Type`
- `If-None-Match`
- `Origin`

If a request contains an additional header not in this list, the request will fail. If you need to send custom headers along with a request, they must be explicitly whitelisted for your route by setting the `config.cors.additionalHeaders`.

```
...
config: {
    cors: {
        origin: ['http://localhost:4000'],
        additionalHeaders: ['x-custom-header']
    }
},
...
```

RESPONSE HEADERS

A server may set one or more custom headers during a cross-origin response:

```
server.route({
    ...
    handler: function (request, reply) {

        reply('A resource').header('x-custom-response', 'value');
    }
});
```

You can try to read the value of this header in the browser script:

```
var header = request.getResponseHeader('x-custom-response');
```

But an exception will occur with an error resembling the following:

```
Refused to get unsafe header "x-custom-response"
```

To allow a browser to read the value of custom response headers, there's another option that must be set in the CORS configuration for the route. The option is `additionalExposedHeaders`:

```
...
config: {
    cors: {
        origin: ['http://localhost:4000'],
        additionalHeaders: ['x-custom-header'],
        additionalExposedHeaders: ['x-custom-response']
    }
},
...
```

Things are a little different yet again when it comes to cookie headers. Let's look at that next.

9.3.4   *CORS and credentials (cookies)*

By default, cookies aren't transmitted in cross-origin requests. But cookies in cross-origin requests have several valid use cases, such as authentication and tracking. To exchange cookies with a server when communicating across origins in a browser, you need to do two things. First you need to indicate to the browser that you want to use credentials in the request. You can do this by setting the `withCredentials` property on an `XMLHttpRequest` object.

Listing 9.17   index.html: setting the XHR `withCredentials` flag

```
var request = new XMLHttpRequest();
request.open('GET', 'http://127.0.0.1:4000/resource', true);
request.withCredentials = true;        ◁── Tells browser to send cookies
                                            with cross-origin AJAX request
```

If you're using a JavaScript library to make HTTP requests on the client side, it should have a corresponding `withCredentials` setting. For example, the following listing shows that jQuery's `$.ajax` function has an `xhrFields` setting where you can set this flag.

Listing 9.18   Setting `withCredentials` using jQuery

```
$.ajax({
    url: a_cross_domain_url,
    xhrFields: {
        withCredentials: true       ◁── Tells browser to send cookies
    }                                    with cross-origin AJAX request
});
```

The other thing you need to do to allow exchanging of cookies is have the server include an `Access-Control-Allow-Credentials` header in its responses. You don't need to add this header manually, though, because hapi has a `credentials` setting in its CORS configuration that you can use, as seen in the following listing.

Listing 9.19   index.js: telling hapi to allow credentials in CORS requests

```
server.route([
    {
        config: {
            cors: {
                origin: ['http://localhost:4000'],
                credentials: true            ◁── Tells hapi to add Access-
            }                                    Control-Allow-Credentials
        },                                       header to responses
        method: 'GET',
        path: '/resource',
        handler: function (request, reply) {
```

```
                    reply('A resource').state('a-cookie', 'yummy');
            }
        }
]);
```

When these two steps have been taken, a browser can freely send and receive cookies with the endpoint. Note that, for security reasons, you can't access or manipulate these cookies directly from JavaScript.

Listing 9.20   Cookies from other domains can't be accessed from JavaScript

```
var request = new XMLHttpRequest();
request.open('GET', 'http://127.0.0.1:4000/resource', true);
request.withCredentials = true;

request.onload = function () {
    var cookie = request.getResponseHeader('set-cookie');    ⟵┐  Attempt to read cookie
    console.log('Loaded successfully');                           header from cross-
    console.log(request.responseText);                           origin request
};
```

If you tried to read a cookie set by a cross-domain request using code like listing 9.20, the browser will refuse to read that header, throwing an exception with an error:

```
Refused to get unsafe header "set-cookie"
```

Despite not being able to directly manipulate the cookies from JavaScript, cross-domain cookies are still extremely useful. When you visit site-a.com, which embeds ads, the ad server can set a cookie for you from adserver.com. When you then go to visit site-b.com, adserver.com can read the same cookie. It now knows that you've been at site-a.com and site-b.com.

9.3.5   *Granularity of CORS settings*

You've seen how to enable CORS in hapi by setting the `cors` options on individual routes. If you have a lot of routes in your application and require CORS on all or many of them, it's rather verbose to have to repeat yourself and set the same configuration on each of them.

There are some other levels at which you can set these options and have them apply to multiple routes. The first one we'll look at is the level of the server. When creating a server, there is a `routes` option. You can use this option to provide a CORS policy that will cascade down and apply to every route on that server, as shown in the following listing.

Listing 9.21   Setting CORS options at server level affects all routes

```
const server = new Hapi.Server({
    connections: {
        routes: {
```

```
        cors: {
            origin: ['*']                    ◁──┐  Set CORS setting
        }                                       │  for entire server
    }
  }
});
```

In a similar way, as shown in the next listing, you can set CORS settings for an entire connection when creating one.

Listing 9.22   Setting CORS options at connection

```
server.connection({
    port: 4000,
    routes: {
        cors: {
            origin: ['*']                    ◁──┐  Set CORS setting for all
        }                                       │  routes on connection
    }
});
```

You can still override CORS configuration for a single route when using this approach, turning it off entirely if you want, as in the following listing.

Listing 9.23   Route-level CORS options override server and connection-level settings

```
server.route([
    {
        config: {
            cors: false                      ◁──┐  Route-level CORS settings
        },                                      │  always take precedence
        method: 'GET',
        path: '/resource',
        handler: function (request, reply) {

            ...

        }
    }
]);
```

My advice is to pick whichever approach leads to cleaner code and less repetition, but more importantly, still provides the level of security that your application needs. Closely related to CORS and cross-origin requests is the concept of cross-site request forgery, which we explore next.

9.4   *Protecting apps against CSRF with Crumb*

A Cross-Site Request Forgery or CSRF attack is a type of exploit of a web application. A CSRF attack occurs when malicious code on a website (site A) forces a user's browser to make a request to another website (site B) for which they're already authenticated.

The user's session cookie is sent along with this forged request, meaning that without proper checks, site B will assume the request to have come from the user. This can be exploited to potentially devastating effect. Let's look at an example of a CSRF attack.

Jim, who hates cats, is logged into Twitter. He browses Twitter for a while, sniggering disdainfully at all the cat pictures. One of Jim's mischievous and feline-loving friends later sends Jim a link to catlove.com, asking him to visit the site. The owners of catlove.com are so passionate about cats that they have included some malicious code on their website to trick people like Jim. See figure 9.10.

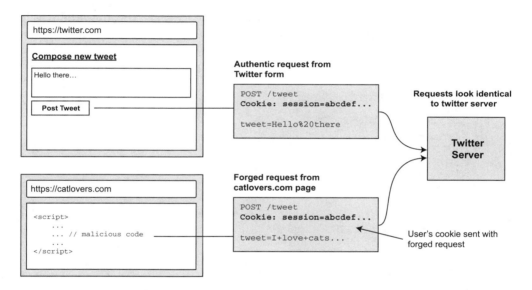

Figure 9.10   Without CSRF protection in place, authentic and forged requests look identical to servers.

The malicious code crafts a request to twitter.com, which posts a tweet saying "I LOVE CATS <3<3<3". Because Jim is already logged into Twitter, his Twitter session cookie will be sent along with the request, so Twitter will think it's him making this request, even though the request was craftily sent from the catlovers.com website.

In this example, Twitter is only checking that the request came from Jim's browser and not enforcing that it was Jim himself who made the request. This is the central weakness exploited by CSRF attacks. It doesn't take much imagination to see how the same process could be used to send requests to banks to forge international money transfers or do about anything evil that you can do on the web.

In reality, the catlovers.com's trick isn't going to work because Twitter knows all about CSRF and has taken steps to prevent CSRF attacks like poor Jim could have suffered. This section shows you how to protect your apps from CSRF exploits.

First we'll build our own little exploit to understand CSRF a little more and then we'll work on fixing this security hole with CSRF tokens using the hapijs plugin Crumb.

9.4.1   *Combatting CSRF attacks with CSRF tokens*

There are several mitigation strategies that web applications can take to protect themselves from CSRF, but by far, the most reliable and simplest way is using CSRF tokens.

The "Compose new Tweet" form on twitter.com has a hidden form field called `authenticity_token`, whose value is a CSRF token. The value of this field is unique for every user and every session. When the form is posted, the server compares the value of the `authenticity_token` it receives from the form submission with the value it sent in the HTML of the form page. If they're not the same, the request isn't allowed. See figure 9.11 for an illustration.

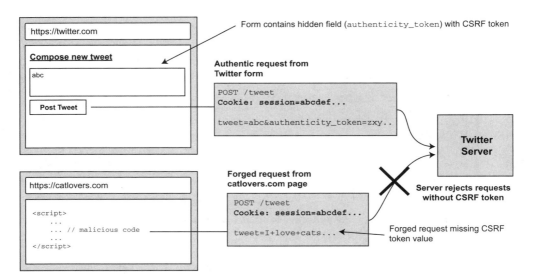

Figure 9.11   CSRF attacks can be prevented by requiring a CSRF token to be present in requests.

Even if catlovers.com is able to send a cross-domain request to twitter.com on behalf of Jim, it has no way of knowing what the correct `authenticity_token` value should be, so the server will reject the request.

9.4.2   *Understanding CSRF by creating our own exploit*

Before learning how to combat CSRF attacks in hapi, as a fun exercise, let's create a quick exploit of our own. We're then going to see how we could have protected against this by using Crumb. You'll then be able to use this as a template for adding CSRF protection to your own apps.

The sample app used in this exploit is a simple hapi website. There's a home page with a personal status message and a form for updating your status. The status for a user is stored in their session, as shown in listing 9.24.

If this were a real app, we'd want to ensure that the status could only be updated by the user filling out the form and hitting submit. But we're not going to add any CSRF protection to start with.

Listing 9.24   index.js: sample app vulnerable to CSRF

```
const Hapi = require('hapi');
const Path = require('path');

const server = new Hapi.Server();
server.connection({ port: 4000 });

server.register([
    require('vision'),
    require('hapi-auth-cookie')
], (err) => {

    if (err) {
        throw err;
    }

    server.views({
        engines: {
            hbs: require('handlebars')
        },
        layout: true,
        path: Path.join(__dirname, 'views'),
        isCached: false
    });

    server.auth.strategy('session', 'cookie', {
        password: 'password-that-is-at-least-32-chars',
        isSecure: false
    });

    server.route([{
        method: 'GET',
        path: '/',
        config: {
            auth: {
                strategy: 'session',
                mode: 'try'                          ← Attempt but don't
            },                                         require authentication
            handler: function (request, reply) {

                const message = request.auth.isAuthenticated ?   ← If user isn't
                    request.auth.credentials.message :             authenticated, create
                    'Feeling great!';                              for them a session with
                request.cookieAuth.set({ message: message });      default status message
                reply.view('index', { message: message });   ← Renders home page with
            }                                                    current status and
        }                                                        update status form
    }
```

```
    }, {
        method: 'POST',
        path: '/change',
        config: {
            auth: 'session',
            handler: function (request, reply) {

                request.cookieAuth.set({ message: request.payload.message });
                reply.redirect('/');
            }
        }
    }, {
        method: 'GET',
        path: '/evil',
        handler: {
            view: 'evil'
        }
    }]);

    server.start((err) => {

        if (err) {
            throw err;
        }

        console.log('Started server!');
    });
});
```

Endpoint to update current
status, requested by form,
but also open to CSRF

Renders view containing
CSRF exploit

This basic app also has two Handlebars views and a layout template, which are both
minimal, as shown in the following listing.

Listing 9.25   views/layout.hbs: the layout template

```
<!DOCTYPE html>
<html lang="en">
<head>
    <meta charset="UTF-8">
    <title>Document</title>
</head>
<body>
    {{{content}}}
</body>
</html>
```

index.hbs shows the status message and contains the form that lets the user update
their status, as shown in the next listing.

Listing 9.26   views/index.hbs: the home page form template

```
<h1>Current Status: {{message}}</h1>

<form action="/change" method="POST">
    <label for="message">Update status: </label>
    <input type="text" name="message"/>
```

```
    <input type="submit" value="Submit">
</form>
```

Now it's time to be a little evil and exploit this unassuming app. We'll add another view called evil.hbs. Inside we'll place some JavaScript that will forge a request to silently update the current user's status, as shown in the following listing.

Listing 9.27 views/evil.hbs: template with ill intent

```
<form id="evilForm" action="http://localhost:4000/change" method="post">
    <input type="hidden" name="message" value="Feeling evil!"/>
</form>

<script>
    document.getElementById('evilForm').submit();      ◁── When page loads, form
</script>                                                   automatically submitted
                                                           without our knowledge
```

Navigating to /evil will show a page that seems to quickly redirect to the home page. What's happening is that it's submitting a forged form with JavaScript in the background. The status message on the home page will be updated to "Current Status: Feeling evil!" If we load the page at http://127.0.0.1:4000/evil, this will work too. We're not performing an AJAX request here, merely submitting a simple form so CORS doesn't apply.

Hopefully this little exploit will have highlighted to you the terrifying possibilities of CSRF exploits. Keen to avoid them in your apps? Keep on reading.

9.4.3 *Protecting HTML forms using Crumb*

Crumb is a hapi plugin that makes protecting your HTML forms from CSRF exploits easy. We'll fix the example now from the previous section using Crumb.

> **NPM PACKAGE**   crumb v6 (www.npmjs.com/package/crumb)

First things first. We need to install Crumb and register it with our server, as seen in the following listing.

Listing 9.28 index.js: add Crumb to the list of plugins

```
...

server.register([
    require('vision'),
    require('hapi-auth-cookie'),
    require('crumb')                        ◁── Include Crumb in list
], (err) => {                                   of registered plugins
...
```

If you were to try the status update form again at this point, you'll find it doesn't work anymore because Crumb is now watching every request your server receives. When Crumb sees an incoming POST request, such as that from an HTML form, it checks whether there's a `crumb` property in the parsed payload. If not, it responds immediately to the request with a 403 Forbidden response.

Great, so no more CSRF exploits are possible. But our form doesn't work anymore. All we need to do to fix that is to make sure the `crumb` value is sent along with our form submission.

As a convenience, the Crumb plugin places a value called `crumb` in our default view context, so we can pop it in a hidden form field and we're done, as shown in the following listing.

> **Listing 9.29   views/index.hbs: add a hidden `crumb` field to the update status form**

```
<h1>Current Status: {{message}}</h1>

<form action="/change" method="POST">
    <input type="hidden" name="crumb" value="{{crumb}}"/>        ◁⎯⎯ Hidden field
    <label for="message">Update status: </label>                     containing crumb
    <input type="text" name="message"/>                              value (the CSRF token)
    <input type="submit" value="Submit">
</form>
```

Now our form will work successfully by passing along the correct `crumb` every time we submit the form. The exploit page at /evil won't work anymore, though, because it won't be submitting the `crumb` value along with the form.

You may be wondering about now whether a would-be attacker could make an AJAX request first to the form page and grab the `crumb` from the form before submitting their forged request along with the scraped `crumb`?

Remember that the browser under the same-origin policy wouldn't allow such a request. It's important therefore that you don't allow CORS requests to pages that display the `crumb` value in their response HTML. Otherwise, you're allowing exactly this kind of circumvention of the CSRF protection to take place.

9.4.4   *Protecting RESTful APIs using Crumb*

You can protect HTML forms from CSRF attacks. Big deal. You're probably sitting there now thinking "HTML forms are sooo last decade. Nowadays it's all about single-page apps and APIs—get with the times, Matt."

Crumb also has a `restful` setting (as you may already know, REST is an architectural style for designing web applications or services). Once enabled, hapi will look for your `crumb` in a request header named `X-CSRF-Token` instead of in a payload, as shown in the following listing. This applies to any request using methods PUT, POST, PATCH, or DELETE.

> **Listing 9.30   index.js: setting the `restful` option in Crumb**

```
...
server.register([
    require('vision'),
    require('hapi-auth-cookie'),
```

```
    {
        register: require('crumb'),
        options: { restful: true }
    }
], (err) => {
...
```
◁─── **Switch on the restful setting for crumb**

We can adapt our example to send the status update request as an AJAX request with a PUT method to illustrate this, instead of the simple `<form>` approach.

Listing 9.31 views/index.hbs: submitting the form via an AJAX request and PUT method

```
<h1>Current Status: {{message}}</h1>

<input name="status" type="text" id="status">
<button id="submit">Update status</button>

<script>

    var submitButton = document.getElementById('submit');
    submitButton.addEventListener('mouseup', function (e) {

        var message = document.getElementById('status').value;

        var req = new XMLHttpRequest();
        req.open("PUT", "http://localhost:4000/change", true);
        req.setRequestHeader("X-CSRF-Token", '{{crumb}}');
        req.setRequestHeader("Content-Type", 'application/json');
        req.send(JSON.stringify({ message: message }));
        req.onload = function () {

            location.reload();
        }
    });
</script>
```

Set an X-CSRF-Token header containing the crumb (CSRF token) value ─▷ (points to `req.setRequestHeader("X-CSRF-Token", '{{crumb}}');`)

To get access to the `crumb` value here, we need to have our script contained within a view, or provided via some global JavaScript variable. If you don't like these methods, another approach is to have a single dedicated endpoint that responds with the crumb value for a user. It's *important*, as previously mentioned, that this endpoint is not accessible from other origins (no CORS settings)—otherwise, you run the risk of undermining the CSRF protection altogether. See the following listing.

Listing 9.32 A dedicated route for generating crumb (CSRF token) values

```
server.route({
    method: 'GET',
    path: '/generate',
    handler: function (request, reply) {

        return reply({ crumb: request.plugins.crumb });
    }
});
```
◁─── **crumb value available in handler at request.plugins.crumb**

It can be easy to forget about CSRF when building apps. You usually want to get stuff working quickly, and security can go by the wayside. Installing Crumb early on in your development is a simple, foolproof way of putting security first.

9.5   *Security headers*

There are several common security-related response headers that can be set by servers. These are all controlled through a single route configuration option in hapi called `security`. The simplest way to set the headers is with the value `true`, as shown in the following listing.

> **Listing 9.33   Setting `security` to `true`, all headers to default values**

```
server.route({
    config: {
        security: true
    },
    method: 'GET',
    path: '/',
    handler: function (request, reply) {

        ...

    }
});
```

Alternatively, a finer-grain of control is possible by setting an object with properties to control each header, as shown in the next listing.

> **Listing 9.34   Individual headers can be controlled by setting an object**

```
server.route({
    config: {
        security: {
            hsts: {
                maxAge: 15768000,
                includeSubDomains: true,
                preload: true
            },
            xframe: 'sameorigin'
        }
    },
    method: 'GET',
    path: '/',
    handler: function (request, reply) {

        ...

    }
});
```

Table 9.1 contains a full list of the headers that `security` controls and the possible values for each setting.

Table 9.1 Headers controlled by `config.security` route option

Setting	Header	Possible setting values	Default value
hsts	`Strict-Transport-Security`	`true`, `false`, or an object with `maxAge`, `includeSubDomains` and `preload` properties	`true` (sets `maxAge` to `15768000`)
	Informs a client that it should only communicate with the server using secure (HTTPS) connections for the period of `maxAge` seconds. Prevents man-in-the-middle attacks when sites may be initially communicated with using HTTP rather than HTTPS. This header is ignored by browsers when a resource is accessed using HTTP.		
xframe	`X-Frame-Options`	`true`, `false`, `'deny'`, `'sameorigin'` or an object with `rule` and `source` properties	`true` (sets header to `deny`)
	Indicates to a browser whether the response content should be allowed to be rendered in a `<frame>`, `<iframe>`, or `<object>` tag. `deny` prevents embedded, `sameorigin` means it can be embedded on the same origin. To allow specific origins, you should use an object with rule set to allow-from.		
xss	`X-XSS-PROTECTION`	`true` or `false`	`true`
	Enables cross-site scripting filter built into browsers.		
noOpen	`X-Download-Options`	`true` or `false`	`true` (sets header to `'noopen'`)
	Internet Explorer-specific header, controlling visibility of Open button on download dialog.		
noSniff	`X-Content-Type-Options`	`true` or `false`	`true` (sets header to `'nosniff'`)
	Helps prevent attacks based on MIME-type mismatches		

9.6   Summary

- Authentication is based around the concepts of schemes and strategies—you can use a pre-made scheme, such as `basic` provided by the hapi-auth-basic plugin, to define your own auth strategy. You then apply the strategy to your routes.
- Authentication scopes provide basic authorization functionality.
- You can use different authentication modes such as `try` and `optional` for routes without mandatory authentication.
- Bell offers a simple way to implement third-party authentication using a choice of providers including Facebook, Twitter, and Google.
- Crumb provides CSRF protection for forms and REST APIs.
- hapi provides a number of options to make dealing with CORS straightforward. These can be set at the route, connection, or server level.

Testing with Lab, Code, and server.inject()

This chapter covers

- Writing and running tests with Lab
- Writing assertions with Code
- Testing hapi servers
- Using test spies, stubs, and mocks

Testing is a fundamental practice in the production of quality software, but there are a lot of dogma and strong opinions around testing. Regardless of whether you believe in test-first development or you write all your tests after you've finished building features, you *should* be writing tests.

The hapi contributors themselves are fully committed to testing every line of code they write. All hapi.js core projects are tested to 100% coverage. This 100% rule is enforced by default by hapi's test runner, called Lab.

Aside from its use in the development of hapi itself, Lab is a tool that can be used by application developers to test their own software. In fact many of the tools that are used to write hapi itself are available for you to use to achieve the same level of quality and confidence in your code. These utilities include Lab (the test runner) and Code (an assertion library). There are also several other features built into hapi to make testing easier, such as the `server.inject()` method. This chapter covers these tools, along with some other important testing-related concepts like spies, stubs, and mocks.

10.1 Introduction to Lab

If you've ever worked with Express or any other Node web frameworks before hapi, it's possible that you've met Mocha. Mocha is a *test runner*. As the name suggests, it runs tests that you write and tells you whether they passed or not.

> **NPM PACKAGE** `lab` v10 (www.npmjs.com/package/lab)

Lab is a tool based on Mocha (in fact, it started out as a direct fork of Mocha) written by the hapi contributors. It's designed to be simpler to use than Mocha, with fewer features and a smaller codebase. If you have prior experience with Mocha, picking up Lab will be a breeze for you.

In this section we're going to write some simple tests and run them using Lab. We're also going to look at a couple of ways to structure your Lab tests to keep them well organized.

10.1.1 Your first test

There are a couple of ways to install Lab. We're going to start with the most convenient way, which is to install it as a global dependency, and then later we'll look at a cleaner way. To install Lab as a global dependency, append the `-g` flag to the command:

```
npm install -g lab@10
```

> **NOTE** npm packages that are installed globally will often link an executable into your PATH space. In the case of Lab, it will link the lab script to the command `lab`.

To use Lab, we'll first need to write a test. We'll start with a simple test, shown in the following listing, that compares the result of an addition of two numbers.

Listing 10.1 The simplest lab test possible

```
                                                          Load Node's built-in
                                                          assertion module
const Assert = require('assert');         ◁
const Lab = require('lab');
                                                       Create, export script object
const lab = exports.lab = Lab.script();   ◁           (required by all Lab test scripts)

lab.test('addition should add two numbers together', (done) => {    ◁

    Assert(1 + 1 === 2);          ◁      Every test case should have        Define a single test case.
    done();                              at least one assertion             Parameters are
});                                                                         description of test case
                                                                            and callback function.
```

Load Lab package → (points to `const Lab = require('lab');`)

Calling done() signifies test case complete → (points to `done();`)

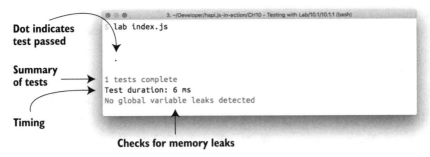

Figure 10.1   Lab's output for a successful test

We can run the test in listing 10.1 by placing this code in a file—for instance, called index.js—and then running `lab index.js` in a terminal window. The output is shown in figure 10.1.

Let's modify the test slightly so it fails instead. We can do this by making a false assertion in a test case, as in the next listing.

Listing 10.2   Test with an incorrect assertion

```
...

lab.test('addition should add two numbers together', (done) => {

    Assert(1 + 1 === 10);          ◁——  An incorrect
    done();                              assertion
});
```

If we run the test again with Lab, we'll get a different output (see figure 10.2). This time our test case has failed. Lab tells us exactly which test has failed by printing out the

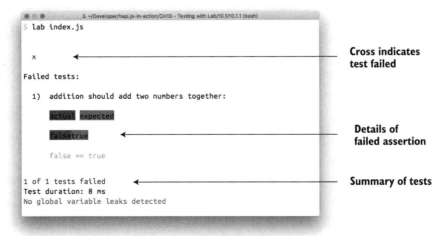

Figure 10.2   Lab's output for an unsuccessful test

description we wrote. Lab also tells us which assertion was incorrect. In this case we were asserting something that was false (that 1 + 1 equals 10) and expecting it to be true.

10.1.2 *Lab as a local dependency*

The previous section mentioned that there was a cleaner way to install Lab and run tests than the global approach. You can install Lab as a local dependency in your project, like any other npm dependency. Typically, Lab is only used in development, so you can install as a dev dependency in a project with a package.json:

```
npm install --save-dev lab@10
```

To run Lab when installed locally like this, you can make use of the powerful npm scripts functionality. npm scripts are simple, aliased commands that you can define in your package.json. For instance, we can define a test script:

```
{
  "name": "my-project",
  "description": "A well tested piece of software",
  "version": "1.0.0",
  "scripts": {
    "test": "lab"
  }
}
```

We can then run this script by typing npm test into a terminal. npm will take care of resolving the lab command within the locally installed dependencies. No need for polluting global dependencies any more.

We can do even better than this, though. We can leave off the filename of our test altogether in our lab command. When there's no file/directory specified when running Lab, it will default to looking for tests in the ./test folder. This is how we'd normally structure our code when using Lab, with all our tests inside ./test.

10.1.3 *Organizing tests with experiments*

We've already seen how to write a test case with Lab by calling the lab.test(description, callback) method. Typically, a real-world test script will contain many of these test cases in order to probe all avenues of your code. You can organize related tests into experiments. An *experiment* is like a container or group of test cases. To create a experiment, we call lab.experiment(description, callback), as shown in the following listing.

Listing 10.3   Grouping test cases with experiments

```
const Assert = require('assert');
const Lab = require('lab');
const lab = exports.lab = Lab.script();

lab.experiment('basic arithmetic', () => {                    Define scope of
                                                              new experiment
```

```
lab.test('+ should add numbers together', (done) => {        ⟵

    Assert(1 + 1 === 2);
    done();
});
                                                                        Test cases
lab.test('- should subtract numbers', (done) => {           ⟵          are within
                                                                        experiment
    Assert(10 - 2 === 8);
    done();
});

});
                                                           Define scope of
lab.experiment('modular arithmetic', () => {      ⟵─┘      new experiment

    lab.test('% should perform modulus', (done) => {         ⟵

        Assert((5 + 3) % 6 === 2);
        done();
    });
});
```

10.1.4 Asynchronous by default

You've probably noticed the required done parameter in each of our test case call-backs. We call this done function once we've made all the assertions that we need to to ensure our test passes. Other test runners have such a concept, and it's usually optional. In Lab, done is required in every test case, even if that test case is entirely synchronous.

All the tests we've written so far have been synchronous tests, but the purpose of the done parameter is to allow for asynchronous tests.

Listing 10.4   Asynchronous test with a problem

```
const Assert = require('assert');
const Lab = require('lab');

const lab = exports.lab = Lab.script();

lab.test('setTimeout() should cause a delay', (done) => {

    const start = Date.now();

    setTimeout(() => {
                                                        Assertion statement
        Assert(Date.now() - start > 1000);    ⟵─┘      executes after test is over
    }, 1000);
                                            done() is called
    done();                          ⟵─┘   too soon
});
```

In this test, we're checking that setTimeout runs the callback function after at least 1 s. But *there's a problem with this test*. If we run the test, the output contains this line:

```
Test duration: 7 ms
```

How can a test that is testing whether something takes longer than a second finish in only 7 ms? The problem is that we're calling done() before our setTimeout callback actually executes. To fix this test, we simply move done() inside the setTimeout, as shown next.

Listing 10.5   Test is fixed

```
setTimeout(() => {

    Assert(Date.now() - start > 1000);          done() is now called once
    done();                                       assertion has been checked
}, 1000);
...
```

This test now takes over 1,000 ms to complete, with the assertion actually taking place. It's important that you remember to conclude your tests with done() at the right point—otherwise you may not be testing everything you thought you were. And don't forget to call done() altogether, or your tests will simply timeout and fail waiting for done() to be called.

10.1.5 *Lab syntax flavors*

A couple of popular styles of writing tests have emerged over the years. We'll call these the BDD (behavior-driven development), or describe/it, and the TDD suite/test (test-driven development) styles. The language they use when writing tests is a little different, but the differences are purely in naming. Lab supports both styles, as shown in listings 10.6 and 10.7.

Listing 10.6   Using the TDD suite/test pattern

```
const Assert = require('assert');
const Lab = require('lab');
const lab = exports.lab = Lab.script();

const suite = lab.suite;          Make aliases for suite
const test = lab.test;            and test to save typing

suite('basic arithmetic', () => {

    test('+ adds numbers together', (done) => {

        Assert(1 + 1 === 2);
        done();
    });
});
```

The BDD styles use the identifiers `describe` and `it` in place of `test` and `suite`.

Listing 10.7 Using the BDD describe/it pattern

```
const Assert = require('assert');
const Lab = require('lab');
const lab = exports.lab = Lab.script();

const describe = lab.describe;
const it = lab.test;

describe('basic arithmetic', () => {

    it('+ adds numbers together', (done) => {

        Assert(1 + 1 === 2);
        done();
    });
});
```

You should recognize that these are entirely stylistic differences. `lab.describe` and `lab.suite` are both aliases for `lab.experiment`. This is shown in table 10.1. Just pick whichever style you prefer or are used to working with from other frameworks.

Table 10.1   Aliases for `lab.experiment` and `lab.test`

Aliases of `lab.experiment()`	Aliases of `lab.test()`
`lab.experiment()`	`lab.test()`
`lab.describe()`	`lab.it()`
`lab.suite()`	

10.2 *Making assertions with the Code assertion library*

At the heart of our tests are assertions. By writing assertions, we probe our apps for unwanted conditions and confirm desired conditions. *Assertions* are simple statements that do one of two things: if a condition is the desired value, the statement does nothing. If the condition is contrary to the desired value, the statement throws an error. The thrown error from an assertion statement is caught by our test runner, and that's how it knows the state of our tests.

So far, we've been using Node's built-in `assert` module to write assertions. This module has some convenient methods for writing assertions, such as the following:

```
Assert(1 + 1 === 2);
Assert.equal(1 + 1, 2);
Assert.notEqual(typeof var, 'object');
Assert.deepEqual([1,2,3], [1,2].concat([3]));
```

But there are many more types of assertion statements that we might want to write that aren't conveniently provided by `assert`. In that case, we can turn to more powerful assertion libraries, such as Code.

10.2.1 *What is the Code assertion library?*

Imagine that we're writing an HTTP parser and want to test whether a value called headers is an object and contains a property called content-type and a property called accept. The assert module doesn't give us any convenient way of writing this assertion. We'd have to write several assertions like so:

```
Assert(typeof headers === 'object');
Assert('content-type' in headers);
Assert('accept' in headers);
```

A property of good tests is that they read almost like prose. Unfortunately, fragmented assertions like the preceding get in the way of that.

> **NPM PACKAGE**   code v2 (www.npmjs.com/package/code)

Code is an alternative assertion library that lets you express an assertion with the same meaning as the previous example in a single statement:

```
expect(headers).to.be.an.object().and.contain(['accept', 'content-type']);
```

Read that statement aloud, and it sounds pretty much like English. When you write assertions like that, tests are a lot easier to read. Another benefit of using an assertion library like Code over Node's built-in Assert library is for the quality of error messages that you get when assertions fail. The following listing compares the two.

> **Listing 10.8   Comparing Assert and Code assertion libraries**

```
const Assert = require('assert');
const Code = require('code');
const Lab = require('lab');

const expect = Code.expect;
const lab = exports.lab = Lab.script();
const test = lab.test;

const headers = {
    accept: '...'
};

test('ensure headers is correct format (using assert)', (done) => {

    Assert(typeof headers === 'object');          Using Assert
    Assert('content-type' in headers);
    Assert('accept' in headers);
    done();
});
```
The same assertion using Code
```
test('ensure headers is correct format (using code)', (done) => {

    expect(headers).to.be.an.object().and.contain(['accept', 'content-type']);
    done();
});
```

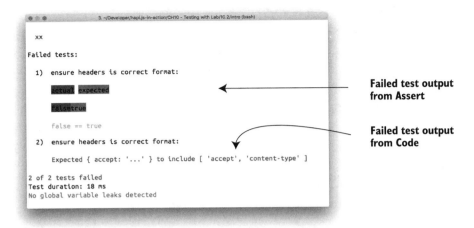

Failed test output from Assert

Failed test output from Code

Figure 10.3   Code's error messages are vastly more helpful for failing tests.

Assert's error message isn't helpful at all, simply telling us something was `false` that should be `true`. Well, duh!

Code's error message tells us what was wrong as you can see in figure 10.3. You could technically use plain old `Assert()` for everything, but the more specific an assertion is written, the better quality the error message—which is invaluable when debugging.

10.2.2 *Code's grammar: structure of an assertion*

Every assertion you write with Code follows a specific structure, as illustrated in figure 10.4.

Flags don't necessarily always come after connecting words. You can add connecting words wherever they make the most sense to create something that reads like an

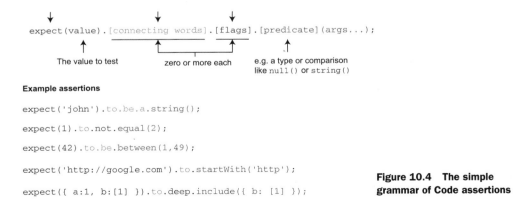

Figure 10.4   The simple grammar of Code assertions

English sentence. For instance, in the following assertion, the flag `not` comes in between other connecting words:

```
expect(1).to.not.be.a.string();
```

We'll now look at the various parts of an assertion and see examples of each.

EXPECT(VALUE)

This statement kicks off the assertion. The value under test can be any valid JavaScript value, including strings, objects, functions, and numbers. Even special built-in object types like `Error` or `Buffer` can be tested. You can also provide a short descriptive prefix, which is then used in error messages for failed tests:

```
expect(err, 'http request err').to.be.null();
```

CONNECTING WORDS

There are several connecting words, which look like properties in assertions (connected by periods):

- a
- an
- and
- at
- be
- have
- in
- to

These exist to make your assertion read like grammatically correct English. They don't have any effect on the meaning of the assertion. Note that the following two assertions behave *exactly* the same way, except for one is missing the connecting words:

```
expect(123).to.be.a.number();
expect(123).number();
```

FLAGS

Flags are similar to connecting words in that they come between the `expect(value)` part of an assertion and the predicate. They shouldn't be confused, though. Flags *do* change the meaning of the assertion. The valid flags are shown in table 10.2.

Table 10.2 Code assertion statement flags

Flag	Meaning

deep	Tells Code to do comparisons deeply rather than strictly.
	
	`const a = { a: 1 };`
	`const b = { a: 1 };`
	
	In the preceding code, a and b aren't strictly equal because they're references to independent objects stored at a different location in memory. But if we look deeper than that, they are equal in the sense that all their properties are the same. We say they're *deeply equal*.

Table 10.2   Code assertion statement flags *(continued)*

Flag	Meaning

deep	```const a = { a: 1 };```
	```const b = { a: 2 };```
	
	In the preceding code, a and b are *not strictly equal* nor *deeply equal* because they're different objects and their properties aren't equal.
	Can be used in assertions like so:
	```expect([{ a: 1 }]).to.deep.include({ a: 1 });```

not	Inverses the assertion outcome. A true assertion becomes a false one and vice-versa: ```expect(1).to.not.be.a.string();```
once	Used with an ```include()``` predicate. Ensures the value is only included *once* in the compared object: ```expect([1,2,2]).to.once.include(1);```
only	Used with an ```include()``` predicate. Ensures the value is the *only* thing included in the compared object: ```expect([1]).to.only.include(1);```
part	Used with an ```include()``` predicate. Allows a partial match: ```expect([1,2,2]).to.part.include([1,5,6]);```

Multiple flags can be used at once—for instance, in the assertion:

```
expect({ name: 'mary', age: 48 }).to.not.deep.include({ age: 24 });
```

PREDICATES

Predicates are the central part of an assertion and come in many flavors. Some accept arguments and some don't. There are predicates to assert that a value is of a specific type. Some examples:

- ```expect(...).to.be.a.string();```
- ```expect(...).to.be.a.number();```
- ```expect(...).to.be.a.object();```
- ```expect(...).to.be.a.array();```
- ```expect(...).to.be.a.function();```

There are also predicates that can check for specific values that we commonly check for in tests:

- ```expect(...).to.be.true();```
- ```expect(...).to.be.false();```
- ```expect(...).to.be.null();```
- ```expect(...).to.be.undefined();```

There are many more for making comparisons. Some examples include:

- ```expect(...).to.have.length(100);```
- ```expect(...).to.be.at.least(21);```

- `expect(...).to.match(/[a-zA-z]+/);`
- `expect(...).to.be.an.instanceof(Error);`

Consult the Code documentation for a full list of predicates.

This section has given you the theoretical background to write powerful and expressive assertions using the Code library. Now you should be ready to put your new superpowers to good use by testing real hapi applications using Code and Lab.

10.3 *Testing hapi servers with server.inject()*

Imagine we have a hapi route that returns the sum of two query string parameters, as in the following listing.

Listing 10.9   A hapi route that adds together query string parameters

```
server.route({
    config: {
        validate: {
            query: {
                a: Joi.number(),        Ensure query parameters are validated
                b: Joi.number()         and coerced to numbers if possible
            }
        }
    },
    method: 'GET',
    path: '/add',
    handler: function (request, reply) {
                                                     Respond with query
        reply(request.query.a + request.query.b);  ◁── params added together
    }
});
```

To test this route, we could write a test that starts our server listening on a port, use Wreck in our test to make an HTTP request, and then inspect the response. This involves quite a bit of overhead, though, and will slow things down for large test suites. When running tests, speed is important.

There's a superb feature in hapi that allows you to test routes without making real HTTP requests. The feature is a method called `server.inject()`.

> **HAPI API**   `server.inject(options, [callback])`   (http://hapijs.com/api# serverinjectoptions-callback)

`server.inject()` is a method that allows you to simulate a request to your hapi server. It pushes a request through your routes without the need for any network interaction. This is incredibly useful for building fast tests.

10.3.1 *Readying servers for testing*

When testing with `server.inject()`, you don't need to start your server to actually listen on a port and make HTTP requests. You interact directly with the `server` object instead.

To be able to test your hapi application with `server.inject()`, you need to be able to load the server object inside your tests and ensure that all the plugins have finished loading. There are various different patterns for doing this, but a simple approach I like, shown in the following listing, is to have a module export a function that I can call asynchronously to prepare and return the server.

Listing 10.10 index.js: encapsulating server construction in a module for easy testing

```
const Hapi = require('hapi');
const Joi = require('joi');

module.exports = function (callback) {        ◁─┐ Export an async function,
                                                 │ returns server object and null
    const server = new Hapi.Server();            │ err argument (to follow
    server.connection({ port: 4000 });           │ standard Node callback pattern)

    server.route({
        config: {
            validate: {
                query: {
                    a: Joi.number(),
                    b: Joi.number()
                }
            }
        },
        method: 'GET',
        path: '/add',
        handler: function (request, reply) {

            reply(request.query.a + request.query.b);
        }
    });

    callback(null, server);
};
```

When running the application, you can have a separate startup script, which loads the server and starts it up, as in the next listing.

Listing 10.11 start.js: startup script for application

```
const Server = require('./index');

Server((err, server) => {

    if (err) {
        throw err;
    }

    server.start((err) => {
```

```
            if (err) {
                throw err;
            }
            console.log('Server started!');
        });
    });
```

We can also use the `before` function in Lab to fetch our server before running our tests. Using this pattern, as the next listing shows, we can ensure we have a fully prepared server object for use in tests.

Listing 10.12 test/index.js: using Lab's `before` feature to load server object

```
'use strict';

const Code = require('code');
const Lab = require('lab');

const expect = Code.expect;
const lab = exports.lab = Lab.script();
const test = lab.test;
const before = lab.before;

let server;

before((done) => {

    require('..')((err, srv) => {

        server = srv;
        done();
    });
});

test('it adds two numbers', (done) => {

    server.inject('/add?a=1&b=2', (res) => {

        expect(res.payload).to.equal('3');
        done();
    });
});
```

Export async function, returns server object and null err argument (to follow standard Node callback pattern)

Get server object

Assign server object to server variable in outer scope

10.3.2 *The server.inject() response parameter*

When we use `server.inject()`, the callback contains a response parameter, named res in listing 10.12:

```
server.inject('/add?a=1&b=2', (res) => {

    expect(res.payload).to.equal('3');
    done();
});
```

This is the response from our application. We can inspect the `res` parameter to confirm that the response matched our expectations in a test. The following is a list of the main properties that you would write assertions for on this response object:

- `statusCode`—The response HTTP status code (200, 404, and so on).
- `result`—The original value passed to reply in the route handler.
- `headers`—An object containing the headers in key-value pairs.
- `payload`—The response payload fully read as a UTF-8 encoded string. Note that no parsing happens here. If the tested route returns JSON, you must parse it yourself to write assertions against property values.
- `rawPayload`—The response payload fully read as a `Buffer` object. Use this for testing binary or non UTF-8 responses.

10.3.3 *Testing with request payloads*

In the previous section we used `server.inject()` in its simplest form to make a GET request to a URL. But `server.inject()` lets you simulate more complex requests to, for example, test POST routes with payloads.

Let's look at testing a more complex route. This route for creating a new user, shown in the following listing, expects a POSTed payload with user info. It assigns a timestamp to the user and responds with the full user object.

Listing 10.13   A route we want to test that processes a POSTed user object

```
const Hapi = require('hapi');
const Joi = require('joi');

module.exports = function (callback) {

    const server = new Hapi.Server();
    server.connection({ port: 4000 });

    const schema = {
        name: {
            first: Joi.string().required(),
            last: Joi.string().required()
        },
        age: Joi.number().required()
    };

    server.route({
        config: {
            validate: {
                payload: schema
            }
        },
        method: 'POST',
        path: '/user',
        handler: function (request, reply) {
            const user = request.payload;
            user.createdAt = Date.now();
```

Validation schema for the expected payload

Add timestamp to user object

```
            return reply(user);                    ⊲┐  Respond with updated
        }                                           │  user object
    });

    return callback(null, server);
};
```

We want to write a couple of tests here. First of all, we want to write a test that confirms that the route responds with the same user data that it is sent. We also want to check for the presence of a `createdAt` field, as in the following listing.

Listing 10.14   Using server.inject() with a payload

```
experiment('Test POST /user', () => {

    test('creates a user', (done) => {

        const user = {
            name: {
                first: 'Craig',               Prepare a test
                last: 'Railton'               payload
            },
            age: 30
        };

        const options = {
            method: 'POST',
            url: '/user',                      Include payload in
            payload: user              ⊲┘     server.inject() options
        };

        const start = Date.now();

        server.inject(options, (res) => {
                                                          Expect response to
            expect(res.statusCode).to.equal(200);         include original payload
            expect(res.result).to.deep.include(user);  ⊲┘
            expect(res.result.createdAt)
                .to.be.greaterThan(start).and
                .to.be.lessThan(Date.now());
            done();
        });
    });
});
```
Expect response to include `createdAt` property ┆──▷ (points to `expect(res.result.createdAt)` lines)

We should also add another test to make sure that our payload is properly validated and, for example, doesn't allow `age` to be a non-numeric string, as shown in the following listing.

Listing 10.15   Testing with an invalid payload

```
experiment('Test POST /user', () => {

    ...
```

```
test('age must be a number or numeric string', (done) => {

    const user = {
        name: {
            first: 'Ana',
            last: 'Railton'
        },
        age: 'potato'
    };

    const options = {
        method: 'POST',
        url: '/user',
        payload: user
    };

    server.inject(options, (res) => {

        expect(res.statusCode).to.equal(400);
        expect(res.result.message).to.include('age').and.to.include('number');
        done();
    });
});
});
```

Include invalid property in payload

Expect 400 Bad Request response code

NOTE I believe that tests are the one place where DRY (*don't repeat yourself*) is less important than having independent, atomic, and self-documenting tests. My test cases often contain lots of repetition or code copied from other tests. That's because I believe that every test should be entirely self-contained and not rely on other test cases or shared or external data.

10.3.4 *Testing authenticated routes*

A couple of different approaches exist for testing routes that require authentication. Let's look at a route requiring HTTP basic authentication. The next code should be familiar to you from previous examples using hapi-auth-basic.

Listing 10.16   Route requiring basic auth

```
const validate = function (request, username, password, callback) {

    if (username === 'john' && password === 'secret') {
        return callback(null, true, { username: 'john' });
    }
    callback(null, false);
};

server.auth.strategy('basic', 'basic', { validateFunc: validate });

server.route({
    config: {
        auth: 'basic'
    },
```

```
    method: 'GET',
    path: '/',
    handler: function (request, reply) {

        reply('hello ' + request.auth.credentials.username);
    }
});
```

The most obvious way of testing this route is simply by emulating a real authenticated request. For instance, if you have a route that you want to test that is protected by HTTP basic authentication, you can test it by adding an appropriate `Authorization` header along with the `server.inject()` request, as in the following listing.

Listing 10.17 Authenticating by an Authorization header with server.inject()

```
test('Authenticates successfully', (done) => {

    const options = {
        method: 'GET',
        url: '/',
        headers: {
            authorization: 'Basic ' +
            ➥ new Buffer('john:secret').toString('base64')       ◁────┐
        }                                                               Manually include a
    };                                                                  properly constructed
                                                                        basic authentication
    server.inject(options, (res) => {                                   Authorization header

        expect(res.statusCode).to.equal(200);
        expect(res.payload).to.equal('hello john');
        done();
    });
});
```

This certainly works, but is authentication strategy dependent. hapi provides a more convenient way of testing authenticated routes. You can specify authentication credentials up front via an extra option with `server.inject()`. When credentials are provided this way, as in listing 10.18, the authentication stage is skipped entirely in the request lifecycle, and the provided credentials are directly set in `request.auth .credentials`. It's also a good idea to test that you can't access your route using a non-existent user.

Listing 10.18 Setting the credentials option with `server.inject()`

```
test('Authenticates successfully', (done) => {

    const options = {
        method: 'GET',
        url: '/',
```

```
        credentials: {
            username: 'steve'                    ⟵─┐ Set the server.inject()
        }                                            │ credentials option
    };

    server.inject(options, (res) => {

        expect(res.statusCode).to.equal(200);
        expect(res.payload).to.equal('hello steve');
        done();
    });
});

test('fails for a non-existent user', (done) => {    ⟵─┐ Check that a nonexistent
                                                         │ user gets a 401 error
    const options = {
        method: 'GET',
        url: '/',
        headers: {
            authorization: 'Basic ' + new Buf-
fer('steve:pass').toString('base64')
        }
    };

    server.inject(options, (res) => {

        expect(res.statusCode).to.equal(401);
        done();
    });
});
```

An advantage of using this approach is that you can change authentication strategies later on without having to alter your tests at all.

The next section dives deeper into more advanced features of Lab.

10.4 *Leveling up Lab*

You know now how to write tests for hapi applications, combining the test runner Lab and the powerful assertion library Code. Well, Lab can actually do a little bit more than run tests. In this section we'll be looking at some of those more advanced features, such as using different reporters, code coverage, and linting.

10.4.1 *Reporters*

Lab comes with support for multiple reporters. You can think about your tests as being Lab's input. The output of Lab depends on which reporter you use. By default, Lab uses the console reporter. The console reporter does as its name suggests and simply prints the result of your tests to the console.

To change reporter, you can use the -r flag when running Lab:

```
lab -r html
```

The console reporter is useful for checking your tests manually—say, before committing your code to source control. The output is designed for humans, though, and isn't convenient for machines to parse. Often test output will need to be integrated with other automated systems, like continuous integration servers or other testing and release tools.

The tap reporter produces output that conforms to the TAP (Test Anything Protocol) protocol. TAP is an attempt to standardize test output across multiple languages and frameworks. The TAP output is extremely simple and despite being designed to be machine parseable, it's also pretty readable by us humans, as the following listing shows.

Listing 10.19   Lab test output when using the TAP reporter

```
TAP version 13
1..2
ok 1 (1)  it adds two numbers
  ---
  duration_ms: 28
  ...
not ok 2 (2)  it does something else
  ---
  duration_ms: 7
  stack: |-
    Error: Expected '3' to equal specified value
  ...
# tests 2
# pass 1
# fail 1
# skipped 0
# todo 0
```

A growing number of testing and CI tools (such as Travis and Jenkins) can consume TAP output.

Table 10.3 contains a full list of the reporters that are available built into Lab and their uses.

Table 10.3   The built-in Lab reporters

Reporter	Description
console	The default reporter. Prints color-coded test output to the console.
html	Prints output as an HTML document. Contains code coverage too.
json	Outputs test results as JSON.
junit	Prints test results in the JUnit format supported by Jenkins, Hudson, and Bamboo.
tap	Prints results in the Test Anything Protocol (TAP) protocol format.
lcov	Print code coverage in lcov format.
clover	Prints code coverage in the clover format supported by Jenkins, Hudson, and Bamboo.

You can use multiple reporters at once, directing the output to different places using the -o flag. For instance, to output tap to the console and html to an HTML file, you can run the following command:

```
lab -r tap -o stdout -r html -o test.html
```

10.4.2 Code coverage

Code coverage is a measure of how well tested your code is. It's normally measured in percentage. If your code has 100% coverage, that means every possible path through your code base has tests associated with it to confirm that it behaves correctly.

Lab comes with a code coverage analyzer built in. Running Lab with the -c flag will enable code-coverage analysis. When using the console reporter, the coverage level will be printed to the console at the end of the tests:

```
$ lab -c

  .

1 tests complete
Test duration: 321 ms
No global variable leaks detected
Coverage: 100.00%
```

When coverage is found to be below 100%, the console reporter will tell you which lines of your code are missing tests—and that's extremely useful:

```
$ lab -c

  .

1 tests complete
Test duration: 284 ms
No global variable leaks detected
Coverage: 95.65% (1/23)
index.js missing coverage on line(s): 22
```

When coverage is enabled with -c flag, a minimum *threshold* for coverage is also set. If the coverage level is below this threshold, the test runner exits with a non-zero exit code. This will be interpreted as a failed build by tools like Travis. By default, the coverage threshold in Lab is 100%. That may sound unrealistically high, but all hapi.js projects have been tested to this level, and it's not as tough as it sounds once you start to think in the mindset of 100% code coverage. You can change this threshold (with -t 90 to set to 90% for example) but I challenge you to always achieve 100% code coverage in all your projects. The subtlest bugs often lie in those final few percentage points.

10.4.3 Linting

Code *linters* are tools that analyze code for syntax errors, confusing and redundant code, and stylistic errors. They help you catch silly mistakes and prevent you from releasing sloppy or incorrect code.

Lab depends on eslint, one such extensible linting tool. You can tell Lab to also run the linter when testing your code by adding the -L flag to your Lab command:

```
lab -L
```

Linting errors will be reported by Lab's console reporter at the end of the test report:

```
$ lab -L

.

1 tests complete
Test duration: 284 ms
No global variable leaks detected
Linting results:
        /Users/mattharrison/.../CH10 - Testing with lab/10.4/10.4.1/index.js:
          Line 1: strict - Use the global form of "use strict".
          Line 25: no-trailing-spaces - Trailing spaces not allowed.
```

As well as syntax errors, Lab's eslint configuration will report on stylistic issues to enforce the hapi.js style guide (http://hapijs.com/styleguide). This is enabled by custom eslint rules loaded by Lab.

10.4.4 Leaking globals

You may have noticed a line in Lab's console output that I haven't mentioned yet:

```
No global variable leaks detected
```

This lines comes from a Lab option that's enabled by default. When running your tests, Lab looks out for any new variables defined in the global space and warns you about them if any are defined. Global variables should be avoided, and if any are detected it's probably because you made a mistake such as forgetting to prefix variable declarations with `const`, `let`, or `var`. If Lab finds any new globals it will tell you about them in the output:

```
The following leaks were detected:name, i, j
```

10.4.5 Parallel test execution

By default, Lab will run in serial mode, executing your tests top down in a file. A test will not start running until the previous one in the test script has finished. Let's look at these two tests in the following listing.

Listing 10.20 Two simple test cases

```
test('it adds two numbers', (done) => {

    console.log('Starting test 1');

    server.inject('/add?a=1&b=2', (res) => {

        expect(res.statusCode).to.equal(200);
        expect(res.payload).to.equal('3');
```

```
        console.log('Finishing test 1');
        done();
    });
});

test('it multiplies two numbers', (done) => {

    console.log('Starting test 2');

    server.inject('/multiply?a=5&b=4', (res) => {

        expect(res.statusCode).to.equal(200);
        expect(res.payload).to.equal('20');
        console.log('Finishing test 2');
        done();
    });
});
```

If we run these tests using the default mode of Lab, the output will resemble the following:

```
Starting test 1
Finishing test 1
Starting test 2
Finishing test 2
```

We can make Lab run our tests in parallel, though, by using the -p flag. If we run our tests in parallel mode, the output will be this:

```
Starting test 1
Starting test 2
Finishing test 1
Finishing test 2
```

So why would we do this? Because it *could* make our tests run faster. And faster tests are always great. Especially when you have loads and your release cycles depend on fast builds.

Why did I say *could* make them run faster though? Is parallel not always faster? No. Remember Node is executing JavaScript in a single thread of execution on your CPU. Lab's parallel mode doesn't do multithreading. But if one of your tests is idle and not using the CPU (for instance, making a HTTP request or waiting on a timer to run to completion), another test can get busy executing.

If all your tests are purely synchronous and don't wait for any I/O or timers, then parallel mode probably won't buy you anything. But if you have tests doing network requests or reading databases, parallel mode could make a big difference to the speed of your tests.

If you do opt for parallel mode, you need to be absolutely sure that there are no race conditions in your tests. You shouldn't ever be doing things like setting a variable in one test and then using the value of that variable in another test—otherwise bad things will happen. You also shouldn't be creating resource conflicts such as reading and writing to the same files or database records when you expect to execute your tests in parallel.

10.5 Testing difficult-to-test code with stubs, spies, and monkey-patching

This section is all about how to test code that seems difficult or impossible to test. Sometimes you want to test code that calls other code that you don't want to test. For instance, you might have a route handler that saves a record to a database. You want to test the handler to make sure it responds with the correct response, but you might not want to actually test the database interaction.

The reason you don't want to test the database might be for one of the following reasons:

- Doing I/O is slow, and you want your tests to be fast.
- You already trust the DB layer, which has been tested well.
- You're testing the DB layer in another test, and there's no need to test it again.

There are several different solutions available to this dilemma, and we'll discuss a few in this section including monkey-patching, stubs, and spies. We'll start with the simplest first: monkey-patching.

10.5.1 Introduction to monkey-patching

By default JavaScript objects are open to modification (you can actually change this behavior using property descriptors, though). If you wanted to, you could modify the native `Math.round()` function to always return 42 no matter what value it's given:

```
Math.round = () => 42;

console.log(Math.round(41.6));          // 42 :)
console.log(Math.round(123.6));         // 42 :o
```

Overwriting existing methods like this is called *monkey-patching* and it's normally a terrible idea. But it can be convenient when testing. The things that make monkey-patching bad (confusing for people using your code, upgrade issues) don't always apply for tests, because they're often small and self-contained. You can also monkey-patch code within your own application or dependencies when testing.

Listing 10.20 shows an example of monkey-patching in a test. In section 10.3, we were trying to test a handler for creating new user objects. Let's try to test the same handler again, except this time the handler stores the new user record in MongoDB, and the response contains the database ID assigned to the record by MongoDB, along with a timestamp.

> **Listing 10.21 index.js: storing the new user record in MongoDB**

```
const Hapi = require('hapi');
const Joi = require('joi');
const MongoDb = require('mongodb');          ←┐  Load mongodb
                                              │  package
module.exports = function (callback) {
```

```
const server = new Hapi.Server();
server.connection({ port: 4000 });

const schema = {
    name: {
        first: Joi.string().required(),
        last: Joi.string().required()
    },
    age: Joi.number().required()
};

server.route({
    config: {
        validate: {
            payload: schema
        }
    },
    method: 'POST',
    path: '/user',
    handler: function (request, reply) {

        const db = request.server.app.db;         ◁──┘  Retrieve db object from
        const user = request.payload;                    server.app namespace
        user.createdAt = Date.now();

        db.collection('users').insertOne(user, (err, result) => {

            if (err) {
                reply(err);
            }

            const document = result.ops[0];
            reply(document);
        });
    }
});

const url = 'mongodb://localhost:27017/app';
MongoDb.MongoClient.connect(url, (err, db) => {

    if (err) {
        return callback(err);
    }
                                                   ◁──┘  Add db object to
    server.app.db = db;                                   server.app namespace
    callback(null, server);
});
};
```

Add timestamp to user object ⊢─▷

Insert user object into MongoDB users collection ⊢─▷

The test in listing 10.21 makes assertions for the following things when a POST request is made to /user:

- The response includes the original user object properties
- The response contains an accurate createdAt timestamp

- The response contains an _id property (generated by MongoDB)

Listing 10.22   test/index.js: A test for the MongoDB powered app

```
test('creates a user object', (done) => {

    const user = {
        name: {
            first: 'Craig',
            last: 'Railton'
        },
        age: 30
    };

    const options = {
        method: 'POST',
        url: '/user',
        payload: user
    };

    const start = Date.now();

    server.inject(options, (res) => {

        expect(res.statusCode).to.equal(200);
        expect(res.result).to.deep.include(user);
        expect(res.result._id).to.be.a.string();
        expect(res.result.createdAt)
            .to.be.greaterThan(start)
            .and.to.be.lessThan(Date.now());
        done();
    });
});
```

When we run this test, it will simulate an HTTP request, which will cause a real database operation inserting a new record into the collection. Instead, in our test, we don't want to actually hit the database. We can simply monkey-patch the server.app.db.collection function with our own replacement.

Listing 10.23   test/index.js: monkey-patching MongoDB's `collection` method

```
test('creates a user object', (done) => {

    server.app.db.collection = function () {

        return {
            insertOne: function (doc, callback) {

                doc._id = 'abcdef';
                callback(null, { ops: [doc] });
            }
        };
```

```
    };

    ...

});
```

Now when the handler for this route executes, it won't actually call into MongoDB—our monkey-patched replacement will be called instead.

Note that this is a permanent replacement of the `server.app.db.collection` function and will affect other tests unless you reload your server for each test. You could do that by using a `beforeEach()` instead of a `before()`, getting a whole new server object for each test:

```
beforeEach((done) => {

    require('..')((err, srv) => {

        server = srv;
        done();
    });
});
```

10.5.2 Using Sinon's spies and stubs

Sinon is a powerful library of test tools that you should add to your testing arsenal.

NPM PACKAGE   sinon v1 (www.npmjs.com/package/sinon)

Sinon provides several utilities that can be used in testing, including spies and stubs. Let's look at each of those now.

SPIES

When testing code, it's helpful to know whether the right methods are being called, and with the expected arguments. Spies gives us this ability. Spies can wrap themselves around methods or functions. They know when they've been called and how many times. They even know which arguments they were called with and what they returned (or if they threw). They can be useful, for instance, to check that a function (such as an async callback) gets called only once and always with the correct options.

The Sinon library includes a `spy` object. The following listing uses this in our test from the previous section that uses the monkey-patch, to check that our patched function is called only once and with the correct arguments.

Listing 10.24   test/index.js: using a spy to check whether/how methods are called

```
test('creates a user object', (done) => {

    server.app.db.collection = function () {          ◁─┐  We expect function to
                                                         │  be called once with
        return {                                         │  'users' as argument
```

```
        insertOne: function (doc, callback) {

            doc._id = 'abcdef';
            callback(null, { ops: [doc] });
        }
    };
};

const spy = Sinon.spy(server.app.db, 'collection');
const user = {
    name: {
        first: 'Craig',
        last: 'Railton'
    },
    age: 30
};

const options = {
    method: 'POST',
    url: '/user',
    payload: user
};

server.inject(options, (res) => {

    expect(spy.calledOnce).to.be.true();
    expect(spy.calledWith('users')).to.be.true();
    spy.restore();
    done();
});
});
```

Annotations:
- `const spy = Sinon.spy(server.app.db, 'collection');` ← **Create new spy from collection method of server.app.db object**
- **restore method returns spied-upon method to original state** → `spy.restore();`
- `expect(spy.calledOnce).to.be.true();` ← **Assert on spy.calledOnce to check method was called only once**
- **Assert on spy.calledWith method to check method was called with correct argument**

STUBS

Sinon stubs allow you to monkey-patch a method and create a spy with a single function call. They have the added benefit that you can restore the method to its original unpatched state. The following listing looks at yet again the same example, but this time using a Sinon stub.

Listing 10.25   test/index.js

```
test('creates a user object (shows use of stub)', (done) => {

    const stub = Sinon.stub(server.app.db, 'collection', (doc, callback) => {

        return {
            insertOne: function (doc2, cb) {

                doc2._id = 'abcdef';
                cb(null, { ops: [doc2] });
            }
        };
    });
```

Annotation:
- **Create stub for server.app.db .collection method** → `const stub = Sinon.stub(server.app.db, 'collection', (doc, callback) => {`

```
const user = {
    name: {
        first: 'Craig',
        last: 'Railton'
    },
    age: 30
};

const options = {
    method: 'POST',
    url: '/user',
    payload: user
};

server.inject(options, (res) => {

    expect(stub.calledOnce).to.be.true();
    expect(stub.calledWith('users')).to.be.true();

    stub.restore();

    done();
});
});
```

Stub exposes same testing
methods/properties as a spy

You can restore original
method using restore().

10.5.3   *Using proxyquire*

Proxyquire gives a clean and simple way to test code that was previously difficult to test. It works by hijacking Node.js's `require()` function to replace real dependencies with mocked versions that you provide.

NPM PACKAGE   proxyquire v1 (www.npmjs.com/package/proxyquire)

The `proxyquire()` function provided by proxyquire works like the standard `require()` function, except you can provide a list of mocks as a second argument. When the module is then loaded, all the real dependencies loaded in the file are replaced with your mocks.

The following listing shows an example of testing a hapi app that uses the `file` handler, provided by Inert. Normally this code would be difficult without actually changing the application code itself.

Listing 10.26   index.js: hapi app that uses the Inert file handler to serve a text file

```
const Hapi = require('hapi');

module.exports = function (callback) {

    const server = new Hapi.Server();
    server.connection({ port: 4000 });

    server.register(require('inert'), (err) => {
```

```
        if (err) {
            throw err;
        }

        server.route({
            method: 'GET',
            path: '/',
            handler: {
                file: 'file.txt'
            }
        });

        server.initialize((err) => {

            if (err) {
                throw err;
            }
            callback(null, server);
        });
    });
};
```

We want to write a test for the GET/route, but we don't want the test to actually hit the filesystem to return the contents of file.txt. We can use proxyquire (`npm install --save proxyquire@1`) to provide a stub for the Inert dependency.

Listing 10.27   test/index.js: using proxyquire with stub for inert module

```
'use strict';

const Code = require('code');
const Lab = require('lab');
const Proxyquire = require('proxyquire');                ◁─┐ Load proxyquire
                                                           │ package
const expect = Code.expect;
const lab = exports.lab = Lab.script();
const experiment = lab.experiment;
const test = lab.test;
const beforeEach = lab.beforeEach;

const Server = Proxyquire('..', {                        ◁─┐ Load server module, specifying
    inert: require('./mocks/inert')                        │ module to mock Inert with
});

let server;

beforeEach((done) => {

    Server((err, srv) => {

        server = srv;
        done();
    });
});
```

```
experiment('Test POST /user', () => {

    test('creates a user object', (done) => {

        const options = {
            method: 'GET',
            url: '/'
        };

        server.inject(options, (res) => {

            expect(res.payload).to.equal('proxyquire');
            done();
        });
    });
});
```

We expect "file" contents to contain the word proxyquire, which is coming from our mock, not a real file in filesystem.

The following listing replaces all instances of Inert in our server file with a mock that we place in ./mocks/inert.js.

Listing 10.28   test/mocks/inert.js: Inert mock used with proxyquire

```
exports.register = function (server, options, next) {

    const file = function (route, options) {

        return function (request, reply) {

            reply('proxyquire');
        };
    };

    server.handler('file', file);
    next();
};

exports.register.attributes = { name: 'inert' };
```

Our stubbed version of Inert's file handler simply returns the string `'proxyquire'` without touching the filesystem.

Proxyquire can be a powerful method of controlling exactly what you're testing and what you're not by stubbing out the dependencies in files that you don't want to test.

In this chapter we've looked at how to use hapi.js testing tools such as Lab and Code to write expressive and thorough tests for applications, including peripheral concerns such as linting, code coverage, and testing difficult code with mocks, spies, stubs, and Proxyquire.

10.6   *Summary*

- Lab is a test runner, similar to proper case but integrated well into the hapi.js ecosystem.

- Lab has multiple reporters including console, TAP, and HTML.
- Lab can check code test coverage. hapi's philosophy is everything is always tested to 100%.
- By using the Code package, you can write more powerful and expressive assertions in your tests that provide more detailed error messages when tests fail.
- Code that looks difficult or even impossible to test might surrender to the techniques of mocking, stubbing, spies, and monkey-patching.
- proxyquire is a non-intrusive way of replacing dependencies with mocked counterparts for testing.

In the next (and final) chapter, we're going to be looking at getting your application into production and keeping it there, touching on issues like debugging, monitoring, and TLS.

Production and beyond

This chapter covers
- Logging and server events
- Documenting with Lout
- Monitoring and application metrics
- Debugging with Node Inspector, Poop, and hapi TV
- Deploying apps with SSL

Picking your framework and developing your app's features are merely the beginning. When you get it into production and have real users, you need to concern yourself with logging, monitoring, user privacy, security, and many other things. You also need to ensure there are adequate methods for debugging when (not if) something goes awry. Documentation is also super-important for the maintainability of your projects.

This chapter contains some pointers on these matters and introduces a few tools and techniques to get you well on your way to having both happy users and coworkers.

11.1 Logging with hapi and Good

When a problem occurs in a production app, logs can be your best friend. So it's important that you think about what makes sense to log in your application. I'm not going to tell you what to log because every app is different. Rather, I'm going to introduce to you the concepts and the tools offered by the framework to produce and manage logs.

11.1.1 Introduction to server events in hapi

First up, before we start looking directly at how to manage logs with hapi, I want to discuss *server events* a little because the two subjects are closely linked. In chapter 7, we looked at using an `EventEmitter` object to communicate events across different parts of a hapi application built with plugins. We used this as an uncoupling strategy to ensure that our plugins were as isolated as possible. If you remember, `EventEmitter` is Node's built-in implementation of the popular Observer pattern, as shown here.

Listing 11.1   Example of the Observer pattern with `EventEmitter`

```
const EventEmitter = require('events').EventEmitter;

const emitter = new EventEmitter();        emitter is an (instance
                                           of) EventEmitter.

emitter.on('myEvent', (payload) => {       We can attach one or more
                                           listeners for named events.
    console.log('Got a myEvent with payload', payload);
});

emitter.emit('myEvent', { some: 'data' });    We can emit events, which will
emitter.emit('myEvent', { other: 'data' });   be passed onto any listeners.
```

You might not have known this but the hapi `server` object we've been working with throughout this book is itself an instance of `EventEmitter`. hapi server objects continually emit many different events throughout the startup and running of your application.

HAPI API   `server events` (http://hapijs.com/api#server-events)

A hapi server object emits nine different types of event types, listed in table 11.1. We're only going to concern ourselves with the events in rows with grey backgrounds in this book.

Table 11.1   Server events

Event	Internal/User	Description
`log`	Internal/User	Generated by calling `server.log()` discussed in section 11.1.2

Table 11.1 Server events *(continued)*

Event	Internal/User	Description
request	User	Generated by calling `request.log()` discussed in 11.1.2
request-error	Internal	Generated internally when a request sends back a 500 error
request-internal	Internal	Generated internally by hapi on various stages of a request
response	Internal	Emitted by server when a response is sent
route	Internal	Emitted when a route is added to a server connection
start	Internal	Generated when a server starts
stop	Internal	Generated when a server stops
tail	Internal	Emitted once a request has finished processing

We can listen to these server events, as we would listen for events on any `EventEmitter` object, by using `.on()`:

```
server.on('request-internal', (request, event, tags) => {

    console.log(event);
});
```

If you run an application with the previous code added, you'll see a flurry of events streaming through your console when you make requests:

```
{ request: '1450624202961:Matts-iMac.local:13185:iieo7025:10000',
  timestamp: 1450624202965,
  tags: [ 'received' ],
  data:
   { method: 'get',
     url: '/',
     agent: 'Mozilla/5.0 (compatible; MSIE 9.0; Windows NT 6.1; Trident/5.0)'
   },
  internal: true }
{ request: '1450624202961:Matts-iMac.local:13185:iieo7025:10000',
  timestamp: 1450624202977,
  tags: [ 'handler' ],
  data: { msec: 2.4473870024085045 },
  internal: true }
```

This should give you a hint at the amount of useful data that is available for your logs, generated by hapi for free. You only need to listen for these events. Even though, as I've shown, you could use plain old `.on()` handlers to get these events into your logs, there are much better ways.

11.1.2 Logging with request.log() and server.log()

We've discussed server events a little bit. You may still be wondering what that has to do with logging, though.

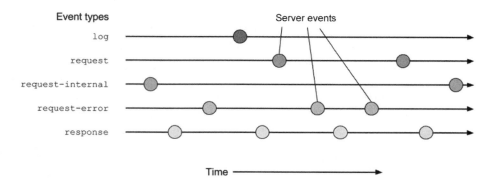

Figure 11.1 Server events are distinct occurrences in time and come in different types.

To get a little abstract for a moment, in hapi, we think of logs as a stream of events across time, as shown in figure 11.1. Those events as a list might look something like the following:

- `1450624201250 - [auth] - User 3415 authenticated`
- `1450624201336 - [mem] - Heap memory usage exceeded 300mb`
- `1450624201389 - [not-found] - Page not found (404)`
- `1450624205469 - [error, database] - DB error`

Each of those single events occurs at a moment in time, indicated by the first time-stamp number, and is tagged with one or more labels between square brackets. A log can be seen as a stream of those events.

Before we look at logs, let's see how to generate log events of our own when something significant happens in our apps.

CREATING LOG EVENTS

There are two methods that we can use to generate our own log events in a hapi app:

- `request.log(tags, data);`
- `server.log(tags, data);`

In both cases, `tags` is an array of tag strings. *Tags* are identifiers that we use to group related log events. For instance, you might use the tag `'database'` for all log events related to your database. Many logging libraries use the concept of log levels such as error, debug, trace, and so on. hapi instead uses this idea of each event being associated with one or more tags.

Remember that I mentioned that logging and server events were closely related? Well, it turns out that `request.log()` and `server.log()` are simple functions that cause a server object to emit `request` and `log` events respectively.

You might be wondering when to use `request.log()` and when to use `server.log()`. The rule of thumb is that whenever you're logging something related to the processing of a specific request, you should use `request.log()`. That's almost anything within a route handler, extension, or pre. This allows you to associate log events with the request, which can be handy later for debugging.

When you want to log something that happened outside the context of a specific request, you should use `server.log()`. An example might be when a shared database connection is unexpectedly closed, or the process receives a signal to restart.

The next listing creates a basic hapi app that uses these two functions to illustrate how they work.

Listing 11.2   A simple app using `request.log()` and `server.log()`

```
'use strict';

const Hapi = require('hapi');

const server = new Hapi.Server();
server.connection({ port: 4000 });

server.route({
    method: 'GET',
    path: '/',
    handler: function (request, reply) {

        request.log(['my-request-tag'], 'Got a request');    ⟵  Log server request event with tag 'my-request-tag'
        reply('Howdy!');
    }
});

server.start((err) => {

    if (err) {
        throw err;
    }
                                                                    Log server log event with tag 'my-log-tag'
    server.log(['my-log-tag'], 'Wohoo, the server has started!');    ⟵
});
```

If you spin this app up and make a request to /, you'll notice that no logging is happening yet. That's because generating log events is one-half of the picture. We also need a way to listen for them and print them out somewhere so we can see them. A quick and easy way to do that is with debug mode.

DEBUG MODE

hapi's debug mode setting is a quick way to get log events printed out to the console. It's only intended to be used in development, though, as a convenient way to preview what your application will log in production.

You can set the debug mode as an option when creating your server, as shown in this listing.

Listing 11.3   Setting debug mode options

```
const server = new Hapi.Server({
    debug: {
```

log is for events logged with server.log().

```
log: ['my-log-tag'],
request: ['my-request-tag']
    }
});
```

request is for events logged with request.log().

You can specify a list of event tags that you're interested in with debug mode, and when matching events occur, they'll be logged to the console:

```
Debug: my-log-tag
    Wohoo, the server has started!
Debug: my-request-tag
    Got a request
```

INTERNAL REQUEST EVENTS

hapi generates a lot of its own request events internally. Rather than being emitted as request events (which are only user-generated events), they are emitted as request-internal events. A slightly confusing thing is that debug mode's request option includes both request and request-internal events, so you can also print out some of these internal events by selecting the appropriate tags. There are many such events, and a full list can be found at http://hapijs.com/api#request-logs. One such example is the internal request event with the tag `handler`:

```
const server = new Hapi.Server({
    debug: {
        log: ['my-log-tag'],
        request: ['my-request-tag', 'handler']
    }
});
```

Every time a route handler has been executed, a handler event will be emitted with the execution time (in milliseconds) of the handler:

```
Debug: my-log-tag
    Wohoo, the server has started!
Debug: my-request-tag
    Got a request
Debug: handler
    {"msec":3.535550996661186}
```

I mentioned earlier that debug mode was designed only for development. So how do we produce logs from log events in production applications? The recommended way is by using Good, the official process monitoring and logging plugin for hapi.

11.1.3 Production logging and process monitoring with Good

To create logs, log events can filtered based on tags and then recorded or reported in some way.

NPM PACKAGE   good v6 (www.npmjs.com/package/good)

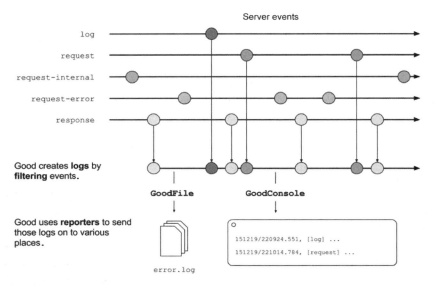

Figure 11.2 Logs are sent to different output locations by reporters such as GoodConsole and GoodFile.

Perhaps you do that by writing them to the console, or a log file, or perhaps forwarding them over a TCP socket to another service. This is the function of the hapi plugin Good, illustrated in figure 11.2.

Good uses *filters* to determine *which* events to include in a log and uses *reporters* to determine *how* to output a log.

NPM PACKAGE GoodConsole v5 (www.npmjs.com/package/good-console)

Let's look at a simple example using the GoodConsole reporter. Listing 11.4 recycles the same example from the previous section, this time using Good instead of the debug mode. You should go ahead and install a few dependencies to run this example: npm install --save good@6 good-console@5.

Listing 11.4 Registering Good and the GoodConsole reporter

```
server.register({
    register: require('good'),
    options: {
        reporters: [
            {
                reporter: require('good-console'),      ←── Select the reporter
                events: {                                    to use
                    log: ['my-log-tag'],
                    request: ['my-request-tag']
                }
```

Specify which tags the reporter should filter for log and request events

```
            }
        ]
    }
}, (err) => {

    if (err) {
        throw err;
    }
    server.start((err) => {

        if (err) {
            throw err;
        }

        server.log(['my-log-tag'], 'Wohoo, the server has started!');
    });
});
```

The GoodConsole reporter prints your chosen events to the console. It formats each log event as a single line containing the date, time, event tags, and any data (such as the message):

```
151219/220924.551, [log,my-log-tag], data: Wohoo, the server has started!
151219/220938.163, [request,my-request-tag], data: Got a request
```

There are many other reporters available for Good. Here are the official reporters under the hapijs GitHub organization:

- good-console
- good-file
- good-http
- good-udp

The names are fairly self-explanatory in terms of how they output the log events. The option of sending logs over UDP and HTTP opens up integration possibilities with almost any third-party service or open source software that provides centralized log aggregation, such as Splunk, Logstash, FluentD, and many others.

11.1.4 *Using multiple reporter instances*

It's possible to use several reporters at once with Good. Each reporter can subscribe to a different set of events if you like. You may, for example, decide to use two instances of the GoodFile reporter (see listing 11.5) and log all `error` events to a log file called error.log.

NPM PACKAGE GoodFile v5 (www.npmjs.com/package/good-file)

You may also want to log all other events to a file called debug.log. Achieving this kind of setup is trivial with Good. You can also select all tags for an event type by specifying the option with an asterisk.

NOTE   The Good error event maps directly to the hapi server request-error event.

> **Listing 11.5   Creating a debug and error log file with the GoodFile reporter**

```
server.route([
    {
        method: 'GET',
        path: '/error',
        handler: function (request, reply) {        Requesting this route
                                                     logs request-error
            throw new Error('An error');            event to error.log file.
        }
    }
]);

server.register({
    register: require('good'),
    options: {
        reporters: [
            {                                        GoodFile requires name of
                config: 'error.log',                 output file as config option.
                reporter: require('good-file'),
                events: {
                    error: '*'        ◁        Asterisk tells Good to
                }                               listen for all tags for this
            },                                  event type (no filtering).
            {
                config: 'debug.log',
                reporter: require('good-file'),
                events: {
                    log: '*',
                    request: '*',
                    response: '*'
                }
            }
        ]
    }
}, (err) => {
    ...
});
```

GoodFile will log much more data than GoodConsole, including request IDs along with request information such as the full set of request headers. Each event will be logged as newline-separated JSON.

11.2   *Documenting your routes*

Producing API documentation is typically a boring and tedious process. hapi has some neat features, though, that allow you to document as you go by adding a little metadata to your routes as you create them. You can then use this metadata along with a plugin called Lout to generate documentation automatically.

11.2.1 Introduction to route tags, notes, and descriptions

We all know how to create routes at this point. But there are three particular properties on the route configuration object that I've not discussed. The following listing uses them all.

Listing 11.6 Creating a route with a description, tags, and notes

```
server.route({
    config: {
        description: 'The home page route',        Documentation
        tags: ['web', 'home'],                      config properties
        notes: ['Remember to add proper functionality']
    },
    method: 'GET',
    path: '/',
    handler: function (request, reply) {

        reply('Hello world!');
    }
});
```

These three properties are for documentation purposes only—they don't affect the behavior of your server in any way. Aside from being useful to read when browsing through your code later, they come into use when you use some additional documentation utilities, as we'll see next.

11.2.2 Autogenerated documentation with Lout

Lout is a plugin that adds an extra route to your application (by default this is found at /docs). Lout crawls all the routes on your server, inspecting each of them, and then produces browsable, detailed HTML documentation, all automatically.

NPM PACKAGE lout v9 (www.npmjs.com/package/lout)

Let's try Lout (npm install --save lout@9) now (see the following listing). It depends on both Vision v4 and Inert v3 plugins, so we must register those along with Lout before starting our application.

Listing 11.7 Register all necessary plugins for Lout to work

```
'use strict';

const Hapi = require('hapi');

const server = new Hapi.Server();
server.connection({ port: 4000 });

server.route({
    config: {
        description: 'The home page route',
        tags: ['web', 'home'],
        notes: ['Remember to add proper functionality']
```

```
    },
    method: 'GET',
    path: '/',
    handler: function (request, reply) {

        reply('Hello world!');
    }
});

server.register([
    require('vision'),         ◁─── Register Lout's
    require('inert'),               dependencies Inert
    require('lout')                 and Vision
], (err) => {                  ◁─── Register
                                    Lout
    if (err) {
        throw err;
    }
    server.start((err) => {

        if (err) {
            throw err;
        }

        console.log('Started server');
    });
});
```

Lout doesn't require any explicit configuration up front because it comes with a set of sensible defaults to ensure that it works out of the box. When your application starts up, you can browse to /docs to view the generated documentation, shown in figure 11.3.

Clicking on a route opens more info

Figure 11.3 Automatic documentation with Lout

Lout shows us the additional documentation fields that we add to our routes (`tags`, `description`, and `notes`), but that's only the beginning. The following listing looks at a slightly more interesting route.

Listing 11.8 A PUT route with validated request parameters and payload

```
server.route({
    config: {
        description: 'Modify a single product',
        tags: ['web', 'products'],
        notes: ['Remember to add proper functionality'],
        validate: {
            payload: {
                name: Joi.string().required(),
                price: Joi.number().required(),
                sku: Joi.string().required().min(5)
            },
            params: {
                id: Joi.number().required().min(1)
            }
        }
    },
    method: 'PUT',
    path: '/products/{id}',
    handler: function (request, reply) {

        reply('Modified a product!');
    }
});
```

If you use Joi schemas for validation on your routes, Lout will also pick up on these when crawling your routes. Lout can then display the expected parameters for a route in its output, as shown in figure 11.4.

Coupled with Lout, the validation power of Joi extends to producing clear expectations to consumers of your API.

Figure 11.4 When coupled with Joi, Lout includes validation information.

11.3   *Monitoring*

If you have an application running in production that is experiencing problems, the next place you're to look after your logs is your other metrics and monitoring data. Where you get this data and what it consists of will vary, depending on things like your hosting provider.

If you're hosting your application on a Platform as a Service like Heroku, you may have a dashboard you can consult. If you're managing your own infrastructure, perhaps on Amazon Web Services, you might jump over to Cloudwatch to check things like CPU consumption and network utilization.

There's a whole host of application metrics that you'll want to know that these platforms don't provide. Things like average request time, number of requests per second, or how long a database query takes—or perhaps even more specific things to your app, such as the number of users that uploaded a new profile picture in the last 30 minutes.

This section looks at a couple of ways to get custom metrics out of your apps into graphs that you can watch update in real time. And who doesn't feel cool and important looking at an array of colored graphs?

11.3.1   *Introducing Graphite and StatsD*

Graphite and StatsD are two indispensable tools in application monitoring. They're both free and open source software products. When you combine them, you can produce extremely useful custom application monitoring dashboards with minimal effort.

GRAPHITE

Graphite is a couple of tools rolled into a single product. It consists of a database and a graphing platform. It stores metrics that you send to it, and then you can plot them seems redundant dynamically and produce custom saved dashboards. It also manages things like automatic purging of old data.

STATSD

StatsD is a simple tool created by Etsy for collecting metrics from applications. StatsD receives metrics from an application (sent over the network) in a simple format and then forwards them onto a Graphite server after some aggregation. There's a package called `node-statsd` for Node.js that we can use to send data to a StatsD server.

GETTING STARTED WITH GRAPHITE AND STATSD

Graphite and StatsD can be difficult to set up from scratch, but the process has been made much easier recently by tools like Docker. You can now get started with Graphite in minutes, as we'll see now. We're going to use Docker to install Graphite and StatsD locally. First you'll need to install Docker on your local machine (https://docs.docker.com/machine/).

To start a Docker container running with StatsD and Graphite installed, execute the following command (it might take a while the first time as it needs to download the hopsoft/graphite-statsd Docker image from the Docker hub):

```
sudo docker run -d \
  --name graphite \
  --restart=always \
  -p 80:80 \
  -p 2003:2003 \
  -p 8125:8125/udp \
  -p 8126:8126 \
  hopsoft/graphite-statsd
```

When the command finishes executing, you should have a full Graphite/StatsD setup running on your local machine. You can confirm this by navigating to the Graphite dashboard. If you're using Docker Machine, first get your Docker host IP address by typing the following:

```
docker-machine ip [machine]
```

I named my machine `default`, so I typed `docker-machine ip default` and got the result `192.168.99.100`. Browsing to http://192.168.99.100/ in a browser will open Graphite.

Now let's send some data its way.

11.3.2 *Measure anything with StatsD*

Before we start sending real application data to StatsD, let's experiment with some fake data. We can use the `node-statsd` package from npm, which offers a simple to use StatsD client.

NPM PACKAGE `node-statsd` v0.1.x (www.npmjs.com/package/node-statsd)

We're going to use the `statsd.timing(key, value)` method from this package to send metrics to StatsD. Despite being called *timers,* these measurements can be any numeric time-series data that you might want to plot: CPU load, memory, response times, and so forth.

The `key` is an identifier we can use to group our measurements over time so that we can plot them on a graph. The simple script in the following listing sends some dummy data for the keys `number_of_connections` and `response_time`. Data is sent every 10 seconds for 10 minutes.

Listing 11.9 Sending dummy data to StatsD every 10 seconds for 10 minutes

```
const StatsD = require('node-statsd');

const STATSD_HOST = '192.168.99.100';         ◁──┐ Use IP obtained from running
const statsd = new StatsD({ host: STATSD_HOST });  ◁──┐ docker-machine ip default

                                                      Create StatsD client
const randomIntBetween = (a,b) => {
```

```
    return a + Math.floor(Math.random() * ( b - a + 1));    ◁── Generate random integer
};                                                               between a and b (inclusive)

const interval = setInterval(() => {                                          ◁──

    statsd.timing('number_of_connections', randomIntBetween(0,100));
    statsd.timing('response_time', randomIntBetween(500,2000));
}, 1000 * 10);                                                         Every 10 seconds
                                                                     send some fake data
setTimeout(() => {                          ◁── After 10 minutes
                                                clean up and exit
    clearInterval(interval);
    statsd.close();
}, 1000 * 60 * 10);
```

By visiting the Graphite dashboard and browsing to /dashboard, we can generate a
custom dashboard containing these metrics. StatsD prefixes our keys so
number_of_connections becomes stats.timers.number_of_connections. We can
use the browser to add multiple charts to the dashboard, as shown in figure 11.5.

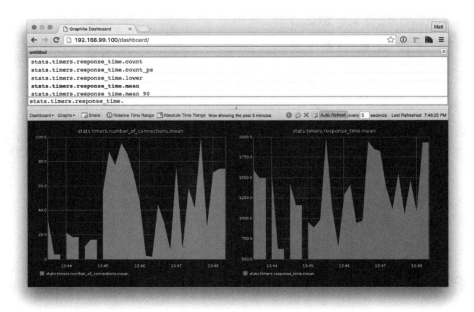

Figure 11.5   A quickly constructed custom Graphite dashboard

11.3.3 *Getting operations data from hapi using Oppsy*

The Oppsy module (npm install --save oppsy@1) provides a whole bunch of useful
metrics you can log or send to StatsD or another monitoring or metrics system, such
as Splunk.

NPM PACKAGE   oppsy v1 (www.npmjs.com/package/oppsy)

When instantiated with a hapi server and started, Oppsy will emit an `ops` event with the frequency you specify. Each event will have a payload containing various useful measurements, as shown in the following listing.

Listing 11.10   Registering a hapi server with Oppsy and printing out `ops` events

```
const Hapi = require('hapi');
const Oppsy = require('oppsy');

const server = new Hapi.Server();
server.connection({ port: 4000 });

const oppsy = new Oppsy(server);          Create Oppsy instance, passing
                                          it a hapi server object

oppsy.on('ops', (data) => {                         Listen for
                                                    ops events
    console.log(data);
});

server.start((err) => {

    if (err) {
        throw err;
    }
                                    Start Oppsy, generating
    oppsy.start(1000);              ops events every second
});
```

Let's see an example of the payload from Oppsy:

```
{
    requests: { '4000': { total: 4, disconnects: 0 ... } },
    responseTimes: { '4000': { avg: 2.5, max: 3 } },
    sockets: { http: { total: 0 }, https: { total: 0 } },
    osload: [ 1.87890625, 1.5078125, 1.3740234375 ],
    osmem: { total: 8589934592, free: 17965056 },
    osup: 2177726,
    psup: 1.409,
    psmem: { rss: 37740544, heapTotal: 20602624, heapUsed: 12133392 },
    concurrents: { '4000': 0 },
    psdelay: 2.1419219970703125,
    host: 'Matts-iMac.local'
}
```

Table 11.2 explains what each of the properties in the Oppsy payload means.

Table 11.2   Oppsy data

Property	Meaning
`requests`	Summary of requests since last `ops` event
`responseTimes`	Summary of response times since last `ops` event

Table 11.2 Oppsy data *(continued)*

Property	Meaning
sockets	Currently connected sockets
osload	Operating system load (1-, 5-, and 15-minute) averages
osmem	Operating system memory (in bytes)
osup	The uptime of the OS in seconds
psup	The uptime of the server process in seconds
psmem	The process's memory stats
concurrents	Number of concurrent connections
psdelay	The Node event loop delay
host	Server host

It's easy to see how useful it would be to take some of this data and ship it off to our dashboard. We can namespace metrics by separating parts of the key with a period character. This helps us to organize our metrics in Graphite:

```
'use strict';

const Hapi = require('hapi');
const Oppsy = require('oppsy');
const StatsD = require('node-statsd');

const STATSD_HOST = '192.168.99.100'; // `docker-machine ip default`
const statsd = new StatsD({ host: STATSD_HOST });

const server = new Hapi.Server();
server.connection({ port: 4000 });

const oppsy = new Oppsy(server);

oppsy.on('ops', (data) => {

    statsd.timing('ops.osmem.free', data.osmem.free);
    statsd.timing('ops.osload', data.osload[0]);
    statsd.timing('ops.psdelay', data.psdelay);
});

server.start((err) => {

    if (err) {
        throw err;
    }

    oppsy.start(1000);
});
```

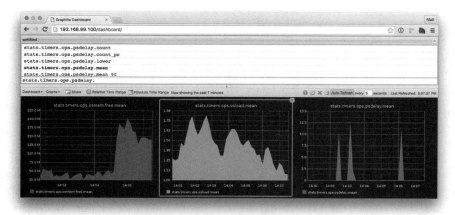

Figure 11.6   Graphite dashboard displaying data from Oppsy

This kind of data is extremely useful on charts. The StatsD Node client buffers and aggregates the metrics you send and transmits them over UDP, meaning minimal overhead, which makes this suitable for production use (see figure 11.6).

11.4   Debugging

When your app isn't behaving how you expect, there are several tools and techniques that you can turn to for debugging. This section looks at a few, increasing in sophistication from `console.log()` to browsing heap dumps.

11.4.1   Don't feel bad about using console.log()

It's quick, it's easy, and for simple debugging tasks, `console.log()` is probably enough.

If, for example, you're expecting an object's property to be set in a route handler, but it isn't, toss a couple of `console.log()`s in there and see what you're working with. `console.log()` is often my first port of call for debugging before looking at fancier and more advanced tools.

Make sure you remove your `console.log()`s before committing your code, or going to production.

11.4.2   Node debug

Node comes with a built-in debugger, which if you've ever worked with gdb (GNU debugger) before, should be familiar. If not, don't fret—it's a simple yet powerful tool.

The following listing shows a hapi route we need to debug.

Listing 11.11   A route that should echo a request header

```
server.route({
    method: 'GET',
    path: '/',
```

```
        handler: function (request, reply) {

            reply(request.headers['X-Custom-Header']);
        }
});
```

This route is supposed to echo to us the value of the X-Custom-Header header in response to a request. But when we make a request using cURL, sending along such a header, all we get back is an empty response:

```
curl -H "X-Custom-Header: Something" localhost:4000
```

Something's clearly not right. We could use console.log() to print out the value of request.headers, but this is a good opportunity to show off Node's debugger instead. The next listing sets a breakpoint by adding a debugger statement to the code. A *breakpoint* signifies some place you'd like execution to stop so you can poke around at the current state of the process.

Listing 11.12 Adding a breakpoint using a debugger statement

```
'use strict';

const Hapi = require('hapi');

const server = new Hapi.Server();
server.connection({ port: 4000 });

server.route({
    method: 'GET',
    path: '/',
    handler: function (request, reply) {

        debugger;
        reply(request.headers['X-Custom-Header']);
    }
});

server.start((err) => {

    if (err) {
        throw err;
    }
    console.log('Started server');
});
```

We can start the debugger by running:

```
node debug index.js
```

Our next steps are as follows:

1 Debugger starts a script and pauses on the first line.
2 Type cont to continue.

3 "Server started" message logged, server waiting.

4 Initiate cURL request from console.

5 Debugger pauses at breakpoint.

6 Switch to repl mode by typing `repl` in debugger pane. You can now execute JavaScript at the current location in the code.

7 Type `console.log(request.headers);` to view all headers in request. See figure 11.7.

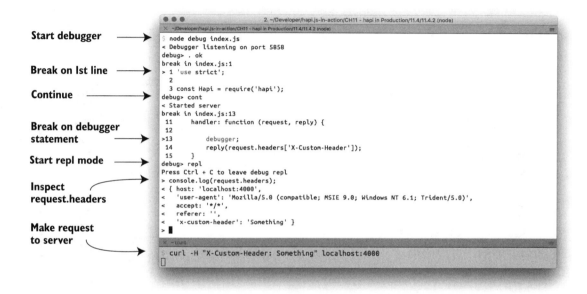

Start debugger

Break on lst line

Continue

Break on debugger statement

Start repl mode

Inspect request.headers

Make request to server

Figure 11.7   A debugger session with Node debug

By printing out the `request.headers` object, we can see now that the issue is that all the header names are lowercase, regardless of the case of the header name sent in the request. This is because Node forces all header names to be lowercase. We can use `node-debug` wherever it's necessary to pause and jump into our code to figure out a problem.

11.4.3 Node Inspector

Node Inspector is probably the number-one most useful debugging tool out there for Node.js, in my opinion. Node Inspector is the power of `node debug` coupled with the friendly interface of the Chrome developer tools debugger.

> **NPM PACKAGE** `node-inspector` v0.12.x (www.npmjs.com/package/node-inspector)

Node Inspector is normally installed globally:

```
npm install -g node-inspector
```

You can add debugger statements to your code as you did with node debug or you can add breakpoints visually in the inspector once it opens.

To start a script with Node Inspector:

```
node-debug index.js
```

Node Inspector will then open in your default browser (see figure 11.8). You can step through code, set breakpoints, and print out variables in your code, as shown in figure 11.8. If you know how to use the Chrome debugger, you can use Node Inspector too.

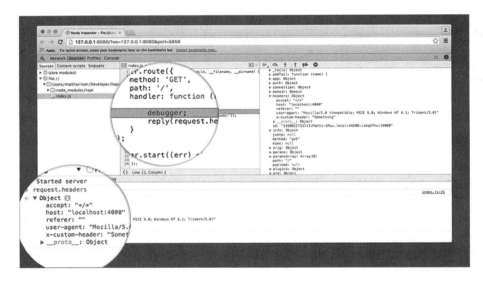

Figure 11.8   The Node Inspector interface

NOTE   There are currently efforts to integrate the V8 inspector into Node.js. When this feature becomes stable it will likely offer a similar but more complete interface as Node Inspector. Find out more here: http://mng.bz/Taje.

11.4.4 *Core dumps with Poop*

Poop (yup, seriously) is a hapi plugin. When registered with your server, it will ensure that a heap memory dump of the process is taken and written to a file when any uncaught error causes your server to crash. You can then collect this file and inspect it in Chrome development tools to attempt to understand the crash situation better.

NPM PACKAGE   poop v2 (www.npmjs.com/package/poop)

Heap dumps are useful tools for *post-mortem* debugging—debugging after a crash has already occurred and the process has ended. They're mainly useful for understanding crashes that occurred due to memory leaks. That's when your app allocates and holds on to memory by accident, not letting the garbage collector do its work.

Often slow memory leaks eventually lead to a process crashing when it runs out of memory altogether. In these situations, you can then check the heap dump to find out where the memory was being leaked. This listing creates a leaky app to illustrate how this works.

Here we're using Poop version 2 (npm install --save poop@2).

Listing 11.13 App that leaks memory and then crashes after a second

```
'use strict';

const Hapi = require('hapi');

const server = new Hapi.Server();
server.connection({ port: 4000 });

server.register(require('poop'), (err) => {          ⊲─ Register Poop
                                                        with server
    if (err) {
        throw err;
    }
    server.start((err) => {

        if (err) {
            throw err;
        }
        console.log('Started server');
    });
});

class MyObject {
    constructor() {

        this.name = 'MyObject';
    }
};
                                               Attach array to global scope,
global.myobjs = [];                         ⊲─ preventing garbage collection

for (let i = 0; i < 1000; ++i) {
                ⊳  myobjs.push(new MyObject());
Create objects  }
and add them
to myobjs       setTimeout(() => {
                                               Simulate a crash after
    throw new Error('Can\'t touch this');      one second by throwing
}, 1000);                                      an uncaught exception
```

In the listing, we cause our app to crash after one second. But first we create a bunch of garbage that can't be collected due to being attached to the global scope.

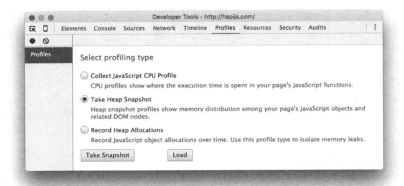

**Figure 11.9
Chrome Developer
Tools Profiles tab**

When the app crashes, Poop will automatically create a heap dump file by default in our current working directory. The file name will be something like heapdump-xxxxx.heapsnapshot. You can then open this file in the Profiles tab of the Chrome Developer Tools, shown in figure 11.9.

Once the dump file has been processed, we can inspect the entire JavaScript heap at the time of the crash. The garbage we created using the MyObject class is clearly visible by its constructor name, as shown in figure 11.10.

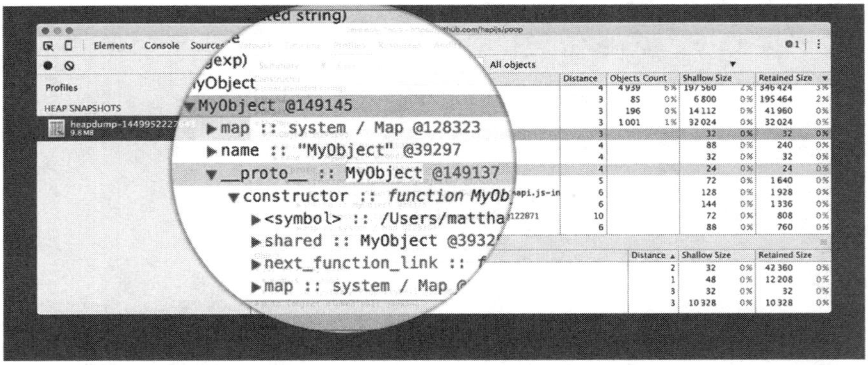

Figure 11.10   A processed heap dump ready for inspection

11.4.5   *Real-time request debugging with hapi TV*

hapi TV (npm install --save tv@5) is an extremely cool plugin that lets you monitor your application's incoming requests in real time, thanks to a websocket-powered dashboard. This is only intended for use in development, though, because it does carry an overhead that could affect performance in production.

NPM PACKAGE   tv v5 (www.npmjs.com/package/tv)

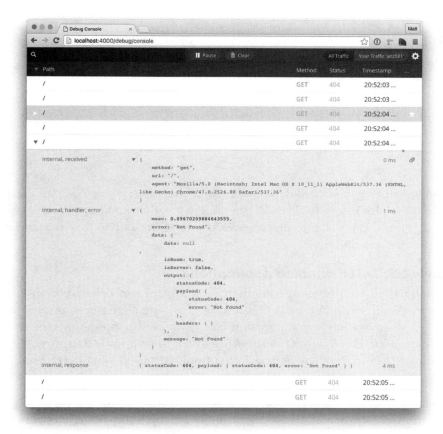

Figure 11.11   Inspecting a request in the TV debug console

You can view each request received to your server, along with status code, payload, handler timings, and more (see figure 11.11). To use TV, install it (npm install --save tv@5) and register it along with Vision and Inert, as shown here.

Listing 11.14   Registering hapi TV and dependencies

```
'use strict';

const Hapi = require('hapi');

const server = new Hapi.Server();
server.connection({ port: 4000 });

const plugins = [
    require('inert'),
    require('vision'),
    require('tv')
];
```

```
server.register(plugins, (err) => {

    if (err) {
        throw err;
    }
    server.start((err) => {

        if (err) {
            throw err;
        }
        console.log('Started server');
    });
});
```

By default, the real-time console is available at the /debug/console path. hapi TV could be useful, for example, if you're developing a mobile app that consumes a hapi-powered API. You can watch requests arrive at your server in real time from your app and inspect their properties.

11.5   *Deploying SSL/TLS-enabled applications*

If you don't allow your users to communicate with your service or website via a TLS (Transport Layer Security) connection, you're providing almost zero privacy to your users. If your application is in the small minority where this doesn't matter, then you can keep on using HTTP only. Otherwise you owe it to your users to protect their privacy online. If you collect any personal data from your users whatsoever, you should use TLS.

> **NOTE**   SSL (Secure Sockets Layer) is a protocol that is now deprecated in favor of the TLS protocol. But you will still hear people (including me) using the term SSL when they mean the newer TLS protocol.

The good news is that TLS isn't as complicated or expensive to implement as you might expect. There are a couple of options on how to set it up. One thing you're definitely going to need, though, is an SSL certificate. There are several providers, and the pricing can vary wildly from free (check out Let's Encrypt) to several hundreds of dollars per year.

You could be tricked into thinking that the more expensive SSL certificates lead to more secure sites and safer users. That's not exactly true. The algorithms and encryption behind a $5/year and a $500/year certificate could be exactly the same. The only difference is the effort that the more expensive provider has gone to to verify who you are. This level of trust between certificate provider and holder may be important for large enterprises, but it's probably not for a small startup or one-person company. For your personal blog, a $5/year or free certificate will probably do fine.

11.5.1   *Options for TLS*

You have two common options (see figure 11.12) for how to run SSL on your hapi application:

1 SSL terminated at a load balancer, reverse proxy or other hardware or software device. All traffic from this intermediate stage to your application server is unencrypted.

2 SSL terminated by Node.js.

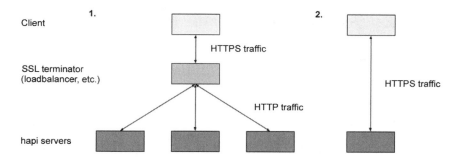

Figure 11.12   Options for a TLS architecture

NOTE   SSL termination refers to the point at which encrypted SSL traffic is decrypted and forwarded from this point as unencrypted data.

If your application is a multi-node app without many servers, the first option will probably be the preferred choice. Typically you will install an SSL certificate on a load balancer or reverse proxy, following the instructions for that software. There's little to no work to do on the hapi side if your setup looks like this.

The other option is to have your hapi application listening for secure connections and managing the TLS termination itself. It's this approach that we'll be looking at for the rest of this chapter.

11.5.2 Setting up a TLS connection with hapi

Every time we create a connection to a server in hapi, it's one of two types: either a TLS connection or a non-TLS connection. Up until now, we've only been creating non-TLS connections in this book. To create a TLS connection, we have to specify the certificate and private key of our SSL certificate when creating a connection, as shown in the following listing.

Listing 11.15   TLS settings when creating a connection

```
server.connection({
    port: 443,
    tls: {
        key: 'XXXX',
        cert: 'XXXX'
    }
});
```

The problem is that if we don't have an SSL certificate yet, how can we test this out?

11.5.3   *Testing SSL with a self-signed certificate*

It's possible to generate an SSL certificate on your own machine, signed by you, rather than a certificate authority (CA). If you put a site on the internet using such a certificate, it will function technically like one with a purchased certificate. All traffic will be encrypted between client and server. The catch is that browsers will warn users about an untrusted server (because the browsers don't see a certificate signed by a trusted CA). This is no problem for your local testing and development, though. You can make an exception for this certificate and continue.

To generate a self-signed certificate, you need to have OpenSSL installed. Follow the installation instructions for your platform. If you're using a Mac, you probably already have it installed.

1 Generate a private key:

```
openssl genrsa -des3 -out server.pass.key 1024
```

2 Remove the passkey from the private key:

```
openssl rsa -in server.pass.key -out server.key
```

3 Generate a certificate-signing request (you can keep all the defaults):

```
openssl req -new -key server.key -out server.csr
```

4 Create the certificate:

```
openssl x509 -req -days 365 -in server.csr -signkey server.key
-out server.crt
```

You will now have a server.key file and a server.crt file. You need to set these files to be used by hapi's TLS connection settings, as shown here.

Listing 11.16   Listing 11.16 Providing SSL private key and certificate to hapi

```
const Hapi = require('hapi');
const Fs = require('fs');
const Path = require('path');

const server = new Hapi.Server();
server.connection({ port: 80 });
server.connection({
    port: 443,
    tls: {
        key: Fs.readFileSync(Path.join(__dirname, 'server.key')),
        cert: Fs.readFileSync(Path.join(__dirname, 'server.crt'))
    }
});

server.start((err) => {
```

**Certificate and private key
provided to hapi through
connection TLS option**

```
    if (err) {
        throw err;
    }

    console.log('Started server!');
});
```

If you start this application (you'll require elevated permissions to run it) and attempt to load your app in a browser (https://localhost), you'll be greeted with a warning likethat in figure 11.13. By clicking the Proceed link (wording could be different in your browser), you can then test your TLS-encrypted site.

When you're finally ready to put your TLS site into production, you'll need to purchase a real SSL certificate from a certificate authority. Once you have

Figure 11.13   The message shown by Google Chrome for an untrusted SSL certificate

your SSL certificate and private key, you need to substitute the self-signed items from the previous section with these.

11.5.4   Forcing HTTPS

Even if you've decided that you want to protect your entire site with TLS, it's still desirable to have a non-TLS connection available on port 80. If people forget to type `https://` into a web browser, and your server isn't listening in non-TLS mode, they won't be able to access your site.

The recommended approach here is to have two connections on your server. One will be a TLS connection and the other a non-TLS connection, and you can redirect all non-TLS traffic to the appropriate TLS URL (see figure 11.14).

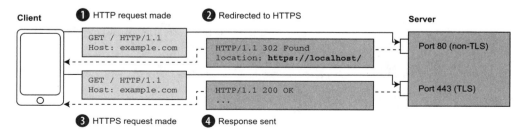

Figure 11.14   Redirecting insecure requests to HTTPS

This functionality isn't built in to hapi, but it's a snap to set up by using the `onRequest` extension point.

Listing 11.17   Redirecting HTTP requests to HTTPS requests

```
server.ext('onRequest', (request, reply) => {

    if (request.connection.info.protocol === 'http') {
        const secureURL = 'https://' + request.info.host + request.url.path;
        return reply.redirect(secureURL);          ◁┐
    }                                                │ If request originated from a
    reply.continue();                                │ non-https connection, redirect
});                                                  │ it to https-equivalent URL
```

A related security issue is that of HTTP Strict Transport Security (HSTS). A web server is able to tell a client via HSTS that it should only communicate with it via HTTPS in the future. The client then remembers this for the specified time. Any future attempts by a user to request the insecure URL will be transparently redirected by the client.

The HSTS header is simple to set in hapi through the `security` route option, as shown in the following isting. This was discussed in chapter 9.

Listing 11.18   Setting HSTS header through the security route `config` option

```
server.route({
    config: {
        security: {
            hsts: {
                maxAge: 15768000,
                includeSubDomains: true
            }
        }
    },
    method: 'GET',
    path: '/',
    handler: function (request, reply) {

        ...

    }
});
```

The setting can also be made the default for an entire server by setting the appropriate option under `connections.routes`, as shown in the following listing.

Listing 11.19   Setting HSTS header as default for all routes on a connection

```
const server = new Hapi.Server({
    connections: {
        routes: {
            security: {
                hsts: true
```

```
            }
          }
        }
});
```

Combining mandatory SSL with HSTS gives your users the best privacy you can offer.

11.6 Summary

- hapi servers are `EventEmitters` that emit a range of events during startup and running.
- We can print out server events in development using debug mode.
- We should use Good for our production logging needs.
- You can automatically generate documentation for your app using Lout by adding some simple metadata to your routes.
- hapi TV is a real-time debugging console that's easy to add to your application.
- If you install Poop, you can get useful heap dumps from your apps if they crash in production, helping you to find memory leaks.
- You should consider serving your content over TLS, so far as enforcing HTTPS by using redirects and HTTP Strict Transport Security (HSTS).

We've come a long way, and I hope you've enjoyed this journey as much as I have. I hope I've equipped you with the skills and knowledge to go out there and confidently build fast, maintainable, and secure applications. I can't wait to see what you build!

appendix A
Getting started with
Node.js and npm

This book is designed to be as welcoming for newcomers as for experienced Node developers. If you're the former, this section is intended to be your onramp into Node.

Throughout the book, I've tried to explain any of Node's peculiarities when and where they make sense. That said, everything could not fit within these pages. As you progress as a Node developer, I recommend you follow up with further material to supplement your knowledge, such as the following two Manning books dedicated to teaching Node:

- *Node.js in Action* by Mike Cantelon, Marc Harter, T. J. Holowaychuk, and Nathan Rajlich (Manning, 2013)
- *Node.js in Practice* by Alex Young and Marc Harter (Manning, 2014)

A.1 What is Node.js?

Node.js was written by Ryan Dahl and a small group of contributors in 2009. Since then it has gained over 800 contributors. It's gone through corporate sponsorship by Joyent, a dramatic fork (the io.js project), a re-merging, and the recent establishment of the Node.js Foundation.

History aside, what *is* Node.js? Simply put, Node.js lets you run programs written in JavaScript outside of the traditional environment of JavaScript—browsers. What kind of environments are we talking about? Well, any really, but mainly as web developers, if we're not building programs for browsers, we're building them for servers. Node lets us write our server-side programs in JavaScript, rather than, say, PHP, Java, Ruby, or any of the other common server-side web programming languages.

Why would we want to write our servers with JavaScript, though? Here are some advantages commonly cited:

- Web developers are already familiar with JS from working with it and the browser, so companies can leverage existing knowledge.
- It's the established language of the web, and that doesn't look set to change anytime soon.
- Code reuse is possible between front and back ends.
- The asynchronous coding style is a good fit for building servers.

Node uses V8, the super-fast JavaScript engine inside Google Chrome to execute your code. If V8 runs our JavaScript, what's Node's role? One way I like to think of Node is as the *standard library that JavaScript never had.*

If you think of some of those other programming languages, like PHP or Ruby, they have large standard libraries that provide APIs for filesystem access, networking, and cryptography, to name a few. JavaScript as a language never had these things originally, because it was designed for the browser, where such functionality is either unsafe or unnecessary. Node extends JavaScript to provide you with all things you'd expect on the server, like the ability to make TCP requests or save a file to disk.

A.2   Getting Node and npm

There are various ways to install Node on your machine. The central place to find the downloads is https://nodejs.org/en/download/.

A.2.1   Installers

Probably the easiest way to get started if you're on Mac or Windows is to use the installer for your platform. The installers will conveniently install both Node.js and npm for you.

For Windows, you'll want the Windows Installer (.msi) download and for Mac it's the Mac OS X Installer (.pkg) download. Once downloaded, the installers will guide you through the setup process. Once complete, you're ready to go.

A.2.2   Linux

The folks at NodeSource have done a tremendous job of making it as easy as possible to find a suitable distribution of Node.js for whichever Linux distro you're using. You can find instructions at https://github.com/nodesource/distributions.

A.2.3   Compiling from source

Another option is to compile and install Node yourself directly from the source on Github:

```
git clone https://github.com/nodejs/node.git
cd node
[git checkout v4.4.1]     # optional step
./configure
```

```
make                      # will take a while...
[sudo] make install
```

A.2.4 *Using a version manager*

If you're on Mac or Linux and find yourself needing access to several different versions of Node on the same machine, a really great solution is using one of the popular Node version managers such as https://github.com/creationix/nvm or https://github.com/tj/n. I'm a big fan of nvm and use it when I need to test my code on several versions of node.

Installing it is as simple as:

```
curl -o- https://raw.githubusercontent.com/creationix/nvm/v0.31.0/install.sh
| bash
```

You can then simply download any version of Node from the command line. For example:

```
nvm install 4.4.1
```

To switch a previously installed version:

```
nvm use 5.0.0
```

A.3 *Hello Node*

Once you have Node and npm installed, you're ready to write your first program. You write Node programs in a file and usually save with the .js extension, just like for the browser. You can keep those files anywhere, but it makes sense to create a dedicated folder for every project that you work on.

Let's make a folder called `hello_node` to store our first Node project. Inside we'll add a file called index.js. It's sort of a convention, but not a requirement, in Node to call the entry point into your application index.js. Let's add some JavaScript to index.js:

```
const hello = function (name) {

    console.log('Hello ' + name + '!');
};

hello('world');
```

To execute a Node program, we use the `node` program, which should be in your PATH after installation. We can run the preceding program now:

```
node index.js
```

You should see this output:

```
$ node index.js
Hello world!
```

Congratulations! You just wrote your first Node application. Good job! Notice how it exited the program and you got terminal control again after printing "Hello world!" That's a feature of Node programs—they exit when there's nothing left to do. Most of the Node programs that we'll write in this book don't exit because they're servers. Servers always have something to do: listen for new connections. Let's write an example of a Node app that doesn't exit by itself, by using a timer:

```
var i = 0;

setInterval(() => {

   console.log('Hello ' + (++i));
}, 1000);
```

If you run the preceding script, you'll notice that it will just keep on going forever:

```
$ node index.js
Hello 1
Hello 2
Hello 3
Hello 4
Hello 5
...
```

We can force the process to exit by hitting Ctrl+C on the keyboard (this sends a signal to the node process to exit).

A.4   *Hello npm*

Back when I used to write lots of PHP, I hardly thought about dependencies. I used a big framework like Zend or CodeIgniter that had a gazillion features, and if I needed something that wasn't in the framework, I probably ended up writing it myself. The dependency management solutions at the time (PEAR/PECL) were difficult to work with. Now, kudos to PHP, this has changed a lot with the advent of better tools like Composer.

Luckily, we're spoiled in Node because we have npm, and it's been with us pretty almost from the start. npm is the biggest open source package registry in the world. As of this writing, there are around 250,000 packages, and this is growing all the time.

npm is a huge part of the success of the Node ecosystem. npm makes it easy to install, manage, and publish packages. npm is a separate program from Node, but it's so integral to Node that it's bundled with all installations.

The ways that we go about creating a package for publishing on npm and creating an application that uses npm dependencies are quite similar. It all starts with creating a package.json file. This file goes at the root of your project. You can create it manually according to the instructions at https://docs.npmjs.com/files/package.json. But a much easier way is by calling the command:

```
npm init
```

You'll be asked a bunch of questions, such as how to name your package—you can skip all these if you like by hitting Enter to accept the defaults and edit the file manually later. If you take a peek at your package.json, it'll probably look a little like this:

```
{
  "name": "my-project",
  "version": "1.0.0",
  "description": "",
  "main": "index.js",
  "scripts": {
    "test": "echo \"Error: no test specified\" && exit 1"
  },
  "keywords": [],
  "author": "",
  "license": "ISC"
}
```

Once you have a package.json file, you're all primed to start installing any dependencies you like. As an example, let's look at the Chalk (www.npmjs.com/package/chalk) package. Chalk lets you style your terminal text with colors.

First we need to install Chalk. We should also make sure to record in the package.json that our project depends on Chalk. We can do this in a single step:

```
npm install --save chalk
```

The `--save` part tells npm to save the record this dependency to your `package.json`. If you take a look there, you'll see a new thing:

```
"dependencies": {
  "chalk": "^1.1.1"
}
```

npm will also download Chalk and install the code in a directory at node_modules/ chalk. Let's make a simple script now that uses Chalk to print some text in a multitude of colors:

```
const chalk = require('chalk');

const colors = [
    'red',
    'green',
    'yellow',
    'blue',
    'magenta',
    'cyan'
];

colors.forEach((color) => {

    console.log(chalk[color]('Hey look I\'m ' + color));
});
```

We run this script exactly the same way with node index.js. Node will resolve your `require('chalk')` call to the dependency installed by npm. This is one way npm and Node work together to make your life easier. See figure A.1.

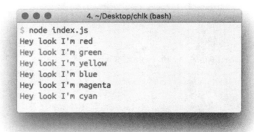

Figure A.1   Console output using the Chalk npm package

You're all set up with now Node and npm, and you're familiar with the package-installation process. We'll be calling on npm a lot throughout the book to include necessary dependencies.

appendix B
npm packages used
in this book

One of the joys of using Node is the huge abundance of brilliant packages, only an `npm install` away from you! This book discusses a large number of packages. I've tried my best to introduce them within the text and point you to the right place to find out a little more. There are so many, though, that you're undoubtedly going to forget some along the way. Therefore, I thought it would be helpful to readers to have a central reference with a list of all the packages used within this book, including the version numbers that work with the examples in the book.

Please come back here anytime you're wondering what on earth Poop does or which version of Inert you're supposed to be installing.

B.1   A quick word about version numbers and Semver

You may be wondering what 2.x.x or 1.0.x means. All packages on npm have a version associated with them, such as 2.4.5. This version number has parts separated by a period. The version numbering for npm packages is supposed to follow the Semver (semantic-versioning) rules (http://semver.org). Here are the basic rules of Semver for package maintainers:

Given a version number MAJOR.MINOR.PATCH, increment the:

1   MAJOR version when you make incompatible API changes,
2   MINOR version when you add functionality in a backwards-compatible manner, and
3   PATCH version when you make backward-compatible bug fixes.

All the modules within the hapi ecosystem follow Semver strictly. You can assume that if your app worked with version 1.0.3 of a dependency, it will work with 1.24.5 if such a version is released. For this reason, I specify all the dependencies from within the hapi ecosystem in this book using:

MAJOR.x.x

Because not every maintainer out there follows Semver quite as strictly as hapi does, we're a extra careful when specifying external dependencies in this book. Instead, we use:

MAJOR.MINOR.x

By pinning to a minor version like this, things are more likely to work faithfully as new versions of the package are released in future.

B.2   The packages

Table B.1 is the complete list of packages used in the book and the version for which the examples have been tested.

Table B.1   Packages used in this book and the the versions tested

Name	Version used	What is it for?
accept	2.x.x	Parsing `Accept-Language` header
bell	7.x.x	Third-party authentication
boom	3.x.x	HTTP-friendly errors
catbox	7.x.x	Multi-strategy caching
catbox-memory	2.x.x	Catbox strategy for in-memory cache
catbox-redis	1.x.x	Catbox strategy for Redis cache
code	2.x.x	Assertion library for testing
confidence	1.x.x	Configuration library
crumb	6.x.x	CSRF Protection
dindin-api	2.x.x	Chapter 1 project as an npm package
glue	3.x.x	Composing hapi apps from config
good	6.x.x	Logging and process monitoring
good-console	5.x.x	Good reporter for console logging
good-file	5.x.x	Good reporter for file logging
handlebars	4.0.x	JavaScript template engine
hapi	13.x.x	HTTP server framework
hapi-auth-basic	4.x.x	HTTP Basic Authentication plugin
hapi-auth-bearer-token	4.x.x	HTTP Bearer Token auth plugin
hapi-auth-cookie	6.x.x	HTTP Cookie authentication plugin

Table B.1 Packages used in this book and the the versions tested

Name	Version used	What is it for?
inert	3.x.x	Static file serving for hapi
joi	8.x.x	JavaScript object validation
lab	10.x.x	Test runner, linter, and coverage tool
lout	9.x.x	Autogenerated documentation
mongodb	2.1.x	MongoDB client library
netmask	1.0.x	IP address utilities
node-statsd	0.1.x	StatsD client library
oppsy	1.x.x	Collecting hapi server ops data
poop	2.x.x	Taking heap dumps on crashes
proxyquire	1.7.x	Mocking dependencies
qs	6.x.x	Querystring utilities
rethinkdb	2.2.x	RethinkDB client library
sinon	1.17.x	Testing spies, stubs, and mocks
sqlite3	3.0.x	SQLite client library
tv	5.x.x	hapi request debugging console
vision	4.x.x	HTML view rendering for hapi
wreck	7.x.x	Making HTTP requests

index

RELATED MANNING TITLES

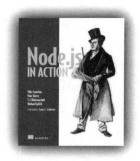

Node.js in Action
by Mike Cantelon, Marc Harter, T.J. Holowaychuk,
and Nathan Rajlich

ISBN: 9781617290572
416 pages, $44.99
October 2013

Node.js in Practice
by Alex Young and Marc Harter

ISBN: 9781617290930
424 pages, $49.99
December 2014

Express in Action
Writing, building, and testing Node.js applications

by Evan M. Hahn

ISBN: 9781617292422
256 pages, $39.99
April 2016

Secrets of the JavaScript Ninja, Second Edition

by John Resig, Bear Bibeault,
and Josip Maras

ISBN: 9781617292859
464 pages, $44.99
August 2016

For ordering information go to www.manning.com